Organisations and Behaviour

Pippa Riley

Viva Books
New Delhi | Mumbai | Chennai | Kolkata | Bengaluru | Hyderabad | Kochi | Guwahati

First Indian Edition 2011

VIVA BOOKS PRIVATE LIMITED

- 4737/23 Ansari Road, Daryaganj, New Delhi 110 002
  E-mail: vivadelhi@vivagroupindia.net, Tel. 42242200
- 76, Service Industries, Shirvane, Sector 1, Nerul, Navi Mumbai 400 706
  E-mail: vivamumbai@vivagroupindia.net, Tel. 27721273, 27721274
- Jamals Fazal Chambers, 26 Greams Road, Chennai 600 006
  E-mail: vivachennai@vivagroupindia.net, Tel. 28290304, 28294241
- B-103, Jindal Towers, 21/1A/3 Darga Road, Kolkata 700 017
  E-mail: vivakolkata@vivagroupindia.net, Tel. 22836381, 22816713
- 7, Sovereign Park Apartments, 56-58, K. R. Road, Basavanagudi, Bengaluru 560 004
  E-mail: vivabangalore@vivagroupindia.net, Tel. 26607409, 26607410
- 101-102 Mughal Marc Aptt., 3-4-637 to 641, Narayanguda, Hyderabad 500 029
  E-mail: vivahyderabad@vivagroupindia.net, Tel. 27564481, 27564482
- First Floor, Beevi Towers, SRM Road, Kaloor, Kochi 682 018, Kerala
  E-mail: vivakochi@vivagroupindia.net, Tel: 0484-2403055, 2403056
- 232, GNB Road, Beside UCO Bank, Silpukhuri, Guwahati 781 003
  E-mail: vivaguwahati@vivagroupindia.net, Tel: 0361-2666386

Published by arrangement with

BPP Learning Media Ltd.
BPP House, Aldine Place
London W12 8AA

ISBN : 978-81-309-1767-2

Published by Vinod Vasishtha for Viva Books Private Limited, 4737/23, Ansari Road, Daryaganj, New Delhi - 110 002.

Printed and bound by Raj Press, R-3, Inderpuri, New Delhi - 110 012.

Contents

Introduction

Viva-BPP Learning Media's Business Essentials range is the ideal learning solution for students studying for business-related qualifications and degrees. The range provides concise and comprehensive coverage of the key areas that are essential to the business student.

Qualifications in business are traditionally very demanding. Students therefore need learning resources which go straight to the core of the topics involved, and which build upon students' pre-existing knowledge and experience. The BPP Learning Media Business Essentials range has been designed to meet exactly that need.

Features include:

- In-depth coverage of essential topics within business-related subjects
- Plenty of activities, quizzes and topics for discussion to help retain the interest of students and ensure progress
- Up-to-date practical illustrations and case studies that really bring the material to life
- A full index, with key terms highlighted in bold

Each chapter contains:

- An introduction and a list of specific study objectives
- Summary diagrams and signposts to guide you through the chapter
- A chapter roundup, quick quiz with answers and answers to actvities

Titles in the Series

- Accounts
- Business Decision Making
- Business Environment
- Business Maths
- Business Strategy
- Economics
- Finance: Management Accounting and Financial Reporting
- Human Resource Development and Employee Relations
- Human Resource Management
- Management: Communications and Achieving Results
- Management: Leading People and Professional Development
- Managing Finance
- Marketing and Promotion
- Marketing and Sales Strategy
- Marketing Principles
- Organisations and Behaviour
- Research Project

Study Guide

This Course Book includes features designed specifically to make learning effective and efficient.

- Each chapter begins with a summary diagram which maps out the areas covered by the chapter. There are detailed summary diagrams at the start of each main section of the chapter. You can use the diagrams during revision as a basis for your notes.
- After the main summary diagram there is an introduction, which sets the chapter in context. This is followed by learning objectives, which show you what you will learn as you work through the chapter.
- Throughout the Course Book, there are special aids to learning. These are indicated by symbols in the margin:

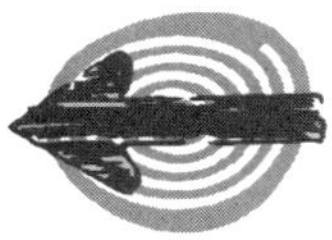

Signposts guide you through the book, showing how each section connects with the next.

Definitions give the meanings of key terms. The *glossary* at the end of the book summarises these.

Activities help you to test how much you have learned. An indication of the time you should take on each is given. Answers are given at the end of each chapter.

Topics for discussion are for use in seminars. They give you a chance to share your views with your fellow students. They allow you to highlight holes in your knowledge and to see how others understand concepts. If you have time, try 'teaching' someone the concepts you have learned in a session. This helps you to remember key points and answering their questions will consolidate your knowledge.

Examples relate what you have learned to the outside world. Try to think up your own examples as you work through the Course Book.

Chapter roundups present the key information from the chapter in a concise format. Useful for revision.

- At the end of each chapter, there is a **chapter roundup** and a **quick quiz** with answers. Use these to revise and consolidate your knowledge. The chapter roundup summarises the chapter. The quick quiz tests what you have learned (the answers often refer you back to the chapter so you can look over subjects again).
- At the end of the book, there is an index.

Part A

Approaches to Management and Leadership

Chapter 1:
WHAT IS MANAGEMENT?

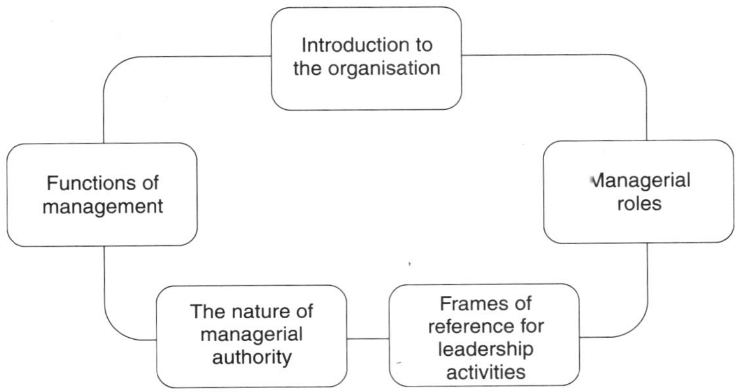

Introduction

Before we can discuss 'approaches to management', we need to consider what 'managing' is. So we begin this introductory chapter by looking at organisations and why they might need managing. We then go on to look at some of the various models of how management 'works', the functions managers perform and the roles they fulfil. When discussing the leadership role, we identify some frames of reference for leadership activities. Finally, we ask a question that is often taken for granted. If the function of management is (partly) to tell people to do things, why should anybody listen? How do managers actually exercise power in the organisation?

Your objectives

In this chapter you will learn about the following:

(a) The term 'organisation' and the need for management of people and activities in business organisations

(b) Some of the activities and roles of a manager, and the range and complexity of the management task

(c) The nature of managerial authority in an organisation, and the difference between the authority, power and responsibility of managers

(d) The different types of leadership activities

(e) The process of delegation of authority

1 INTRODUCTION TO THE ORGANISATION

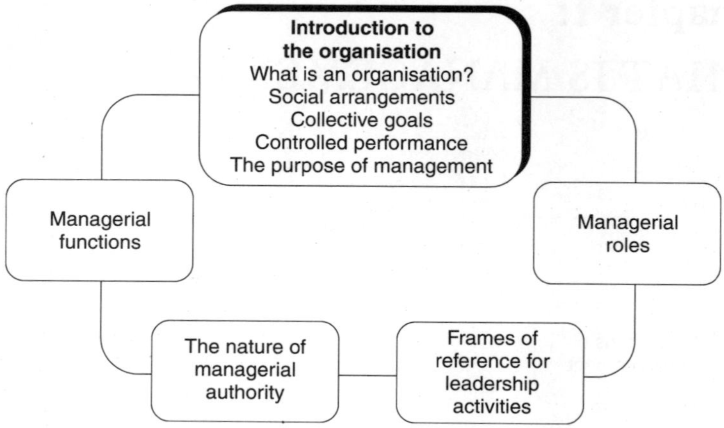

1.1 What is an organisation?

Before we look at formal definitions of what an organisation might be, let's approach the question from a purely practical angle. The writer Chester Barnard (1938) used the example of a man trying to lift a stone which is too heavy for him. By getting together with another person, and combining their efforts, the man is able to move the stone.

FOR DISCUSSION

Suppose that you are the person wanting to move the stone. Consider how you would go about getting other people to help you: what could you offer them? What are they offering you? Who will be in charge of the operation? What will need organising? Will it make a difference if you are using (a) brute strength, (b) a lever and fulcrum or (c) a bulldozer? You are, in effect, dealing with organisational issues of planning, organising, resourcing, controlling and people management.

Chester Barnard (1938) described an organisation as 'a system of co-operative human activities'. Another writer described organisations as 'systems of behaviour designed to enable humans and their machines to accomplish goals'. Can you identify in these definitions the features of our rock-rolling organisation?

A simple but precise definition may be given as follows.

Definition

> **Organisations** are 'social arrangements for the controlled performance of collective goals'. (Buchanan and Huczynski, 1991)

1.2 Social arrangements

An organisation is made up of individuals brought together to carry out different roles within it to enable them to achieve its goals and objectives. This is achieved through the inter-relationships, co-operation and, on occasion, conflict between these individual members.

Banding together in organisations offers:

(a) A greater ability to achieve individual and organisational purposes, by allowing people to pool their knowledge, experience, special expertise and resources

(b) The satisfaction of the individual's need for relationships with other people

In order to achieve the goals and objectives, the business organisation must formalise the 'social arrangements' to provide a 'controlled performance' (see Paragraph 1.4). This involves the allocation of functions, tasks and activities to individuals or groups along with clearly defined responsibilities, levels of authority and communication channels. These factors will determine the structure of an organisation.

Organisational structure

We will be discussing organisation structure in detail in Chapter 3. Broadly it implies a framework intended to:

(a) **Link individuals** in an established network of relationships so that authority, responsibility and communications can be controlled

(b) **Group together the tasks** required to fulfil the objectives of the organisation, and allocate them to suitable individuals or groups; this may be done on the basis of function (sales, production, personnel and so on), geographical area (eg for regional sales territories), product or product type – or whatever is appropriate

(c) Give each individual or group the **authority** required to perform the allocated functions, while controlling their behaviour and use of resources in the interests of the organisation as a whole

(d) **Co-ordinate** the objectives and activities of separate units, so that overall aims are achieved without gaps or overlaps in the flow of work

(e) **Facilitate** the flow of work, information and other resources through the organisation

We will be discussing some related issues of organisation structure a bit later in this chapter, when we consider the nature of a manager's authority. However, you should be clear in your own mind that 'controlled performance of collective goals' is almost impossible without some kind of deliberate organisational structure. We call this a formal organisation.

Definitions

A **formal organisation** is one which is deliberately constructed to fulfil specific goals. It is characterised by planned division of responsibility and a well-defined structure of authority and communication. The organisation structure provides for consistent functions and roles, irrespective of changes in individual membership.

An **informal organisation** is one which is loosely structured, flexible and spontaneous, fluctuating with its individual membership. Examples of an informal organisation are colleagues who tend to lunch together and 'cliques'. Informal organisations always exist within formal organisations.

Activity 1 **(10 minutes)**

Jason, Mark, Gary and Robbie set up in business together as repairers of musical instruments – specialising in guitars and drums. They are a bit uncertain as to how they should run the business, but when they discuss it in the pub, they decide that attention needs to be paid to three major areas: taking orders from customers, doing the repairs (of course) and checking the quality of the repairs before notifying the customer.

Suggest three ways in which the boys could structure their business.

Organisational culture

Again, we will be discussing this in detail later on (Chapter 5), but basically the 'culture' of an organisation consists of the shared assumptions, values and beliefs of its members; its collective self-image; its sense of 'the way we do things round here'; its general 'style'. Some aspects of culture are as follows.

(a) **Underlying assumptions**: belief in quality or the importance of the customer; trust in the organisation to be loyal and provide good rewards; freedom to make decisions, and even mistakes – and so on. These basic ideas guide the behaviour of individuals and groups.

(b) **Beliefs and values** expressed by the organisation's managers and members, in sayings, slogans or mottoes; in-jokes, stories about past successes, heroic failures or breakthroughs, legends about past figures and so on. Managers can encourage the values they want (care for quality, use of initiative, loyalty and so on) by example, by giving the right messages, by rewarding the right attitudes and punishing (or simply not employing) those who are not prepared to be part of the culture.

(c) **Visible signs**, such as the style of the offices or what people wear, the formality or informality of communication between managers and staff and so on.

1.3 Collective goals

All organisations have collective or shared goals, over and above the individual goals of their members. A chess club, for example, may believe in promoting excellence in the game of chess, or making chess more accessible to ordinary people. It may also have more specific objectives to do with being successful in inter-club chess tournaments, attracting new members, or raising money. Or it may simply fulfil the need for its members to get together with fellow enthusiasts, and to improve their game. In other words, there are different types of goal.

(a) **Ideological goals** are to do with beliefs and values, and what the organisation has defined as its 'mission'. (For example, the mission or ideological goal of a telecommunications organisation may be to 'get the world talking'.)

(b) **Formal goals** are those set for the organisation by a dominant individual (the organisation's founder, say) or group (the shareholders or management team). Members work to attain these goals because it is also a means to their personal goals (such as earning pay).

(c) **Shared personal goals** are pursued when the individual members agree on what they want from the organisation (eg a discussion group, or a group of academics deciding to pursue research).

Activity 2 **(10 minutes)**

In what areas do you think business organisations might wish to set themselves goals or specific objectives? Suggest five areas

---

FOR DISCUSSION: CASE EXAMPLES

Here are some ideological goals or 'mission statements' of well-known organisations.

GlaxoSmithKline (GSK) mission is 'to improve the quality of human life by enabling people to do more, feel better and live longer'.

IBM: 'IBM is the world's largest information technology company, with 80 years of leadership in helping businesses innovate. Drawing on resources from across IBM and key Business Partners, IBM offers a wide range of services, solutions and technologies that enable customers, large and small, to take full advantage of the new era of e-business. As the world's leading information technology services organisation, we have unparalleled experience in all of the fundamental issues associated with planning, implementing, deploying and operating SAP.com solutions with expertise and industry specific package enhancements in more than a dozen industries.'

Apple Computers: 'Our goal has always been to create the world's friendliest, most understandable, most useable computers – computers that empower the individual...'

Whose goals are these? Who will benefit (inside and outside the organisation) if these organisations achieve their stated goals? (People who stand to gain or lose by the activities of an organisation are called its 'stakeholders': they have a 'stake' or interest in it.)

1.4 Controlled performance

An organisation is responsible to its owners (or shareholders) and other stakeholders for the achievement of its collective goals. It clearly has to find reliable, systematic ways of ensuring that:

(a) Its collective goals are known and understood by all members.

(b) The necessary resources (including members' time and effort) are secured and utilised in such a way that goals will be reached without undue risk, disruption or waste.

(c) They can tell whether, or to what extent, they have reached their goals – and if not, why not, and what can be done.

This is called control – hence 'controlled performance'.

Definition

> **Control** is the overall process whereby goals and standards are defined, and performance is monitored, measured against the goals and adjusted if necessary, to ensure that the goals are being accomplished.

1.5 The purpose of management

Let's look again at our definition of an organisation as 'a social arrangement for the controlled performance of collective goals'. What does it suggest about the purpose of management?

(a) Collective goals have to be set for the organisation, and communicated to its members.

(b) These goals have to be met, and somebody has to ensure that this happens.

(c) The collective goals of the organisation have to be harmonised with the individual goals of its members, in order to secure their co-operation.

(d) Social arrangements – organisational structures and systems – have to be designed and maintained, so that:

  (i) The individual members 'pull' together without gaps or duplicated effort

  (ii) Available resources are used to best effect

  (iii) Uncertainty and risk are reduced as far as possible

(e) The organisation needs a collective or corporate identity in its dealings with its employees and other stakeholders. Somebody has to create and sustain this corporate identity and the shared values or culture that accompany it.

(f) Somebody has to look after the interests of the organisation's stakeholders, especially its owners (if they are not involved in the day to day running of the organisation themselves).

Management can be regarded as the catalyst which is essential for converting the inputs of the operation into valued outputs and, in the process, ensuring that stakeholders' needs are satisfied.

We will now look at what the management process means in terms of its basic functions.

2 FUNCTIONS OF MANAGEMENT

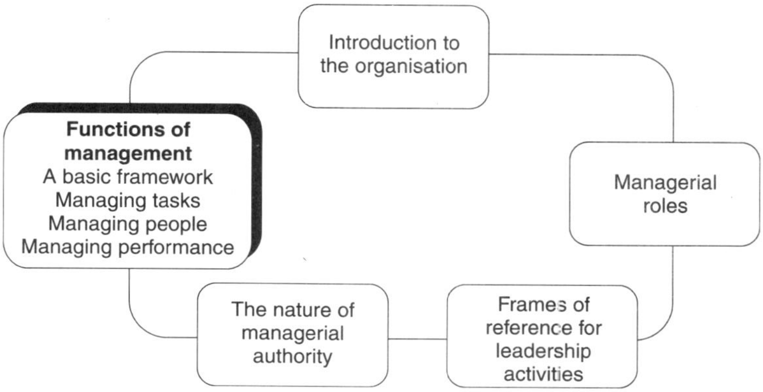

2.1 A basic framework

The process and functions of management have been analysed in various ways by different writers. One of the first, and most influential, accounts of management functions was provided by the French industrialist Henri Fayol. Fayol (1967) listed the functions of management as follows.

(a) **Planning**. This essentially means looking to the future. It involves selecting the 'ends' which the organisation wishes to achieve (its objectives) and the 'means' (plans, policies, programmes and procedures) it will adopt in order to achieve them.

(b) **Organising**. The work to be done (in order to fulfil the plans) must be divided and structured into tasks and jobs, within a formal structure of authority and communication. Organising includes work scheduling (what is to be done when) and work allocation (who is to do what).

(c) **Commanding**. Fayol called this 'maintaining activity among the personnel'. It involves instructing and motivating subordinates to carry out tasks.

(d) **Co-ordinating**. This is the task of harmonising the activities of individuals and groups within the organisation, reconciling differences in approach, timing and resource requirements in the interest of overall organisational objectives.

(e) **Controlling**. This is the task of monitoring the activities of individuals and groups, to ensure that their performance is in accordance with the plans, standards and objectives set for them. Deviations must be identified and corrected.

Activity 3 **(10 minutes)**

Using Fayol's functions of management, indicate under which of the five headings the five activities below fall.

1 Ensuring that the sales department does not exceed its budget.

2 Deciding which products will form the main thrust of advertising during the next financial year.

3 Ensuring that new working practices are communicated to the workforce.

4 Ensuring that the sales department liaises with production on delivery dates.

5 Changing work schedules to reduce idle time.

2.2 Managing tasks

A number of the functions listed by Fayol concern the management of tasks. Planning, controlling, organising and co-ordinating are closely inter-linked in the process of mobilising and managing the resources of the organisation: labour, time, information, materials, finance and so on.

Why plan and organise?

If individuals and groups within an organisation are to be effective in working for the achievement of the organisation's objectives they need to know what it is they are expected to do. Planning allows managers to identify:

(a) The objectives for which they are responsible
(b) What actions will serve towards achieving those objectives
(c) How far they are being successful in achieving those objectives

Planning and organising are important functions in an organisation for the following reasons.

(a) **Uncertainty**. Organisations cannot deal with things ad hoc, as they occur, without chaos. The future cannot be foreseen with certainty in any case, and even the best-laid plans will go wrong to a greater or lesser degree (which is where 'control' comes in). Nevertheless, plans and structures give some direction and predictability to the work of the organisation: in other words, they are a form of risk management.

(b) **The need for co-ordination**. Organisations are collections of individuals and groups (or sub-systems): each will perceive its own part of the organisation's activity, and work towards its own objectives accordingly. Planning and organising ensures that:

  (i) Sub units of the organisation know what it is they need to achieve, and when

  (ii) Work 'flows' from one process (or department) to another without holdups or clashes, and without idle time or overwork for staff and machinery

  (iii) The resources required for a task are available where and when they are required

  (iv) Required work is being done by somebody – but not being duplicated by others, with a waste of effort

  (v) All of the above are achieved in such a way that products/services of the required quality are available to customers at the right place, at the right price and at the right time

---

FOR DISCUSSION

Suggest examples of the planning/organising needed in each of the areas given in (i) to (v) above, and what would happen if planning was not carried out.

(c) **The need for objectives.** Human beings are 'purposive': they like to feel that their actions have a point. If the organisation doesn't set objectives, people will set their own, according to their own interpretation of the situation: chaos ensues. Objectives are also important in learning and motivation, so people can target and adjust their behaviour according to what they want to achieve.

Types of plan

Planning involves decisions about:

- What to do in future
- How to do it
- When to do it and
- Who should do it (this is also the area covered by 'organising').

Such questions are relevant at all levels of organisational activity:

(a) At a **strategic** level – deciding what business the organisation should be in, and what its overall objectives should be

(b) At a **tactical** level – deciding how it should go about achieving its overall objectives: what products it should produce, how it will organise work and so on

(c) At the **operational** level – deciding what needs to be done from day to day and task to task

There are therefore a number of different types of plan, which can be categorised as follows.

Objectives

Objectives are the end goals, towards which all the organisation's activities will be directed: to earn a profit, say, or provide a certain service.

Strategies

Strategies are long-term plans for the activities and resources which will achieve the organisation's objectives. (A human resource strategy, for example, is a plan for the number and types of staff to be acquired and maintained in the long term.)

Policies

Policies are general statements or 'understandings' which provide guidelines for management decision making. (It might be company policy, for example, to offer five year guarantees on all products, or to promote managers from within the organisation.) Policy guidelines allow managers to exercise their own discretion and freedom of choice, but within certain acceptable limits.

Procedures

Procedures are chronological sequences of actions required to perform a task: they exist at all levels, but become more extensive lower down in an organisation's hierarchy, where the work is more routine. They have three main advantages.

(a) **Efficiency**. Procedures (ideally) prescribe the most efficient way of doing a job.

(b) **Routine**. Procedures remove the need for the exercise of discretion, where fresh decisions are not necessary.

(c) **Standardisation** of work makes output more predictable and more consistent throughout the organisation.

Rules

A rule (or regulation) prescribes a specific, definite action that must be taken in a given situation. It allows no discretion – unlike a policy. For example:

(a) 'Employees in department X are allowed 10 minutes exactly at the end of their shift for clearing up and cleaning their work-bench'.

(b) 'Employees with access to a telephone must not use the telephone for personal calls'.

Programmes

Programmes are co-ordinated groups or series of plans which together achieve a particular objective; for instance, a company might undertake a programme of expansion, computerisation or customer care, involving different aspects and stages of planning.

Budgets

A budget is a formal statement of expected results set out in numerical terms, usually summarised in money values. It is a plan for carrying out certain activities with specified resources within a given period of time, in order to achieve certain targets.

Planning and control

Activity 4 **(10 minutes)**

Dial-a-Video Limited offers home video rental service to subscribers. Subscribers choose a video from a catalogue, phone Dial-a-Video Limited and the video is delivered by a despatch rider. The Chairman, Rajiv Bharat, says to you: 'I hope to expand the business. I've discovered a market for art movie videos. I've had to knock the directors' heads together to develop plans for building a distribution system: they've agreed a number of stages: for a new catalogue, market research and that sort of thing. We'll charge £4 per video per day including delivery. It is a premium price, but people who like that sort of movie will pay for it. We'll tell the despatch riders not to accept tips though.'

What sort of plans has Rajiv Bharat described to you?

Planning is the process of deciding what should be done. Control is the process of checking whether it has been done, and if not, doing something about it. The combined processes of planning and control are known as a control cycle, see Figure 1.1.

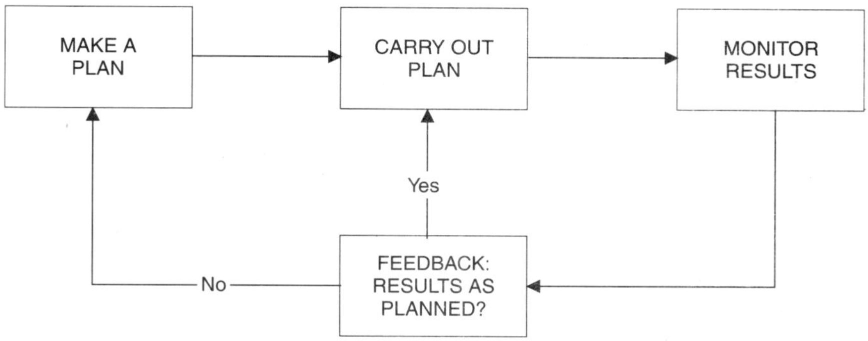

Figure 1.1 A control cycle

In more detail, the control cycle in management has six basic stages.

(a) **Making** a plan: deciding what to do and identifying the desired results. The plan should include:

   (i) **Aims,** which dictate

   (ii) **Priorities,** or 'key results' (objectives which must be achieved for the aims to be fulfilled) and 'key tasks' (things that must be done on time and to the required standard if the key results are to be achieved), for which there should be

   (iii) **Performance standards,** the definition of how well key tasks must be performed in order to achieve key results (acceptable quality, cost or amount of output, say)

   (iv) **Specific short-term goals** for key tasks, against which progress can be monitored; so that

   (v) **Action plans,** specifying 'what, how, who, when, where and how much' can be formulated

(b) **Carrying out** the plan, or having it carried out by subordinates.

(c) **Monitoring and measuring** actual results achieved.

(d) **Comparing** feedback on actual results against the plans.

(e) **Evaluating** the comparison, and deciding whether further action is necessary to ensure the plan is achieved. If results are worse than planned (negative feedback), the activity will have to be adjusted to get it back on course. If they are better than planned (positive feedback), it may be desirable to maintain the deviation from the plan, or to adjust the plan itself to take advantage of the situation.

(f) **Implementing** corrective action where necessary.

2.3 Managing people

You may have noticed that Fayol's framework does not give particular priority to the 'people' aspects of management. By including 'commanding', however, he does recognise the important fact that managers perform their functions and achieve their objectives (or not) with and through the efforts of other people.

You may feel that Fayol's term – 'commanding' – barely does justice to this process. Later writers, recognising more fully the interpersonal (as opposed to purely administrative) dimensions of management, pointed out that management involves many complex human relations functions.

(a) **Managers are also leaders.** Team members may be willing to comply with the procedures and rules of the task, but they will (arguably) be more effective if they can be encouraged to commit themselves to its objectives.

(b) **Managers are communicators.** Managers are collectors, disseminators and users of information. Leadership requires communication skills such as the ability to inspire, influence, persuade or resolve conflict.

(c) **Managers are human resource mobilisers.** Managers are responsible for obtaining, retaining, developing, allocating and (where necessary) shedding labour resources: that is, staff members.

(d) **Managers have superiors, peers and colleagues.** Managers have to maintain co-operative relationships with other managers, and individuals not within their power to 'command', in order to obtain resources and achieve shared objectives.

(e) **Managers represent the organisation** to other people, inside and outside the organisation.

Activity 5 **(10 minutes)**

Brainstorm some alternative terms to replace or add to the term 'commanding' to describe management's 'people' function.

2.4 Managing performance

Peter Drucker worked in the 1940s and 1950s as a business adviser to a number of US corporations. He argued that the manager of a business has another, overarching function: economic performance. In this respect, the business manager is different from the manager of any other type of organisation. The managers of a business can only justify their authority by the economic results they produce, even though as a consequence of their actions significant non-economic results occur as well: employee satisfaction, for example, or an attractive image in the community.

Drucker (1993) described the jobs of management within this overarching function as:

(a) **Managing a business***:* creating customers, innovation

(b) **Managing managers***:* creating a sound culture and structure of management, setting objectives, developing future managers; and – coming in third!

(c) **Managing the workers and work**

The writer Henry Mintzberg argued that looking at managerial functions was in itself misleading, because managerial work, the actual day-to-day life of a manager, is much more complex and subject to disruption than a functional view suggests. We'll look at Mintzberg's alternative view.

3 MANAGERIAL ROLES

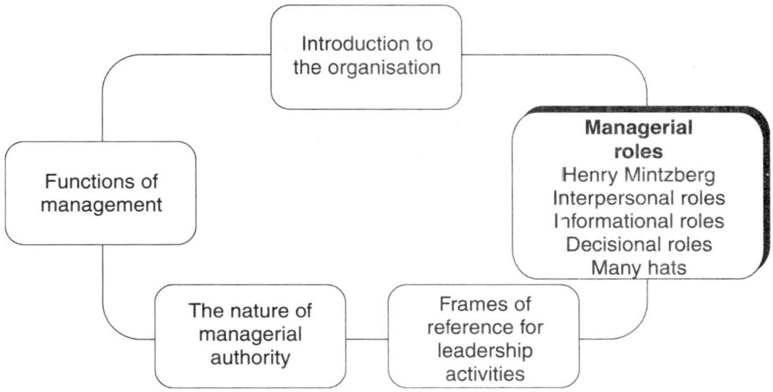

3.1 Henry Mintzberg

Henry Mintzberg (1980) carried out research into how managers actually do their work, and argued that: 'The classical view says that the manager organises, co-ordinates, plans and controls; the facts suggest otherwise.' Managers do not spend scheduled chunks of time analysing formal reports and systematically planning events: managerial work is disjointed and fragmented, and planning is often conducted on a day to day basis, in between more urgent tasks. Managers have to wear different 'hats', depending what is going on at the time.

Mintzberg identified ten managerial roles, three interpersonal, three informational and four decisional roles. These may be taken on as appropriate to the personality of the manager and his subordinates, and to the nature of the task in hand.

3.2 Interpersonal roles

Mintzberg recognised that management is an interpersonal process, and outlined three basic roles which managers adopt in relation to other people.

(a) **Figurehead**. Performing ceremonial and social duties as the organisation's representative, for example at conferences. This is mainly the role of senior figures.

(b) **Leader**. Selecting and training team members, and uniting and inspiring the team to achieve its objectives.

(c) **Liaison**. Communicating with people outside the work unit (eg in inter-departmental meetings) or the organisation: building up an informal system of information exchange.

3.3 Informational roles

According to Mintzberg, 'the manager does not leave meetings or hang up the telephone in order to go back to work. In a large part, communication is his work.' A manager is likely to have a wider network of contacts within and outside the organisation than his subordinates, so he is the best person to gather and spread information.

(a) **Monitor**. Receiving information from the environment and from within the organisation. Much of this may be obtained informally, say from chatting with contacts or subordinates: managers do not rely solely on formal reports.

(b) **Disseminator**. Passing on information to subordinates.

(c) **Spokesman**. Transmitting information to interested parties outside the work unit or organisation.

3.4 Decisional roles

The manager's formal authority and access to information put him in a strong position to take decisions.

(a) **Entrepreneur**. Being a 'fixer', mobilising resources to get things done and to seize opportunities.

(b) **Disturbance-handler**. Coping with the unexpected, rectifying mistakes and getting operations and relationships back on course when necessary.

(c) **Resource allocator**. Distributing limited resources in the way that will most efficiently achieve defined objectives.

(d) **Negotiator**. Bargaining – for example, for resources and influence.

3.5 Many hats

The manager needs to have all these 'hats', putting on the right one(s) for each task and situation. A manager will wear some hats more than others: senior officials, for example, are more likely to be called upon to act as figureheads than team managers, who will be more concerned with resource allocation and disturbance-handling. In modern management theories, particular emphasis has been placed on leadership and entrepreneurship, at team level as well as organisational level: involving and committing employees to achieving goals, and focusing on creative action and resource mobilisation to get things done.

Activity 6 **(15 minutes)**

The *Telegraph Magazine* asked a cinema manager: 'What do you actually do?' The answer was as follows.

'Everything, apart from being the projectionist and cleaning the lavatories. My office is also the ticket office. If there's a big queue at the confectionery kiosk, I'll help serve and I'll usher people to their seats if we're really busy. Sometimes I go into the cinema before a show and tell the audience about any special events, such as a director coming to give a talk.

'I get in around lunchtime, deal with messages and ensure that the lights and heating are working. I write orders for posters and publicity pictures, popcorn and ice cream and deal with the correspondence for the 2,000 members on our mailing list. I'll brief the projectionist, ushers and kiosk staff and at about 1.45pm the first matinee customers arrive. Our afternoon audience is mainly elderly people and they take some time to settle, so I'll help them to their seats and only start the film when everyone is comfortable. In the evening, more ushers and bar staff arrive and I'll brief them about the programme, seating and timing. While the film is on, I'm selling tickets for the other screen, counting the takings and planning tomorrow. If I get a moment I try to grab something to eat.'

Which of Mintzberg's roles does this manager take on in his 'average' day?

Fayol, Drucker and Mintzberg did not suggest that managerial functions were only carried out by 'managers': they could be performed to an extent by any member of the organisation. In most Western companies, however, a separate group of people is responsible for planning, resourcing, co-ordinating and controlling their own work and the work of others. So what gives these people the right to make decisions about people and resources they do not own? Why should anybody listen to them or obey them?

4 THE NATURE OF MANAGERIAL AUTHORITY

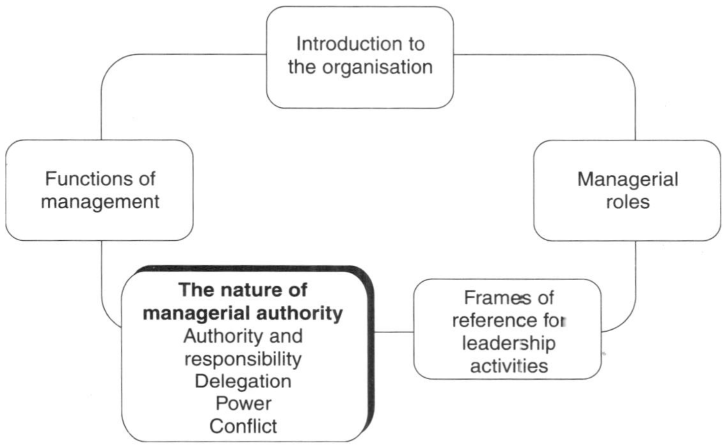

4.1 Authority and responsibility

Definitions

> **Authority** is the right to do something, or to get others to do it.
>
> **Responsibility** is the liability of a person to be called to account for the way he has exercised the authority given to him. It is an obligation to do something, or to get others to do it.

In an organisation, the authority or 'legal' right of managers to manage is given to them, or bestowed on them, by the organisation or its owners or stakeholders. A manager is usually given authority from above, by virtue of the position in the organisation hierarchy to which he has been appointed. On the other hand, an elected team leader, for example, is given authority from below. Either way, the scope and amount of the authority being given to a person should be clearly defined.

Authority is, in effect, 'passed' down the organisation structure, by a process called delegation.

Definition

> **Delegation** is the process whereby superior A gives subordinate B authority over a defined area which falls within the scope of A's own authority.

Note from our definition that managers cannot bestow on others the right to make decisions which are outside the scope of their own authority. Managers are simply sharing their own authority. They are also sharing their responsibility – but not giving it away: A remains responsible (and accountable to his own boss) for the results of the tasks and decisions which have been delegated to B.

Definition

> **Accountability** is the duty of the individual to report to his superior to account for how he has used his delegated authority and fulfilled his responsibilities.

The delegated authority of a manager of a subordinate in a direct line down the chain of command is sometimes called **line authority**.

4.2 Delegation

In any large or complex organisation, a manager will have to delegate some authority to subordinates because:

(a) There are physical and mental limitations to the work load of any individual

(b) Routine or less important decisions can be passed 'down the line', freeing the superior to concentrate on more important aspects of the work (like planning) which only (s)he has the authority to perform

(c) Employees in today's organisations have high expectations with regard to job satisfaction, including participation in decision-making

(d) The continuity of management depends on subordinates gaining some experience of management processes in order to be 'groomed' for promotion

However, in practice many managers are reluctant to delegate and attempt to perform routine tasks and decision-making which could be handed down to subordinates. Among the reasons for this reluctance one can commonly identify:

(a) Low confidence and trust in the abilities of the subordinates: the suspicion that 'if you want it done well, you have to do it yourself

(b) The burden of responsibility and accountability for the mistakes of subordinates

(c) A desire to stay in touch with the department or team – workload and people: particularly if the manager does not feel at home in a management role and/or misses aspects of the subordinate job, or camaraderie

(d) Unwillingness to admit that subordinates have developed to the extent that they could perform some of the manager's duties: the threat of redundancy

(e) Poor control and communication systems in the organisation, so that the manager feels (s)he has to do everything personally, if (s)he wants to keep track of what is going on

(f) Lack of understanding of what delegation involves: that is, not giving subordinates total control

(g) A desire to operate with one's personal 'comfort zone', doing familiar, easy jobs and thereby avoiding risky and difficult management tasks

Activity 7 **(20 minutes)**

Suggest four ways in which senior management (or the organisation) can encourage managers to delegate more.

4.3 Power

Definition

Power is the ability to do something, or get others to do it.

You may have noticed that there is a difference between authority and power. It is quite possible for a person to have the right to do something – but not to be able to: to have the right to ask subordinates to perform a task – but to lack the power to make them do so. Within organisations, there may be respect for the authority of a manager's position, but this needs to be backed up by power. Any individual in the organisation may have power, of one or more of the following types.

(a) **Physical power** – the power of superior force. This is not usually used in organisations, but you might recognise elements of it, for example, in the armed forces or prison service – or in cases of physical intimidation or harassment at work.

(b) **Personal power** – the personal charisma and popularity of a particular individual.

(c) **Position power** – the power associated with a particular job or position in the organisation. As well as delegated authority, this may include power from:

  (i) Access to information

  (ii) Access to other powerful people and groups in the organisation

  (iii) Control over rules and procedures, conditions of working and other influential factors

(d) **Resource power** – control over resources which are valued by others. Managers, for example, control promotions and pay; trade unions control the availability of labour. (Think of strike action.) The amount of a person's power depends on how far he or she controls the resource, how much the resource is valued by others, and how scarce it is.

(e) **Expert power** – possessing knowledge and expertise which is recognised and needed by others. Many people in organisations have no direct line authority over operational functions, and have to rely on expert power to influence operational managers in matters which fall within their specialist area. For example, a personnel manager has no direct authority over sales staff, but when disciplinary action is required in the sales department, the personnel manager may have more influence than the sales manager, because of his or her training and experience in this area. This is sometimes called **staff authority**. If it is formalised in the organisation, so that the personnel manager (say) is responsible for disciplinary action in all departments of the organisation, this is called **functional authority**.

Activity 8 **(10 minutes)**

What kind of authority – line, staff or functional – do the managers have to secure compliance with their wishes in the following cases?

(a) The chief accountant tells the production manager that she would like a report on the production department's expenditure on raw materials and wages.

(b) The production director tells the production manager that he would like the production department's shift-working changed to a more efficient system.

(c) The personnel director tells the production director that she would like the production department's shift-working changed to something less stressful to the staff.

4.4 Conflict

One of the managerial roles that Mintzberg outlined was that of disturbance or conflict handling. Conflicts exist between individuals, groups and departments; between workers and management; between different levels of management; between different plants within the same company and between different companies.

Definition

Organisational conflict arises from behaviour intended to obstruct the achievement of some other person's goals.

Some people consider that conflict is **avoidable,** caused by disruptive elements (troublemakers) and detrimental to organisational effectiveness. Others take the view that conflict is **inevitable,** part of change, caused by structural factors, for example the class system, and is useful (in small doses) if constructively handled.

The '**happy family' view** presents organisations as **essentially harmonious.**

(a) They are co-operative structures, designed to achieve agreed common objectives, with no systematic conflict of interest.

(b) Management power is legitimate.

(c) Conflicts are **exceptional** and arise from aberrant incidents, such as misunderstandings, clashes of personality and external influences.

This view implies a **unitary perspective** of the organisation. With the unitary approach, the organisation is viewed as a team with a common source of loyalty, one focus of effort and one accepted leader. Conflict can be explained, for example, by bad management, lack of leadership, poor communications, personality clashes or the work of agitators.

In contrast, **the conflict view,** or pluralistic approach to work organisations, sees conflict among competing sub-groups as inevitable. Members battle for limited resources, status, rewards and professional values. Organisational politics involve constant struggles for control, and choices of structure, technology and organisational goals are part of this process. Individual and organisational interests will not always coincide. Management has to create a workable structure for collaboration, taking into account the objectives of all the stakeholders in the organisation.

Conflict can be managed in different ways.

(a) **Avoidance** – one party may recognise that a conflict exists but choose to withdraw from it or to suppress it – hoping that it will go away. This style involves putting problems on hold, invoking slow procedures to stifle the conflict and using secrecy to avoid confrontation. The clarification and continual refinement of goals and objectives, role definitions and performance standards will help to avoid misunderstandings and conflict.

(b) **Smoothing** emphasises the areas of agreement and common goals and glosses over disagreements. Avoidance and smoothing tend to perpetuate a *status quo*.

(c) **Compromise** means agreeing in part with the other person's view or demand. No one wins and no one loses. This type of conflict-handling orientation involves negotiation, looking for deals and trade offs and finding satisfactory or acceptable solutions. Unfortunately it also has a slightly negative tone because it assumes that the parties involved have given up something and therefore that neither is completely happy with the outcome.

(d) **Confrontation/collaboration** – in this approach differences are openly confronted and the issues are analysed as objectively as possible. It is characterised by a problem-solving stance and involves searching for integrative solutions that go beyond just accommodating different points of view.

(e) **Forcing** is a way of pushing one's own view on others – forcing a submission from the other party. The individuals who are in conflict will try to use their own power base to achieve a result that is favourable to them regardless of the impact this may have on others. This involves the creation of a win-lose situation. A cartoon example shows a chairperson calling for a vote by stating 'All in favour say **yes** and all opposed say **I resign**'.

Activity 9 **(15 minutes)**

Look at the following situations and decide which type of conflict handling style would be most appropriate.

(a) When potential disruption outweighs the benefits of resolution

(b) When issues are more important to others than yourself – to satisfy others and maintain co-operation

(c) To merge insights from people with different perspectives

(d) When opponents with equal power are committed to mutually exclusive goals

(e) To allow subordinates to develop by learning from mistakes

(f) When an issue is trivial, or more important issues are pressing

(g) When quick decisive action is vital (eg in emergencies)

(h) When you perceive no chance of satisfying your concerns

(i) To gain commitment by incorporating concerns into a consensus

(j) When harmony and stability are especially important

(k) When others can resolve the conflict more effectively

(l) On important issues where unpopular actions need implementing (eg in cost cutting, enforcing unpopular rules, discipline)

(m) When goals are important, but not worth the effort or potential disruption of more assertive modes

(n) To find an integrative solution when both sets of concerns are too important to be compromised

(o) When your objective is to learn

(p) To achieve temporary settlements to complex issues

5 FRAMES OF REFERENCE FOR LEADERSHIP ACTIVITIES

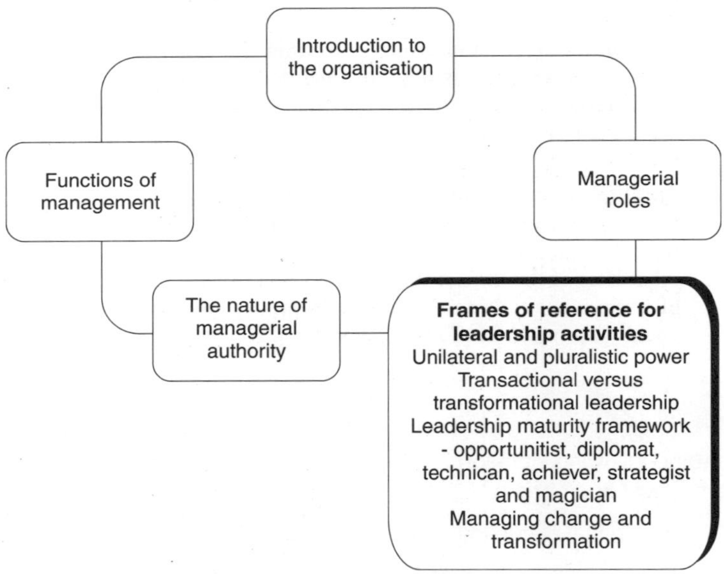

5.1 Unilateral and pluralistic power

As we have already noted, power is the capability of doing or affecting something. It implies the ability to influence others. In its most general sense power denotes either the ability (exercised or not) to produce a certain occurrence or the influence exerted by a person, through whatever means, over the conduct of others in intended ways.

We can talk about two kinds of power: 'Unilateral Power'- where one person controls another, and 'Pluralistic Power' – where each person influences the other, resulting in 'give and take.'

Unilateral power – is power based on a system of rewards or punishments. Examples of sources of organisational power include structure, formal authority, rules and regulations, control of the decision-making process, control of resources and technology and control of information or knowledge.

Pluralistic power – describes a system in which the right to make decisions is divided among different specialists. Power is distributed through social structures, although some individuals may have more power than others. Individual power reflects a degree of influence, rather than a state of domination.

The major beliefs of pluralism are:

(a) Resources and hence potential power are widely scattered throughout society;

(b) Some resources are available to nearly everyone;

(c) No one is all-powerful – an individual or group that is influential in one realm may be weak in another.

Pluralistic leaders believe and are committed to leadership that reaches all constituents, accepting all people for who they are and what they bring to the situation. They have vision and values that support diversity across all dimensions, working to eliminate discrimination and having an ethical commitment to the fair treatment of all.

5.2 Transactional versus transformational leadership

Effective leadership is crucial for any organisation. But as we all know, there are different types of leaders using different types of power. Some abuse their positional power; others have an ability to draw on their own sense of personal powerfulness; most vary in their talent of drawing the best from their people.

Transactional leadership – is familiar to us all. It is based on legitimate authority within the bureaucratic structure of the organisation. The emphasis is on the clarification of goals and objectives, tasks and outcomes and rewards and punishment. Followers are motivated by the leaders' promises, praise and reward or, they are corrected by negative feedback, reproof, threats, or disciplinary actions. Predominantly, transactional leaders rely on organisational power – they are interested in control, in outputs and in performance.

Transformational leadership – is differentiated from transactional leadership in that transformational leaders do more than set up simple exchanges or agreements. Transformational leaders – the leaders who really touch others lives and transform them totally – are charismatic and inspiring, and they create excitement at work. By virtue of the nature of their relationship with followers, they motivate others to do more than they originally intended, more than they thought possible, and to move beyond self-interest and focus on the larger goals of the group or organisation.

The difference between transformational leadership and transactional leadership is given in the table below.

Transactional leadership	Transformational leadership
Clarify goals and objectives and the focus is on short term	Establish long-term vision
Focus on control mechanisms	Create a climate of trust
Solving problems	Make people solve their own problems by empowerment
Maintain status quo or improve current situation	Change the current situation. Every threat is seen as an opportunity
Plan, organise and control	Train, coach, counsel and mentor people
Guard and defend existing culture	Change culture

Transactional leadership	Transformational leadership
Positional power exercised	Power comes from relationships and influencing people. The pressure exerted is subtle and has greater finesse.

The best of leadership is both transformational and transactional. Transformational leadership augments the effectiveness of transactional leadership; it does not replace transactional leadership.

5.3 Leadership maturity framework

The leadership maturity framework (sometimes called the leadership development framework) was developed by Bill Torbert and Susan Cook-Greuter to address the question of 'how can persons develop the capabilities required to exercise transforming power?' This developmental model describes progressive changes, or transformations in how a person interprets events, or 'makes-meaning' of the world. It reveals six stages of human development and shows that these stages unfold in sequence and that later stages may only be arrived at by journeying through earlier stages. Once a stage has been experienced it becomes a permanent part of a person's repertoire. At each stage people make sense of their world in fundamentally and subtly different ways. How they make sense then goes on to impact how they behave – how their 'action logic' is shaped.

The six stages are opportunist, diplomat, expert, achiever, strategist and magician. The characteristics of each stage of development are outlined below.

(a) *Opportunist*

The opportunist is characterised by a **strong reliance on power** that is authoritarian, hierarchical, and inflexible, focussing on immediate needs and opportunities and seeking short-term advantage. Opportunists use **unilateral power** to get from life what they want. They see the world as a series of confrontations or battles. The outside world is to be mastered, defeated, or subjected. They have very short time horizons, are manipulative and deceptive, reject feedback, externalise blame, are mistrustful, have fragile self-control, use hostile humour, flaunt power and sexuality, view rules as loss of freedom, punish according to 'an eye for an eye' and treat what they can get away with as legal. Self-interest and self needs rule the opportunist's world view.

(b) *Diplomat*

The diplomat is characterised by a strong reliance on **pluralistic power** ie, **power through consent**, displaying socially expected behaviour and trying to be 'nice' and cooperative. He or she fears breaking rules and any sort of conflict and provides social glue, seeks conformity, belonging, loyalty and pleasant low stress relationships.

(c) *Expert*

The expert believes in the **'right way' to do things**, seeking to develop own **skills and expertise** to become a 'craft master'. He or she values efficiency over effectiveness, consistency, incremental improvement and perfection.

Experts are interested in problem solving, seek causes, are critical of self and others based on craft logic, accept feedback only from 'objective' craft masters, see contingencies and exceptions, want to stand out and be unique and have a sense of obligation to a wider, internally consistent moral order.

(d) *Achiever*

Achievers seek effectiveness and results through **application of strategies, plans and actions** – breaking rules if necessary. They work towards given goals – feel like initiators, but are more likely to take on given goals than self-create. They see the future as vivid and inspiring, appreciate complexity but try to minimise it, seek reasons for action, set high standards for themselves and others, seek feedback and feel guilt if they fail to meet these standards. Achiever stage managers look for the most direct route through problems, their tendency is always to seek to clarify and simplify.

(e) *Strategist*

The strategist enjoys complexity inherent in people's differing worldviews and capabilities, delighting in paradoxes, anomalies and unique events. He or she **sees the big picture** and holds long-term perspective and values integrity, principles and freedom in creating positive change. Strategists seek to harness diversity, they are guided by deeply held principles within a personal moral code, see the world as a dynamic of inter-related processes and relationships and play many roles in these. Key to these principles and built on the understanding of the relativity of viewpoints is the desire for mutuality and an inclusive rather than exclusive order of things. An important principle is that the use of power should tend towards inclusion and mutuality – that each individual should be given opportunities to self-maximise. The strategist is engaged in striving to comprehend the worldviews of others and to engage in participative, rather than unilateral, meaning-making. This in turn leads to an inclusive way of operating in the world based upon inquiry.

Strategists can equally quickly re-frame circumstances in order to transform action. When Brian Keenan was held hostage in Beirut he went on hunger strike to stop one of his captors physically beating him. This was a way of reframing the situation so that he gave himself power from his previous totally disempowered position.

(f) *Magician*

The focus of the magician is **transformation of society, organisation and self**. He or she seeks common good, enjoys interplay of purposes, actions and results and seeks the motivational challenge of each situation in its uniqueness. Magicians appreciate polarities and acknowledge the ongoing relation between them (dark and light). They are illusive, chameleon-like and may be powerful but may possibly be saddened by the inevitability of paradox in human affairs.

Gandhi, more than any other person in the 20th century developed a new mechanism of social change – non-violent protest. Faced with grave injustices he sought to develop resistance based upon honourable principles. In the face of the prevailing orthodoxy he taught the dispossessed that they held power – moral power to do what was right and that, with courage they could succeed. By making himself vulnerable as a leader in non-violent protests and on hunger strikes he helped make the unthinkable – non-violence in the face of extreme violence – thinkable.

5.4 Managing change and transformation

We can make a distinction between change and transformation. Change is gradual and small, whereas transformation is change on a significant scale.

Change, in the context of organisation and management, could relate to a number of matters:

(a) Changes in the **environment**: these could be changes in what competitors are doing, what customers are buying, how they spend their money, changes in the law, changes in social behaviour and attitudes, and economic changes.

(b) Changes in the **products** the organisation makes, or the services it provides: these are made in response to changes in customer demands, competitors' actions and new technology.

(c) Changes in **technology** and changes in **working methods**: these changes are also in response to environmental change such as the advent of new technology and new laws on safety at work.

(d) Changes in **management** and **working relationships**: for example, changes in leadership style, and in the way that employees are encouraged to work together. Also changes in training and development.

(e) Changes in **organisation structure or size**: these might involve creating new departments and divisions, greater delegation of authority or more centralisation, changes in the way that plans are made, management information is provided and control is exercised, and so on.

Organisational transformation includes major changes in structure, procedures and jobs. Transformation in the way the system operates involves major changes in communication patterns and working relationships and processes. Transformation in employee consciousness involves major changes in the way that things are viewed, involving shifts in attitudes, beliefs and myths.

Leaders of change recognise shifts in the environment and guide their organisation to be responsive to those changes. They take the initiative, anticipate and recognise changes and begin to explore possible courses of action to respond to those changes.

Rooke (1998) argues that only managers at the strategist stage of development and later, can steer transformational change in organisations. Managers at earlier stages would either not see the need, or seeing it, would not have the inclusive frame-making ability to realise it. The strategist stage manager inquires by asking questions such as: 'How do you see this?' 'What sense can we make of it?' 'How would you like to proceed?' 'Can we view this in a different way?' 'What can we learn from that experience?' and so on. They can quickly re-frame circumstances in order to transform action.

Chapter roundup

- An organisation is a social arrangement for the controlled performance of collective goals.
- The structure of an organisation establishes how work is allocated and controlled; how people and activities are grouped together; and the channels through which authority and communication are distributed within the organisation.
- The functions of management traditionally include: planning, organising, commanding, co-ordinating and control. More people-centred approaches prefer the terms 'leadership' and 'motivation' to 'commanding' and add functions such as communication. In business organisations, the overall function of management is economic performance.
- A manager's job is not clear-cut and systematic in practice. Managers must be prepared to switch between a number of roles. Mintzberg classified managerial roles as interpersonal, informational and decisional. (If you want to remember the ten roles, you might try the following mnemonic, using the first letter of each: Few Likely Leaders Make Dull Speeches, Especially During Reward Negotiations!)
- Authority is the right of someone to perform a task. It is bestowed formally by virtue of election, position or delegation. Authority may be delegated by one individual or team to another, but only within the scope of their own authority and on the understanding that they remain responsible for the results.
- Authority must be distinguished from power, which may come from informal sources such as charisma and knowledge.
- The Leadership Maturity Framework reveals six stages of human development and describes progressive changes, or transformations in how a person interprets events, or 'makes-meaning' of the world. The six stages are opportunist, diplomat, expert, achiever, strategist and magician.

Quick quiz

1 Why might people band together to form organisations?

2 What is an informal organisation?

3 Give three examples of things that identify an organisation's culture.

4 Why is management necessary for an organisation?

5 What is the management function of 'control'?

6 What is delegation?

7 Give an example of (a) physical power, (b) expert power and (c) resource power.

8 What is (a) line authority, (b) staff authority and (c) functional authority?

9 List Mintzberg's 'decisional' roles of a manager.

Answers to quick quiz

1 To achieve personal and organisational goals and to fulfil personal needs.

2 An informal organisation is a loosely structured, flexible and spontaneous group, such as colleagues who have lunch together.

3 Assumptions, beliefs and values, self image, style.

4 To plan, organise, direct, co-ordinate, control.

5 To plan and monitor activities and correct any deviations.

6 The passing of tasks and responsibilities for which, the manager remains accountable.

7 (a) The army or prison service
(b) A personnel manager's knowledge of employment legislation
(c) Management's control over pay awards.

8 (a) That of a manager over subordinates

(b) Advice/services offered by a specialist

(c) Authority over policies or procedures that affect all departments of the organisation.

9 Entrepreneur, disturbance-handler, resource allocator, negotiator.

Answers to activities

1 The boys have identified three major functions of their business (sales, repairs and quality control) and two main product areas (guitars and drums). They might decide to structure the business in the following ways.

(a) Have one 'general manager' (whose responsibilities may include quality control) and three 'operatives' who share the sales and repair tasks.

(b) Divide tasks by function: have one person in charge of sales, one quality controller and two repairers (perhaps one for drums and one for guitars).

(c) Divide tasks by product: have a two-man drums team (who share sales/repair/ control tasks between them) and a similar guitars team.

Since there are only four individuals, each (we assume) capable of performing any of the functions for either of the products, the lads may decide to have a looser social arrangement. They may prefer to discuss who is going to do what, as and when jobs come in. A larger organisation would not have this luxury ...

2 Corporate objectives might be formulated for:

(a) Profitability

(b) Market standing (being a leader in the market, in relation to competition, and/or having a good reputation)

(c) Productivity (efficient use of resources)

(d) Innovation (new product development)

(e) Public responsibility (involvement in community affairs, compliance with regulations eg on pollution or safety and so on)

3 Fayol's functions would define the activities: 1 = controlling; 2 = planning; 3 = commanding; 4 = co-ordinating; 5 = organising.

4 The plans Dial-a-Video Limited propose are a strategy to exploit the 'art movie' market segment. A programme for the build-up of the distribution. The £4 charge is a tactic or policy. The 'no-tips' plan is a rule or regulation.

5 Some possibilities include: communicating, leading, inspiring, motivating, empowering, influencing/persuading, role-modelling, representing, peace-making, challenging…brainstorm on!

6 Your answer may well be that the cinema manager takes on all of Mintzberg's roles, although (a)(i) and (c)(iv) play a very minor part in his day.

7 To aid delegation, the organisation could:

(a) Increase the perceived 'quality' of staff through selection and training, so the manager can have greater confidence

(b) Encourage open communication, through organisation culture ('It's good to talk!') or mechanisms such as meetings; if information is freely available to staff and the manager is aware of what is going on, the manager can have more confidence in the staff's decisions and his or her own control

(c) Ensure that efficient control systems are in place, so that results are monitored at all levels: the 'risks' attached to delegation are lessened

(d) Make delegation part of the organisation culture by setting the example at senior management level, and by rewarding effective delegation with praise, pay or promotion

8 Your answer should be similar to ours. Managers secure compliance using:

(a) Functional authority. (The chief accountant is likely to have a formal entitlement to this information, for the benefit of organisational control. It falls within her specialism of financial control, despite having to be prepared by the production department.)

(b) Line authority (within a department, down the chain of command).

(c) Staff authority. (The Human Resources director is unlikely to have any jurisdiction in the production department in such a matter – although her advice, as an expert in human resource management, may carry some weight.)

9
(a) Avoidance
(b) Smoothing
(c) Confrontation
(d) Compromise
(e) Smoothing
(f) Avoidance
(g) Forcing
(h) Avoidance
(i) Confrontation
(j) Smoothing
(k) Avoidance
(l) Forcing
(m) Compromise
(n) Compromise
(o) Soothing
(p) Compromise

Chapter 2:

THE DEVELOPMENT OF MANAGEMENT THOUGHT

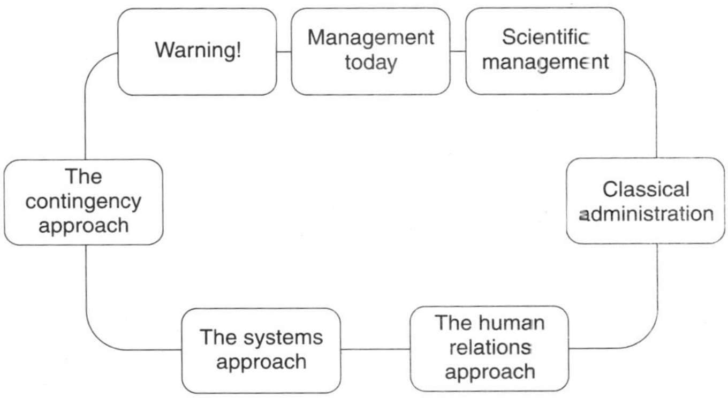

Introduction

In Chapter 1, we looked at the nature of management and managerial authority. We now look at some of the ideas people have formulated about what it is to be a manager. You will find that managers and writers on management have, over the years, come up with different ideas about how organisations work and what is necessary in order for them to be as efficient and effective as they can be. We look briefly at the five main strands of thinking – the hallmarks of which you may identify in the principles and techniques covered in the rest of this Course Book – and at some of the current 'fashions' in management and organisation.

Your objectives

In this chapter you will learn about the following:

(a) The principles of the scientific management, classical, bureaucratic, human relations and contingency schools of thought

(b) The organisation as an open socio-technical system

(c) Trends in modern management practice, including flexibility, multi-skilling, teamworking and empowerment

(d) The contribution of different schools of management thought

(e) Current trends in management thought

1 SCIENTIFIC MANAGEMENT

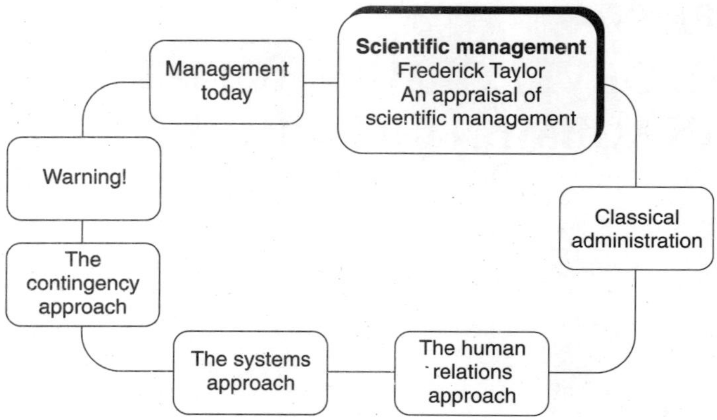

1.1 Frederick Taylor

Frederick W Taylor (1911) was among the first to argue that management should be based on 'well-recognised, clearly defined and fixed principles, instead of depending on more or less hazy ideas'. He pioneered the '**scientific management**' movement which suggested that systematic investigation could indicate 'proper' methods, standards and timings for each operation in an organisation's activities. The responsibility of management was to select, train and help workers to perform their jobs 'properly'. The responsibility of workers was simply to accept the new methods and perform accordingly.

The practical application of this approach was to break each job down into its smallest and simplest component parts or 'motions': each single motion in effect became a separate, specialised 'job' to be allocated to a separate worker. Workers were selected and trained to perform such jobs in the most efficient way possible, eliminating all wasted motions or unnecessary physical movement.

A summary of scientific management, in Taylor's own words, might be as follows.

(a) 'The man who is fit to work at any particular trade is unable to understand the science of that trade without the kindly help and co-operation of men of a totally different type of education.'

(b) 'It is one of the principles of scientific management to ask men to do things in the right way, to learn something new, to change their ways in accordance with the science and in return to receive an increase of from 30% to 100% in pay.'

How well received do you think Taylor's comments would be by the workers in a modern factory?

1.2 An appraisal of scientific management

Alterations to poor work methods and inefficient movements are used today, both to increase productivity and to reduce physical strain on workers. However, it has now been recognised that performing only one 'motion' within a job is profoundly unsatisfying to workers: operations need to be re-integrated into whole jobs. It has also been recognised that workers can and should take more responsibility for planning and decision-making in connection with their work, as we will see later in this chapter.

Looking back on scientific management as an approach, Hicks writes: 'by the end of the scientific management period, the worker had been reduced to the role of an impersonal cog in the machine of production. His work became more and more narrowly specialised until he had little appreciation for his contribution to the total product... Although very significant technological advances were made... the serious weakness of the scientific approach to management was that it de-humanised the organisational member who became a person without emotion and capable of being scientifically manipulated, just like machines'.

Definition

> A **job** is a grouped set of tasks allocated to a given worker.

FOR DISCUSSION

'The job is an historical artefact. Put simply, it was created about 200 years ago to carry out the tasks required by the emerging industrial and commercial sectors. These activities could easily be "boxed up" and given to separate workers. Workers with jobs needed supervisors to watch over them, who in turn needed managers watch over them, creating a hierarchy of responsibility and skills...

It wasn't a very efficient world. There were always things that fell between the job boxes and didn't get done. It was a world that was good at making things, but not good at manipulating information.' (Bridges (1995))

In today's world, where manipulating information is the primary business activity, and traditional jobs are often too inflexible to keep up with constant changes in tasks and skills, what personnel policies do you think need to be put in place to (a) efficiently utilise and (b) protect the interests of the 'de-jobbed' worker?

Scientific management was concerned primarily with tasks and techniques, but it was an early attempt to address the need for more controlled performance, in response to the increasing pace of change and industrial development in the Western world. A more balanced set of principles for management and organisation was put forward by the founders of modern organisation: the 'classical' school.

2 CLASSICAL ADMINISTRATION

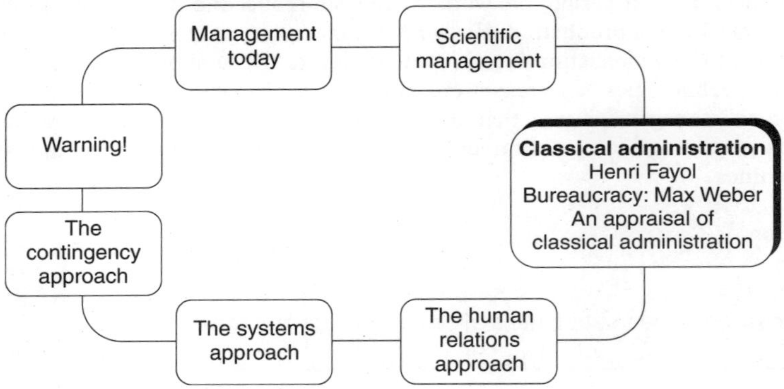

2.1 Henri Fayol

Henri Fayol (1841–1925) was a French industrialist who put forward and popularised the concept of the 'universality of management principles': in other words, the idea that all organisations could be structured and managed according to certain rational principles. Fayol himself recognised that applying such principles in practice was not simple: 'Seldom do we have to apply the same principles twice in identical conditions; allowance must be made for different changing circumstances.' Among his principles of rational organisation, however, were the following influential ideas.

(a) **Division of work**, or specialisation. The most effective performance could be obtained by organising activities according to the expertise or resources required – allowing people, in effect, to 'stick to what they do best'. This encouraged functional organisation structures, with separate departments responsible for production, marketing, distribution and so on.

(b) **Matched authority and responsibility**. Managers should be given the authority or official 'right' to carry out the tasks assigned to them. They should always be held responsible for the exercising of that authority.

(c) **The scalar chain of command**. This is a term used to describe a formal organisation structure with a hierarchy from the highest to the lowest rank. Authority passes down the chain, as superiors give orders and instructions to subordinates: subordinates report back up the chain to their superiors. This creates the traditional view of the organisation structure as a pyramid-shaped chain or tree, as depicted in Figure 2.1.

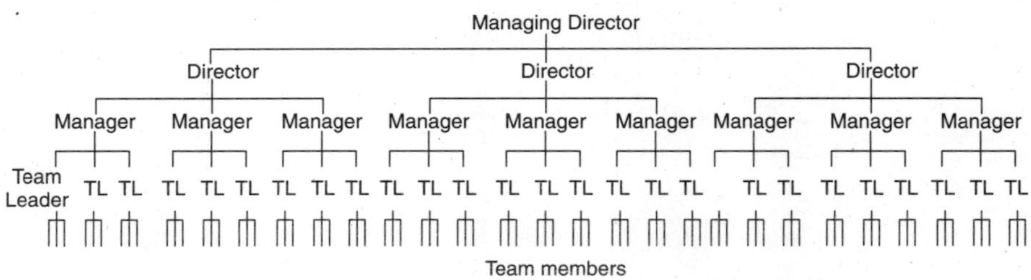

Figure 2.1 Organisation chart

(d) **Unity of command**. For any given activity, a subordinate should receive orders from only one boss. Overlap between departments, or missing out a link in the scalar chain causes uncertainty and wasted effort. Similarly, as far as the organisation is concerned, there should be unity of direction: one head and one plan for each area of activity, so that sub-units of the organisation are not pulling in different directions.

(e) **Subordination of individual interests**. The interest of one employee or group of employees should not prevail over the general interest of the organisation.

Fayol also emphasised the qualities of discipline (or outward signs of respect), equity (fairness, or justice towards employees), 'esprit de corps' (unity and a sense of belonging in the workforce) and initiative, which he thought should be encouraged and developed to the full.

Activity 1 **(10 minutes)**

Borderline Computers use project teams to carry out research, deal with customer needs and to introduce new systems. Identify which of Fayol's principles would clash with this method of working.

2.2 Bureaucracy: Max Weber

The sociologist, Max Weber (1947) developed the notion of bureaucracy. It is similar to Fayol's in its concern with hierarchy, but also develops the idea that the best way to secure efficient administration is to design procedures to reduce individual initiative.

Weber regarded an organisation as an authority structure. He was interested in why individuals obeyed commands, and he identified three grounds on which legitimate authority could exist.

(a) **Charismatic leadership**: a leader has some special power or attribute and expects personal, sycophantic devotion from staff and followers.

(b) **Traditional, or patriarchal leadership**: authority is bestowed by virtue of hereditary entitlement, as in the family firm, or the monarchy.

(c) **Bureaucracy**: authority is bestowed by dividing an organisation into jurisdictional areas (production, marketing, sales and so on) each with specified duties. Authority to carry them out is given to the officials in charge, and rules and regulations are established in order to ensure their achievement. Leadership is therefore of a 'rational-legal' nature: managers get things done because their orders are accepted as legitimate and justified.

Weber specified several general characteristics of bureaucracy, which he described as 'a continuous organisation of official functions bound by rules'.

(a) **Hierarchy**: each lower office is under the control and supervision of a higher one.

(b) **Specialisation and training**: there is a high degree of specialisation of labour. Employment is based on ability, not personal loyalty.

(c) **Impersonal nature**: employees work full time within the impersonal rules and regulations and act according to formal and impersonal procedures.

(d) **Professional nature of employment**: an organisation exists before it is filled with people. Officials are full-time employees, promotion is according to seniority and achievement; pay scales are prescribed according to the position or office held in the organisation structure.

(e) **Rationality**: the 'jurisdictional areas' of the organisation are determined rationally. The hierarchy of authority and office structure is clearly defined. Duties are established and measures of performance set.

(f) **Uniformity** in the performance of tasks is expected, regardless of whoever is engaged in carrying them out.

(g) **Technical competence** in officials, which is rarely questioned within the area of their expertise.

(h) **Stability** – it is stable partly because of its rigid adherence to its rules and procedures and the chain of command, but this rigidity also makes it:

- Very slow to respond to customer/consumer demands
- Very slow to respond to change in its business environment - new technology, competitors, market trends
- Very slow to learn from its mistakes

2.3 An appraisal of classical administration

Many organisations continued to be managed on the 'rational' lines of classical theory. However, as we shall see in Sections 5 and 6 of this chapter, such organisations have certain drawbacks.

The fast-changing business environment of the late 20th century made it very difficult for classical organisations to compete. Flexibility and innovation began to challenge stability; diversity began to challenge 'universal', 'one-size-fits-all' principles of management; multi-skilled project teams were seen to be more responsive to consumer demands than specialised, one-man-one-boss structures; the scalar chain of command was decimated by 'delayering' in response to economic recession and other forces.

Nevertheless, classical thinking allowed practising managers to step back and analyse their experience in order to produce principles and techniques for greater efficiency and effectiveness.

In the 1930s, scientific management was heavily criticised for dehumanising workers and treating them like a mere cog in the machine of production. This reflected not just a more enlightened philosophy of work, but a renewed understanding that organisations are made up of people – not just functions. By robbing the worker of any sense of contribution to the total product or task, the organisation was losing out on an important source of energy and creativity. A new approach set out to redress the balance.

3 THE HUMAN RELATIONS APPROACH

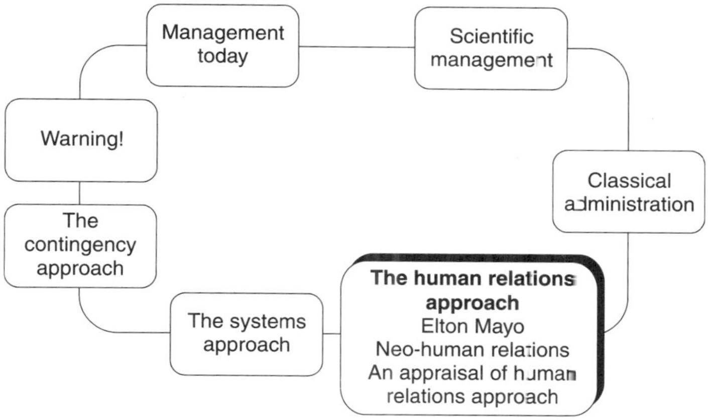

3.1 Elton Mayo

The 'human relations' approach emphasised the importance of human attitudes, values and relationships for the efficient and effective functioning of work organisations. Its pioneer, Elton Mayo (1975) wrote: 'We have thought that first-class technical training was sufficient in a modern and mechanical age. As a consequence we are technically competent as no other age in history has been, and we combine this with utter social incompetence.'

Early work focused on the idea that people need companionship and belonging, and seek satisfaction in the social relationships they form at work. This emphasis resulted from a famous set of experiments (the Hawthorne Studies) carried out by Mayo and his colleagues for the Western Electric Company in the USA. The company was using a group of girls as 'guinea pigs' to assess the affect of lighting on productivity: they were astonished to find that productivity shot up, whatever they did with the lighting. Their conclusion was that: 'Management, by consultation with the girl workers, by clear explanation of the proposed experiments and the reasons for them, by accepting the workers' verdict in several instances, unwittingly scored a success in two most important human matters – the girls became a self-governing team, and a team that co-operated wholeheartedly with management.'

3.2 Neo-human relations

Mayo's ideas were followed up by various social psychologists – including Maslow, Herzberg and McGregor – who emphasised that people have more than merely physical and social needs. Attention shifted towards their 'higher' psychological needs for growth, challenge, responsibility and self-fulfilment. Herzberg suggested that only these things could positively motivate employees to improved performance: work relationships and supervisory style, along with pay and conditions, merely ward off dissatisfaction (and then only temporarily). Only the itself could provide lasting satisfaction, and Herzberg, in particular, concentrated on ways of designing jobs for greater worker satisfaction.

This phase was known as the neo-human relations school.

Definitions

> **Job enlargement** is a way of increasing the satisfaction available in a job by adding tasks, for greater variety and interest.
>
> **Job enrichment** is a way of increasing the satisfaction available in a job by adding responsibility and challenge, for greater scope and involvement.

3.3 An appraisal of the human relations approach

The human relations approach contributed an important awareness of the influence of the human factor at work on organisational performance (and particularly in the work group) and the need to offer job satisfaction to employees. Most of its theorists attempted to offer guidelines to enable practising managers to satisfy and motivate employees and so, theoretically, to obtain the benefits of improved productivity.

However, the approach tends to emphasise the importance of work to the workers without really addressing the financial issues: there is still no proven link between job satisfaction and motivation, or either of these and productivity, or the achievement of organisational goals. Employee counselling (prescribed by Mayo) and job enrichment (prescribed by Herzberg) have, for example, both proved at best of unpredictable benefit to organisations applying them in practice.

> **Activity 2** **(10 minutes)**
>
> Think of any job you have had. How important were the 'human factors' for you in this job? Were you motivated by something else such as money or achievement?

FOR DISCUSSION

Peter Drucker (1993) warned that human relations thinking could manipulate workers just as effectively as bureaucratic rules, dictatorial management or scientific management techniques. It could be used as 'a mere tool for justifying management's actions, a device to 'sell' whatever management is doing. It is no accident that there is so much talk in Human Relations about "giving workers a sense of responsibility" and so little about their responsibility, so much emphasis on their "feeling of importance" and so little making them and their work important.'

Do you think managers only pay lip service to 'enlightened' human relations approaches? If so, why?

As we have seen, early theorists saw the organisation primarily as a structure of tasks and authority which could be drawn in an organisation chart. But that is like a snapshot of an organisation, showing what it looks like frozen at a particular moment in time. In fact, organisations are neither self-contained nor static: they are open systems.

4 THE SYSTEMS APPROACH

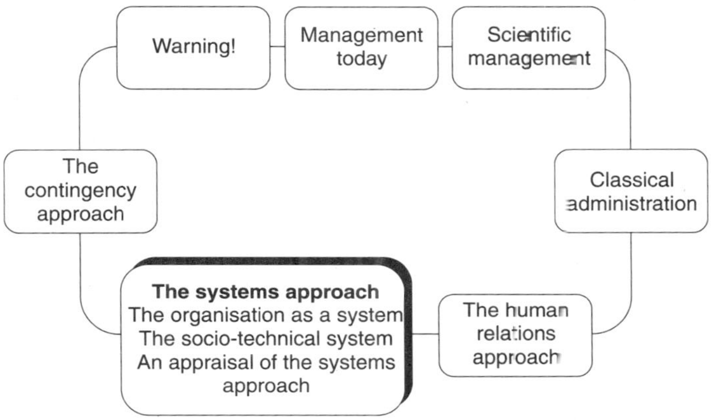

4.1 The organisation as a system

The systems approach to organisations was developed at the Tavistock Institute of Human Relations in the 1950s, although General Systems Theory was pioneered in the 1930s.

There is no universally accepted definition of a system, but it can be described as 'an entity which consists of interdependent parts'. Every system has a 'boundary' which defines what it is: what is 'inside' and what is 'outside' the system. Anything outside the system is said to be its 'environment'.

In systems theory, it is possible to have a closed system, which is shut off from the environment and independent of it. An open system, however, is one which is connected to and interacts with its environment. It takes in influences from the environment and itself influences the environment by its activities, Figure 2.2.

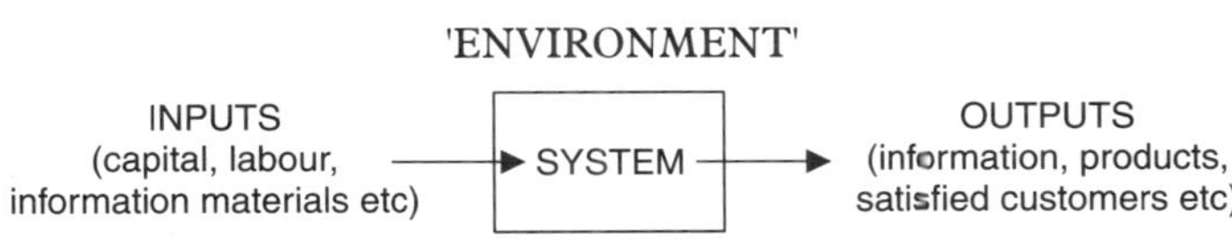

Figure 2.2 An open system

Organisations are open social systems. Why? They are social systems because they are comprised of people. They are open systems because those people participate in other social systems in the environment (such as the family or the class system) and bring with them all sorts of influences from the environment: advertising messages, family pressures, government demands (eg for tax), social attitudes and so on. In addition, the organisation itself takes in a wide variety of inputs, or resources, from the environment, and generates outputs to it as a result of its activities.

Activity 3 **(45 minutes)**

Apply the systems approach to a bank, by completing the table below. You can then try the same approach with an organisation that you have worked for.

Inputs from the environment	Organisational structure/ methods of operation	Outputs to the environment
1 Customers' expectations	1 Financial advisers	1 Business start-up loans
2 Interest rates	2	2 Security of savings
3	3	3
4	4	4
5	**Technology**	5
	1 Cashpoint machines	
	2	
	3	
	4	
	Social structure and individual psychologies	
	1 Job security	
	2	
	3	
	4	
	Management control system	
	1 Policies on staff dishonesty	
	2	
	3	
	4	
	Organisation's goals	
	1 Maximising profits	
	2	
	3	
	4	

4.2 The socio-technical system

The systems approach also emphasises the existence of sub-systems, or parts of the bigger system.

Trist and Bamforth (1951) developed an approach which suggested that an organisation can be treated as an open 'socio-technical' system. That is, a system consisting of at least three sub-systems:

(a) A **structure,** (division of labour, authority relationships and communication channels)

(b) A **technological system** (the work to be done, and the techniques and tools used to do it)

(c) A **social system** (the people within the organisation, the ways they think and interact with each other)

These sub-systems are linked and the system design and management must find a 'best fit' between the needs of the social and technical sub-systems.

Technology does not determine organisation: decisions can and must still be made about job and task design, work place layout and other factors, so that the needs of people (not to be isolated from other workers, to find some meaning or satisfaction in the job) can be met. For example, telephone banking is a new way of banking but the technology does not define how to organise a telephone banking operation. If the use of telephone headsets, and the lack of person-to-person contact with customers, tends to isolate bank workers, other means of meeting their social needs – such as team meetings or opportunities for social interaction during work breaks – might be provided.

Andrew Mayo (1998) argues that today's 'knowledge-based' organisations – where 'products' are knowledge, communication and innovation, and whose chief asset is therefore the knowledge, experience and creativity of its members – are supremely socio-technical systems. He suggests a system diagram which illustrates the organisation's task of **managing knowledge** (Figure 2.3).

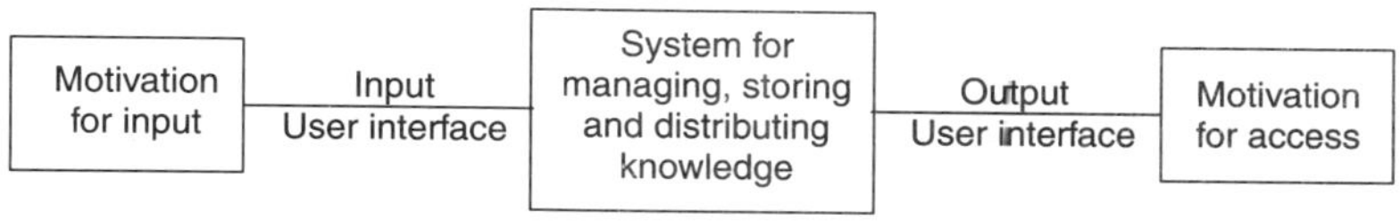

Figure 2.3 Knowledge-management as a socio-technical system

4.3 An appraisal of the systems approach

Looking at the organisation as a system helps managers to remember that:

(a) The organisation is not a static structure as conventional organisation charts suggest: it is continuously reacting to internal and external changes

(b) Sub-systems of the organisation each have potentially conflicting goals which must be integrated, often with some compromise

(c) An awareness of the environment of the organisation (including competitor activity, technological change and customer needs) is vital if the organisation is to survive

Activity 4 **(10 minutes)**

Below are a number of statements. Indicate whether they apply to the systems approach. Mark alongside T for True or F for False.

(a) The organisation is static.

(b) People, technology, organisation structure and environment are equally important in the systems approach.

(c) All sub-systems are in complete agreement.

(d) It is important that all employees are happy in their work.

(e) The organisation is aware of change affecting business.

(f) There is interdependence between all aspects of the organisation.

Once you see the organisation as a system, it becomes clear that there can be no 'one best way' to design and manage such dynamic and varied processes. This is where 'contingency theory' comes in.

5 THE CONTINGENCY APPROACH

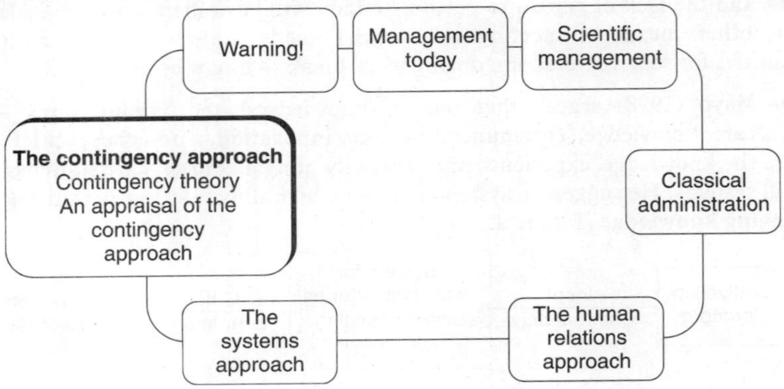

5.1 Contingency theory

The contingency approach to organisation developed as a reaction to the idea that there are 'universal principles' for designing organisations, motivating staff and so on. Newer research indicated that different forms of organisational structure could be equally successful, that there was no inevitable link between classical organisation structures and effectiveness, and that there were a number of variables to be considered in the design of organisations and their style of management. Essentially, 'it all depends' on the total picture of the internal factors and external environment of each organisation. Managers have to find a 'best fit' between the demands of:

(a) The tasks
(b) The people
(c) The environment

in their own particular situation.

We will note contingency approaches to various aspects of management as we proceed through this module.

5.2 An appraisal of the contingency approach

Management writer Tom Lupton (1963) noted that:

'It is of great practical significance whether one kind of managerial 'style' or procedure for arriving at decisions, or one kind of organisational structure, is suitable for all organisations, or whether the managers in each organisation have to find that expedient that will best meet the particular circumstances of size, technology, competitive situation and so on.'

Awareness of the contingency approach will be of value in:

(a) Encouraging managers to identify and define the particular circumstances of the situation they need to manage, and to devise and evaluate appropriate ways of handling them;

(b) Encouraging responsiveness and flexibility to change.

Activity 5 **(30 minutes)**

Cobble and Carter is an accountancy practice. The partners now find that their present, highly bureaucratic methods of organisation are unsatisfactory. Customer needs are wide and varied, decision making is too slow and the staff are becoming demotivated. The partners now have to consider changing their methods to overcome the present difficulties and have decided to use a new approach. This would involve partners being responsible for various companies and they would be assisted by small teams.

(a) Give three advantages if they adopt this approach.

(b) Identify three areas they would need to consider and investigate before making a final decision.

6 MANAGEMENT TODAY

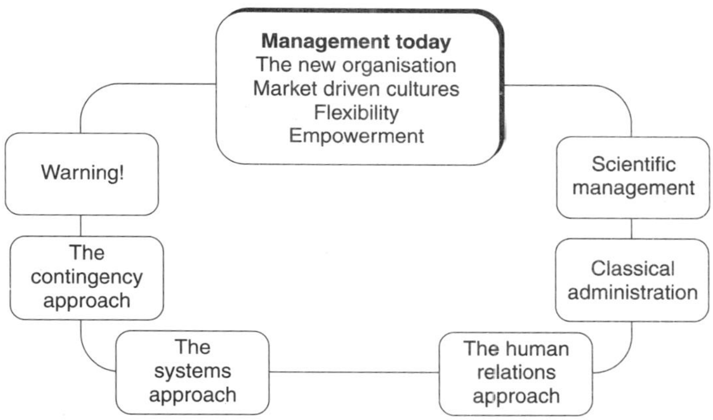

6.1 The New Organisation

In the past, the adoption of classical management principles meant that organisations developed the following characteristics.

(a) **Hierarchical** control through the chain of command.

(b) **Tall structure** with many layers of management and close supervision at each level.

(c) **Single function specialisms** like production and sales, with departments and careers concentrated in these single areas.

(d) **Focus on tasks and responsibilities** within well-defined jobs (as laid out in formal job descriptions) rather than on more flexible concepts such as customer service or using initiative.

(e) **Systems** which were reactive and procedure-bound ('sticking to the rules').

However, the economic downturn or recession, experienced across the world in the late 1980s and early '90s, reduced demand for many organisations' goods and services. This reduced the ability of organisations to carry superfluous staff (people who in Japan are known as 'window-watchers'), under-developed and under-utilised. It also created buyers' markets, where the power was on the side of the consumer, who could take their business elsewhere if their needs were not being met.

Meanwhile, the problems associated with the management and performance of large classical organisations were highlighted: such organisations were incapable of the kind of flexibility and responsiveness required in constantly-changing, customer-driven markets.

Nowadays:

(a) **Everything is international** – thanks to travel and information technology, we work in what has been described as a 'global village', with a global economy and marketplace

(b) **Everything is new** – organisations have come to appreciate that they are unlikely to survive unless they are responsive to the changing – and more demanding – expectations of their customers

(c) **Everything is faster** – you can order a tailor-made Toyota from a Tokyo car showroom and have it delivered 24 hours later

(d) **Everything is turbulent** – there is no going back to the peace and quiet of organisational stability in a world of slow social and technological change. Organisations must continue to cope with an essentially chaotic environment

The New Organisation involves structures and cultures which can adapt swiftly to change and respond flexibly to customer demands.

6.2 Market-driven cultures

In the New Organisation values and cultures have changed.

From 'protective' to 'productive'.

Workers are encouraged to believe that, ultimately, they work for their customers, not their bosses. Instead of seeing themselves as performing functions, following procedures or holding down jobs, they are urged to focus on the task objectives, and issues such as quality, innovation, customer care and 'added value'.

Definition

Added value is an accounting term for the difference between the cost of raw materials and the sales price of the finished product: in other words, the value that is perceived to have been added to inputs by processing within the organisational system.

There is a focus on ends rather than means – so the means can be as flexible as the ends require.

From competitive individualism to teamwork and co-operation

Individual differences and self-interest are (theoretically) submerged in the focus on collective goals and objectives. This is partly possible because individuals' own needs are (theoretically) being satisfied by the increased challenge, responsibility and autonomy at work.

The basic work units of organisations have traditionally been specialised functional departments. In the New Organisation, they are more likely to be small, flexible teams. '**Chunking**' is a term coined to describe the breaking up of the organisation into smaller, more autonomous, more responsive, units.

Teamworking allows work to be shared among a number of individuals, so it gets done faster than by individuals working alone, without people:

(a) Losing sight of their 'whole' task, or

(b) Having to co-ordinate their efforts through lengthy channels of communication.

A team may be called together temporarily, to achieve specific task objectives (a project team), or may be more or less permanent, with responsibilities for a particular product, product group or stage of the production process (a product or process team).

FOR DISCUSSION

We have used the word 'theoretically' about the benefits of team spirit. Do you think people basically 'look after Number 1', even within a close-knit team culture?

We will look more closely at teamworking below, and in detail in Chapter 11.

From security to flexibility

Workers are being taught to thrive on loose job descriptions, career mobility, continuous learning, training and retraining and so on. Recognition of organisations' need for constant innovation and creativity in order to keep pace with change has led to the development of the concept of the learning organisation.

A learning organisation culture encourages:

(a) Continuous learning and knowledge generation at all levels
(b) The free exchange and movement of knowledge around the organisation
(c) The transformation of new knowledge into new action

This is not just about individual creativity, learning and development: it embraces the idea of groups – and the organisation as a whole – learning together. It also implies the involvement of all members, at all levels of the organisation, in the business of learning and developing in ways required by the market environment.

EXAMPLE

A middle ranking execugtive was called to the office of Tom Watson, the founder of IBM. The executive had lost IBM $10,000,000 on some ill-advised venture. When the executive offered his resigation, Tom Watson retorted, 'You must be joking. I've just spent $10,000,000 educating you.'

As we have seen, the new cultural values are directed towards flexibility, co-operation and seeing the 'big picture'. We will now look at ways in which managers can organise for flexibility in its labour resource.

6.3 Flexibility

Re-integration of jobs

In the New Organisation, jobs are changing from simple, well-defined tasks (set out in job descriptions) to more flexible, multi-dimensional work. This new approach recognises that:

(a) Performing a whole meaningful job is more satisfying to a worker than performing only one of its component tasks (as in 'scientific' job design)

(b) Allowing workers to see the big picture enables and encourages them to contribute information and ideas for improvements, which might not otherwise have come to light

(c) The focus on the task and overall objectives reduces the need for tight managerial control and supervision over work processes and practices

Multi-skilling

Multi-skilling is the opposite of specialisation, with its tendency towards rigid job descriptions and demarcation lines between one job and another. It involves the development of versatility in the labour force, so that individuals can perform more than one task if required to do so: workers are being encouraged, trained and organised to work across the boundaries of traditional jobs and crafts. This has been difficult to achieve historically, because craft and occupational groups (such as trade unions) have supported demarcation in order to protect jobs and maintain special skills, standards and pay differentials. This situation is changing now that multi-skilled, flexible labour is highly prized in today's labour market.

The benefits of multi-skilling to the organisation are as follows.

(a) It is an efficient use of manpower.

  (i) It smoothes out fluctuations in demand for different skills or categories of worker.

  (ii) It may be possible to maintain a smaller staff, because you would not need specialists in each skill area.

(b) It puts an end to potentially costly demarcation disputes, where one category of worker objects to others 'invading' their area of work, as defined by narrow job descriptions.

(c) On the other hand, it is less likely that a task will be left undone because it does not explicitly appear on anybody's job description.

Activity 6 **(10 minutes)**

What does multi-skilling offer the employee?

Flexible working

In the New Organisation there is also increased flexibility in the deployment of the labour resource. With the shrinking demand for some categories of labour, ideas about full employment, full-time employment, 'one man, one job' and the '9 to 5' working day have had to be revised. When the demand for labour drops (permanently, seasonally or at random), organisations may be faced either with overmanning and idle time – or with having to lay people off or make them redundant. There are various ways of avoiding this.

(a) The employment of people on **short- or fixed-term contracts**, or annual hours contracts (an agreement of the number of hours to be worked per year instead of per day or week).

(b) The employment of **non-permanent, non-career labour**. This was a major growth sector in the 1980s and the trend seems to be continuing. Part-time work, casual labour, temporary working ('temping'), freelancing and consultancy are popular options, both for the workers and for the organisations who benefit from their services without long-term contractual obligations.

(c) **Flexitime**. Typically, the working day is split into two time zones: a 'core time', when employees must be at their job (commonly 10.00 to 16.00 hours) and a flexible time at the beginning or end of the day, when it is up to the employee to choose which hours to work. Employees may be asked to work a certain number of hours per day ('arrive late, work late'), or per week ('day off, make up the hours'). Annual hours and term-time contracts (allowing parents time off during school holidays) are even more flexible versions of the system.

Activity 7 **(10 minutes)**

Suggest three advantages to the organisation and to the worker of implementing a flexitime system.

FOR DISCUSSION

How flexible are you ready to be when it comes to:

(a) Specialising in a particular knowledge or skill area in your career?
(b) Having full-time, long-term employment?
(c) Doing more training and learning throughout your working life?

6.4 Empowerment

Definition

Empowerment is the current term for making workers (and particularly work teams) responsible for achieving, and even setting, work targets, with the freedom to make decisions about how they are to be achieved. (In France, empowerment is called '*responsibilisation*'.)

Empowerment goes hand in hand with:

(a) **Delayering,** since responsibility previously held by middle managers is, in effect, being given to operational workers;

(b) **Flexibility**, since giving responsibility to the people closest to the product and customer encourages responsiveness – and cutting out layers of communication, decision-making and reporting speeds up the process;

(c) **New technology**, since there are more 'knowledge workers' in the New Organisation. Such people need less supervision, being better able to identify and control the means to clearly understood ends. Better information systems also remove the mystique and power of managers as possessors of knowledge and information in the organisation.

FOR DISCUSSION

'The people lower down the organisation possess the knowledge of what is going wrong with a process but lack the authority to make changes. Those further up the structure have the authority to make changes, but lack the profound knowledge required to identify the right solutions. The only solution is to change the culture of the organisation so that everyone can become involved in the process of improvement and work together to make the changes.' (Max Hand).

What does this suggest about the changes needed in the function of managers?

The change in organisation structure and culture as a result of empowerment can be shown as in Figure 2.4.

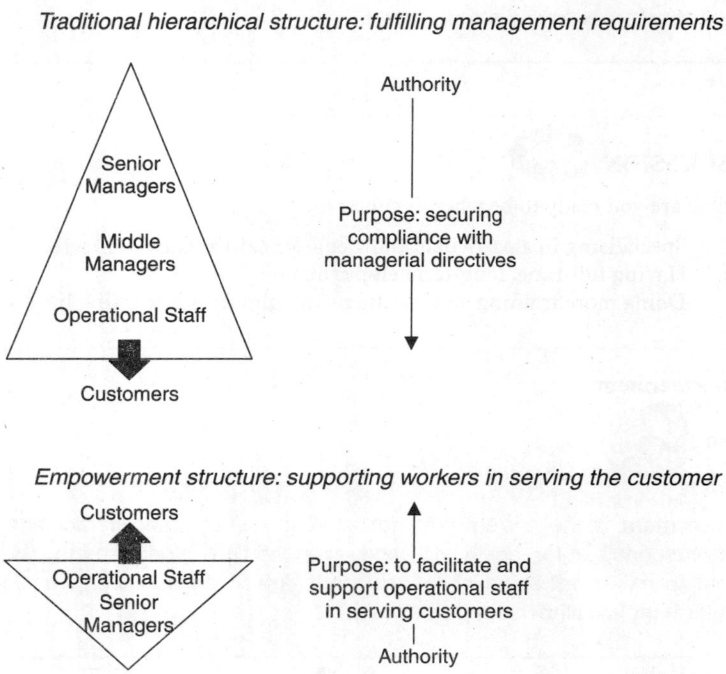

Figure 2.4 Hierarchical and empowerment structures

Activity 8 **(30 minutes)**

Semco is a Brazilian company which makes pumps, dishwashers and cooking units. The company has attracted enormous media and business interest. Here's why.

(a) All managers are rated by their subordinates every six months, on a scale of 1 to 100. Those managers who consistently under-perform are squeezed out.

(b) Workers elect their own boss: 'In a plant where everyone has a financial stake in its success, the idea of asking subordinates to choose bosses seems an eminently sensible way to stop accidents before they are promoted.'

(c) Workers set their own salaries – but they know they might price themselves out of the department's budget if they aim too high.

(d) The workers decide how much of the profits to share and how much to re-invest in the business.

(e) Workers are encouraged to work from home.

(f) Everyone 'from the cleaner upwards' has access to the company's books.

Semco's boss, Ricardo Semler, believes that democracy has been introduced to the work place: this is a radical departure from 'classical' organisation theory, but at a time when firms like IBM are being overtaken by smaller, more flexible competitors, his ideas are gaining currency. 'The trouble is that the corporate world is run by people not exactly busting keen to lose their parking lots, let alone to subject themselves to monthly scrutiny by people whom, currently, they can hire and fire. Even corporate turkeys don't vote for Christmas.' (Victor Keegan, *The Guardian*).

Compare Semco with a typical 'classical' organisation.

Read points (a) to (f) again and list how the classical organisation would deal with each.

EXAMPLE

The validity of this view and its relevance to modern trends appears to be borne out by the approach to empowerment adopted by Harvester restaurants, as described in *Personnel Management*. The management structure comprises a branch manager and a 'coach', while everyone else is a team member. Everyone within a team has one or more 'accountabilities' (these include recruitment, drawing up rotas, keeping track of sales targets and so on) which are shared out by the team members at their weekly team meetings. All the team members at different times act as 'co-ordinator' – the person responsible for taking the snap decisions that are frequently necessary in a busy restaurant. Apparently, all the staff involved agree that empowerment has made their jobs more interesting and has hugely increased their motivation and sense of involvement.

7 WARNING!

This chapter has to conclude with a caveat about the danger of reading too much into changes which, when one looks at them carefully, apply to only a small minority of organisations (albeit a highly visible minority). Currently, corporate fashions dictate lean and mean structures, decentralisation of authority, autonomy for teams and a single-minded concentration on innovation and customer needs. But one might be entitled to assume (based on the evidence of the past few decades) that these are only fashions, and will not last forever. In future editions of this course book, we may well be talking about the return to impressive corporate headquarters, the folly of fragmented management, the wasting of time on 'the quality of working life' when there is little work to be had, and the way information systems empower managers for closer supervision and control! Keep your eyes and ears open – and a pinch of salt handy.

Chapter roundup

- Classical organisation and management theories emphasise issues of:
  - hierarchy and structure of authority
  - control by managers and technical specialists over workers and work
  - principles of 'good' organisation.
- Human relations approaches reacted against the impersonal rationality of classical theories and emphasised the importance of people, their relationships and attitudes at work.
- Later theories emphasised the organisation's openness to environmental influences, and its internal complexity. The organisation could be viewed as an open socio-technical system. Given this dynamic, complex nature, there could be no 'one best way to manage': the contingency approach basically says, 'It all depends ...'
- Most of the fashions in management today (including delayering, teamworking, multi-skilling, integrated job design and empowerment) are based on the need for more flexible organisation and management, in the face of change.
- Empowerment is the giving of responsibility or autonomy to workers, and specifically work teams.

Quick quiz

1. Which management theory did Frederick Taylor write about?
2. What is the principle of 'specialisation'?
3. What did the 'human relations school' recognise?
4. Draw a diagram of the organisation as an open system, listing inputs and outputs.
5. Why is the contingency approach useful?
6. What does a learning organisation culture encourage?
7. List four ways in which management can deploy the employee resource more 'flexibly'.

8 What are the benefits of multi-skilling to the organisation?

9 Why is empowerment particularly appropriate for teams?

Answers to quick quiz

1 Scientific management

2 Organising activities according to the expertise or resources required

3 The importance of people and their needs at work

4 'ENVIRONMENT'

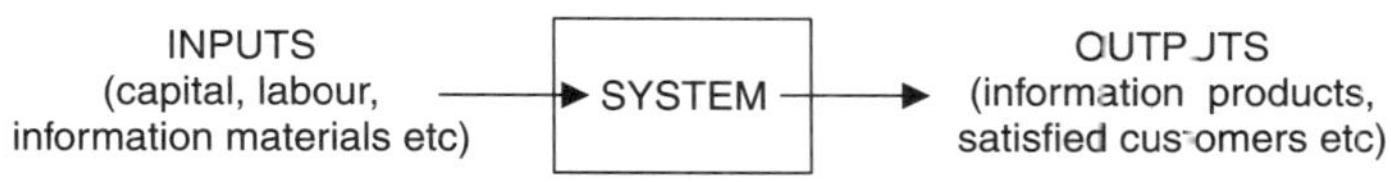

5 It encourages the organisation to be flexible

6 Continuous learning and knowledge at all levels

7 Short-or fixed term contracts; using part-time, casual or temporary labour; flexitime; freelance workers

8 It smoothes out fluctuations in demand for different skills. It is possible to employ smaller numbers. It ends demarcation disputes

9 They are totally involved in improvement, they work together to make changes, they become more flexible and they have power to make decisions

Answers to activities

1 Borderline Computers' methods would conflict with Fayol's principles of specialisation, the scalar chain of command, and unity of command. Sticking to those principles would prevent rapid decision-making and communication and reduce the efficiency of the teams' performance.

2 The answer will be individual to each one of you as you consider the human factors in a job. It is important to recognise that people do have different dominant needs: McClelland defined these as the needs for power, affiliation and achievement. Maslow said your dominant need would be the one which was currently unfulfilled. Thus, it is not enough to say that people pay most attention to human factors at work, although these are clearly important, as Mayo's work demonstrated.

3 Systems approach ideas for a bank might include the following.

Inputs from the environment:	exchange rates, government incentives to businesses, regulation of independent financial advisers.
Organisational structure etc:	flattening hierarchies, Saturday opening, overdraft arrangements.
Technology:	computerisation, home banking, left-handed cheque books.
Social structure etc:	staff mortgages, defined career paths, fast-track graduates.

Management control system:	trade unions, performance related pay, managers' power.
Organisation's goals:	improved public image, customer service focus, careful investment.
Outputs to the environment:	ethical investments, interest rates, employment.

4 Systems approach methods, applied to the given statements (True or False), are as follows. (a) F; (b) T; (c) F; (d) F; (e) T; (f) T.

5 Your answer, concerning Cobble and Carter's proposed change from the classical approach, should have included some of the following.

(a) The advantage of the new approach is that they would be able to respond to different companies in relevant and effective ways. Decision making would be quicker. The smaller teams would feel more responsible for their work, thus increasing motivation. With the improved efficiency, cost savings would be increased.

(b) They would need to consider staffing levels and redeployment, a logical division of customers, the specialist knowledge required, limits of authority and costs.

6 The erosion of rigid specialisation and fragmented job design can offer:

(a) A higher degree of job satisfaction, through variety of work and a greater understanding of its purpose and importance

(b) Job security and material benefits, since a versatile, flexible employee is likely to be more attractive to employers, and have a higher value in the current labour market

(c) Personal skill development

7 Benefits to the organisation include: improved staff morale (because of flexibility); less stressed/distracted staff (because problems outside work can be solved without the guilt attached to lateness); less absenteeism (because of the 'I'm late for work: I'd better not go at all' syndrome).

Benefits to the workers include: less frustration in rush-hour commuting; less pressure over needs like the dentist or school sports days; time to shop, socialise etc in off-peak times; satisfaction of choice.

8 Under the classical system (a): managers would be appraised by their managers; (b) managers would be appointed by the board or senior management; (c) salary levels would be set by top management; (d) this would be decided by the board/senior management; (e) this would not be encouraged (lack of management control); (f) not likely! Trade Union officials may be given information prior to wage negotiations.

Part B

Organisational Structure and Culture

Chapter 3:
ORGANISATIONAL STRUCTURE

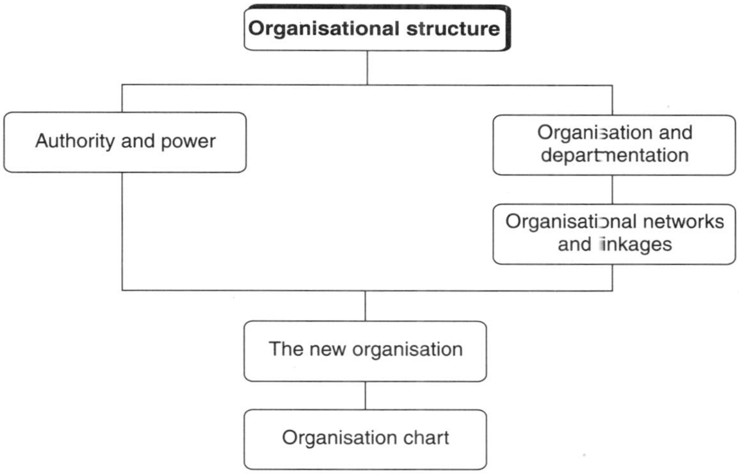

Introduction

In Chapter 1, we introduced the organisation, in general terms, as 'social arrangements for the controlled performance of collective goals'. We suggested that those social arrangements were formalised in an organisation structure. In this chapter, we look in more detail at what that involves.

Your objectives

In this chapter you will learn about the following:

(a) The nature of and influences on both formal and informal organisation

(b) Different organisation structures and networks, and organisation charts

1 ORGANISATIONAL STRUCTURE

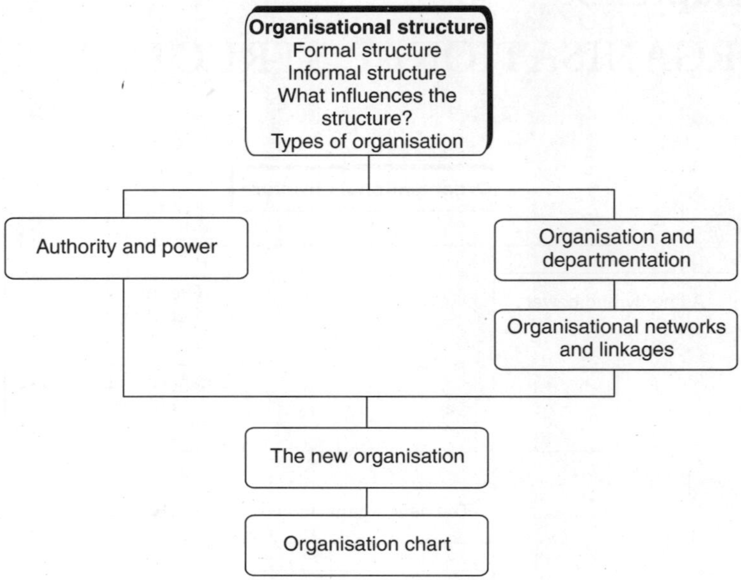

1.1 Formal structure

In Chapter 1, we noted that the formal organisation structure is deliberately constructed to fulfil specific goals. The following table will help to refresh your memory, as well as help you begin to think about your own work or study organisation in terms of its structure.

Objective of organisation structure	Reason	Your organisation
To link individuals in an established network of relationships	So that authority, responsibility and communications can be controlled.	There will be individuals in certain roles in your organisation who you have to deal with regularly in order to do your job. Can you identify them?
To group together the tasks required to fulfil the objectives of the organisation as a whole, and to allocate them to suitable individuals or groups	This must be appropriate – it may be done on the basis of function (sales, production, accounting and so on), geographical area (regional sales territories, for example), product or product type.	What departments exist in your organisation? Why?

Objective of organisation structure	Reason	Your organisation
To allocate to individuals or groups the authority they require to perform their functions, as well as the responsibility to account for their performance to their superiors	This creates a hierarchy or chain of command, whereby authority flows downwards from senior management (a chief executive, managing director or board of directors) to each level of the organisation, and your accountability flows back up.	Can you identify the levels of authority in your own department? Who is your immediate superior, to whom you are responsible for your work? To whom is that person accountable?
To co-ordinate the objectives and activities of separate units	So that overall aims are achieved without gaps or overlaps in the flow of work.	What other departments or areas of the organisation do you have to liaise with regularly?
To enable the flow of work, information and other resources through the organisation, via clear lines of co-operation and communication	So that all the different parts of the organisation are able to meet their objectives.	Where do you get the information and resources you require to do your job? To whom do you supply information and resources in return?

Formal structure is discussed in detail in Sections 2-4 of this chapter.

1.2 Informal structure

Because organisations are made up of people, there is also an informal organisation, the network of relationships, communication and ideas that links people. This is a loosely structured, flexible and spontaneous form of organisation, which alters according to its membership at any given time.

The informal organisation is made up of:

(a) People who form social groups or cliques, or temporary networks, communication or alliances, colleagues who get together over coffee, or e-mail each other at work

(b) Informal customs and ways of getting things done which become unwritten rules or 'the way we do things round here'. (This is why newcomers have to 'learn the ropes' from established members.)

(c) Informal channels of communication (sometimes called the 'grapevine') which by-pass official channels. This is often faster than official communication, though less accurate

The informal organisation always exists alongside the formal structure. Informal methods may supplement and improve aspects of formal organisation, by-passing communication blockages, for example, or speeding up procedures, as well as giving employees the satisfaction of interpersonal relationships.

However, if employees are dissatisfied with aspects of the formal organisation (for example, they feel they never get enough information or they dislike their bosses) the informal organisation can 'take over', being relied on more and more heavily. This can begin to undermine the formal organisation, as short-cuts are taken, gossip abounds and cliques gain power. Managers need to try and harness the informal organisation's power, by encouraging the flow of information, initiative and constructive work relationships – in pursuit of shared performance goals.

1.3 What influences the structure?

(a) Its **size**. As an organisation gets larger, its structure gets more complex: specialisation and subdivision are required. The process of controlling and co-ordinating performance, and communication between individuals, also grows more difficult as the 'top' of the organisation gets further from the 'bottom', with more intervening levels.

(b) Its **task**, ie the nature of its work. Structure is shaped by the division of work into functions and individual tasks, and how these tasks relate to each other. Depending on the nature of the work, this can be done in a number of ways (discussed in Section 3 below). The complexity and importance of tasks will affect the amount of supervision required, and so the ratio of supervisors to workers.

(c) Its **staff**. The skills and abilities of staff will determine how the work is structured and the degree of autonomy or supervision required.

(d) Its legal, commercial, technical and social **environment**. One example is the way new technology is reducing overall staff requirements by increasing specialisation.

(e) Its **age** – the time it has had to develop and grow: whether it is very set in its ways and traditional, or experimenting with new ways of doing things and making decisions.

(f) Its **culture and management style** – how willing management is to delegate authority at all levels, whether teamwork is favoured, or large, impersonal structures are accepted by the staff.

You may have recognised a 'contingency approach' to organisation structure (see Chapter 2 if you need to refresh your memory). Organisations can be very different from each other, according to their circumstances, and different structures may – as we will see later – be appropriate. Let's look briefly at some of the ways in which organisations differ.

1.4 Types of organisation

The business organisation and its owners

One way of classifying business organisations is by their *legal status* and *ownership*.

(a) A **sole trader** is a person carrying on a business: a greengrocer, say, or a hairdresser. The **law does not make any distinction** between the individual and the business: the individual's own money can be used to settle business debts.

(b) A **partnership** is a group of individuals carrying on a business by agreement: a medical or legal practice, say. As with the sole trader, the law does not distinguish between the 'partners' and the 'business'.

(c) A **public sector organisation** is owned by the state. Most state organisations (such as National Health Service Trusts) are financed by public funds (mainly via taxation), and exist to provide cost-efficient services.

(d) A **limited company is a separate legal entity or 'person' in its own right**: it may, in its own name, acquire assets, incur debts and enter into contracts. The company is owned by **shareholders** who have invested in it by purchasing shares, and is **controlled** on their behalf by the **managers** of their company. Normally, the shareholders are not personally liable for the debts of the business.

Types of business activity

How many **organisations** can you think of? Here are a few examples.

(a) A newsagent's shop
(b) A hospital
(c) A school
(d) A business that manufactures soap powder
(e) A business that builds power stations
(f) A chain of supermarkets
(g) A firm of solicitors
(h) A charity
(i) A hotel
(j) A warehousing and distribution firm
(k) A regional development agency

Activity 1 **(15 minutes)**

Continue our list of organisations from (l) to (z). Try to make your examples as varied as you can.

There are many different types of business activity. Some organisations make and build things, others sell and distribute things, while others offer information and services.

Type of business activity	Examples	What do they do?
Manufacturers	Makers of soap powder	They buy in raw materials and components, and co-ordinate labour, machinery and processes to convert these into more complex components or finished products, which can then be sold.

Type of business activity	Examples	What do they do?
Contractors	Builders of power stations, designers of information systems	They are brought in to carry out operations or projects for clients, according to the terms of a contract or agreement about what is to be done, at what price and by what date. Contractors may make similar agreements with **sub-contractors.**
Distributors, wholesalers and retailers	Warehousing and distribution firms, newsagent's shops, chains of supermarkets	They buy things which others have made, and then sell them to customers. A **greengrocer** sells low-priced items, which perish quickly, it needs to make regular sales at fairly high volume. An **art dealer** sells extremely high-priced items, which do not perish but appreciate in value over time, to wealthy connoisseurs: its transactions may be comparatively rare.
Service organisations	Schools, hospitals, solicitors, or development agencies	They 'buy' (employ people with) knowledge and expertise, which is 'sold' to customers and clients. **Entertainment** is a service, as is the **provision of information and advice**.
Not-for-profit organisations	Charities. Public Sector Organisations	These perform a full range of business transactions, but do not have the primary aim of making money for their owners. A **charity,** for example, exists to obtain donations from the public to fund some perceived social need.

Let's now look at some of the 'nuts and bolts' of organisation structure. what gives it its 'shape'?

Activity 2 **(15 minutes)**

See if you can now list five different ways of distinguishing between different kinds of organisation.

2 AUTHORITY AND POWER

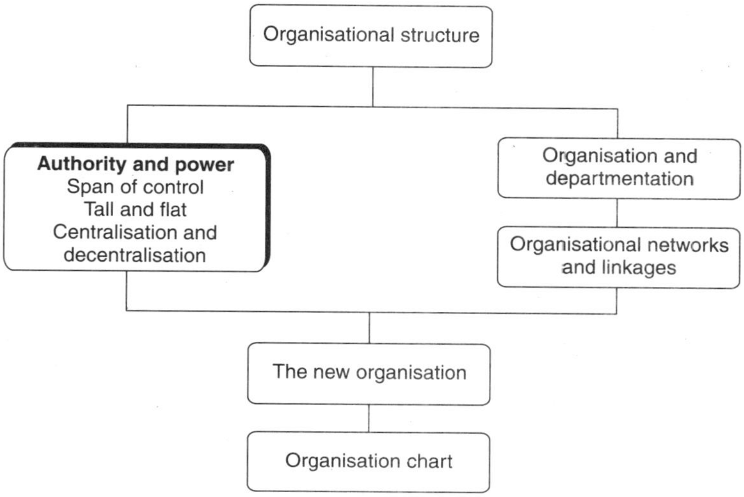

2.1 Span of control

Definition

> The **span of control** refers to the number of subordinates immediately reporting to a superior official.

In other words, if a manager has five subordinates, the span of control is five. If the span of control is too wide, the manager may not be able to supervise adequately. (S)he may spend too much time supervising and handling routine problems, and too little time on higher-level management functions/roles.

On the other hand, if the span is too *narrow*, there may be a tendency to interfere in or over-supervise the work that is delegated to subordinates.

So what is the 'right' span of control? Essentially, it all depends.

(a) A manager's **capabilities** limit the span of control. There are physical and mental limitations to any single manager's ability to control people and activities.

(b) The **nature of the manager's work load**

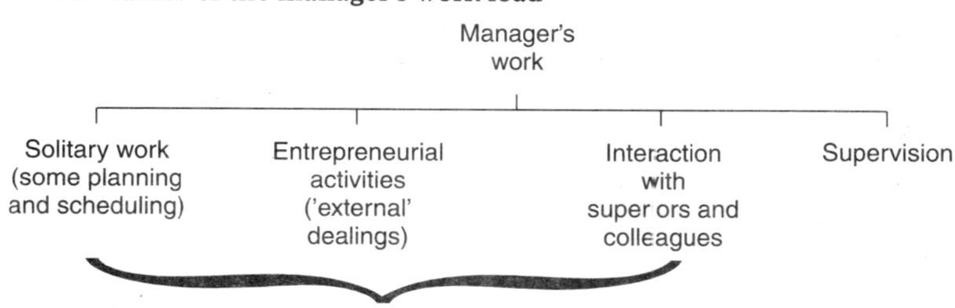

The more non-supervisory work in a manager's workload:

- The narrower the span of control
- The greater the delegation of authority to subordinates

(c) **Subordinates' work**: if all subordinates do similar tasks, or the task is substantially automated or computerised, a wide span is possible. Difficult or complex work, posing time-consuming problems suggests a narrow span of control.

(d) The degree of **interaction between subordinates.** If subordinates can help each other, a wide span is possible. However, if *close group cohesion* is desirable, a narrow span of control might be needed.

2.2 Tall and flat

The span of control concept and the scalar chain of command, or organisation hierarchy, have implications for the 'shape' of an organisation.

Definitions

> A **tall organisation** is one which, in relation to its size, has a large number of levels of management hierarchy. This implies a *narrow* span of control.
>
> A **flat organisation** is one which, in relation to its size, has a small number of hierarchical levels. This implies a *wide* span of control.
>
> **Delayering** is the reduction of the number of management levels from bottom to top.

An organisation with a narrow span of control will have more levels in its management hierarchy than an organisation of the same size with a wide span of control: the first organisation will be narrow and tall, while the second will be wide and flat. (See Figure 3.1.)

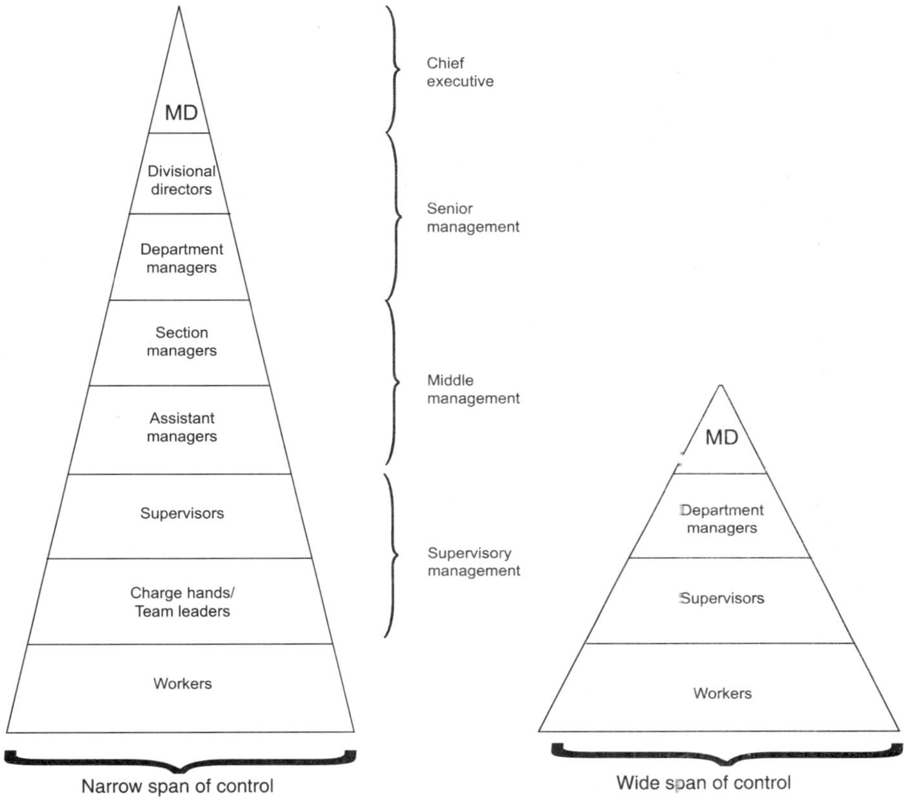

Figure 3.1 Tall and flat organisation

There are good and bad points to both tall and flat.

Tall organisation

For	Against
Narrow control spans	Inhibits delegation
Small groups enable team members to participate in decisions	Rigid supervision can be imposed, blocking initiative
A large number of steps on the promotional ladders – assists management training	The same work passes through too many hands
	Increases administration and overhead costs
	Communication problems, as decisions take time to 'filter down'.

Flat organisation

For	Against
More opportunity for delegation	Implies that jobs **can** be delegated. Managers may only get a superficial idea of what goes on. If they are overworked they are more likely to be involved in crisis management
Relatively cheap	Sacrifices control
In theory, speeds up communication between strategic apex and operating core	Middle managers are often necessary to convert the grand vision of the strategic apex into operational terms

Many organisations have recently been 'delayering.' Middle line jobs are vanishing. Organisations are increasing the average span of control, reducing management levels and becoming flatter. Why?

(a) **Information technology** reduces the need for middle managers to process information.

(b) **Empowerment.** Many organisations, especially service businesses, are keen to delegate authority down the line to the lowest possible level. Front-line workers are allowed to take decisions, which is often the best way to stay flexible and responsive to customers demands.

(c) **Fashion**. Once senior managers believe that tall structures are inflexible they seek to delayer, which convinces other senior managers!

'Tall' and 'flat essentially reflect the amount of delegation in an organisation structure. Another way of putting this is 'centralisation' and 'decentralisation'.

2.3 Centralisation and decentralisation

'Centralisation' and 'decentralisation' refer to the degree to which authority is delegated in an organisation, and therefore the level at which decisions are taken in the hierarchy.

Definitions

> **Centralisation** is the concentration of authority for making most decisions at the top levels of the organisation.
>
> **Decentralisation** is the dispersion of authority to make decisions throughout all levels of the organisation.

We can look at centralisation in two ways.

(a) **Geography**. It used to be the case in Russia that trivial decisions in the province had to be referred thousands of miles away to a Ministry in Moscow. In some firms decision might have to be constantly referred to head office. In this sense, too, office filing or photocopying might be 'centralised' in an organisation (if all the files are kept in the Filing Department, say) or decentralised (if each department stores its own files).

(b) **Authority**. Centralisation also refers to the extent to which people have to refer decisions upwards to their superiors. Decentralisation implies delegation.

The table below summarises some of the key issues.

Arguments in favour of centralisation and decentralisation			
	Pro centralisation		*Pro decentralisation/delegation*
1	Decisions are made at one point and so are easier to co-ordinate.	1	Avoids overburdening top managers, in terms of workload and stress.
2	Senior managers in an organisation can take a wider view of problems and consequences.	2	Improves motivation of more junior managers who are given responsibility-important since job challenge and entrepreneurial skills are highly valued in today's work environment.
3	Senior management can keep a proper balance between different departments or functions – eg by deciding on the resources to allocate to each.	3	Greater awareness of local problems by decision makers. Geographically dispersed organisations should often be decentralised on a regional/area basis.
4	Quality of decisions is (theoretically) higher due to senior managers' skills and experience.	4	Greater speed of decision making, and response to changing events, since no need to refer decisions upwards. This is particularly important in rapidly changing markets.
5	Possibly cheaper, by reducing number of managers needed and so lower costs of overheads.	5	Helps junior managers to develop and helps the process of transition from functional to general management.
6	Crisis decisions are taken more quickly at the centre, without need to refer back, get authority etc.	6	Separate spheres of responsibility can be identified: controls, performance measurement and accountability are better.
7	Policies, procedures and documentation can be standardised organisation-wide.	7	Communication technology allows decisions to be made locally, with information and input from head office if required.

FOR DISCUSSION

'There should be just two roles in an organisation. Either directly serving the customers, or serving the people who do, so that they can serve customers better.' (Daft, 2001). What would this kind of organisation look like? What would it be like to work for?

The power/authority structure, which shapes the organisation, is one factor in organisation design. The other is task structure or organisation itself: how are tasks (and the people who do them) grouped together.

3 ORGANISATION AND DEPARTMENTATION

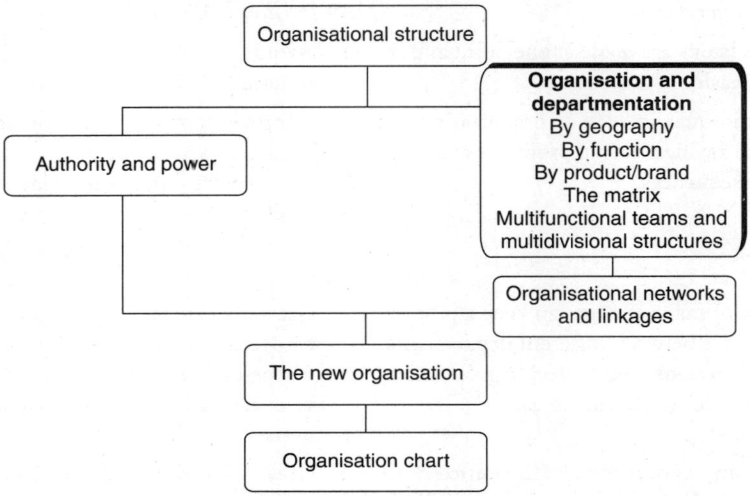

3.1 By geography

In a structure of geographical, regional or territorial departmentation, *some* authority is retained at Head Office, but day to day operations are handled on a territorial basis (eg Southern region, Western region). Within many sales departments, sales staff are organised this way (see Figure 3.2).

(a) *Advantages*

   (i) There is **local decision-making** at the point of contact between the organisation (eg a salesperson) and its customers, suppliers and other stakeholders.

   (ii) It may be **cheaper** to establish local factories/offices than to service markets from one location (eg costs of transportation and travelling may be reduced).

(b) *Disadvantages*

   (i) **Duplication** and possible loss of economies of scale might arise. For example, a national organisation divided into ten regions might have a customer liaison department in each regional office. If the organisation did all customer liaison work from head office it might need fewer managerial staff.

   (ii) **Inconsistency in standards** may develop from one area to another.

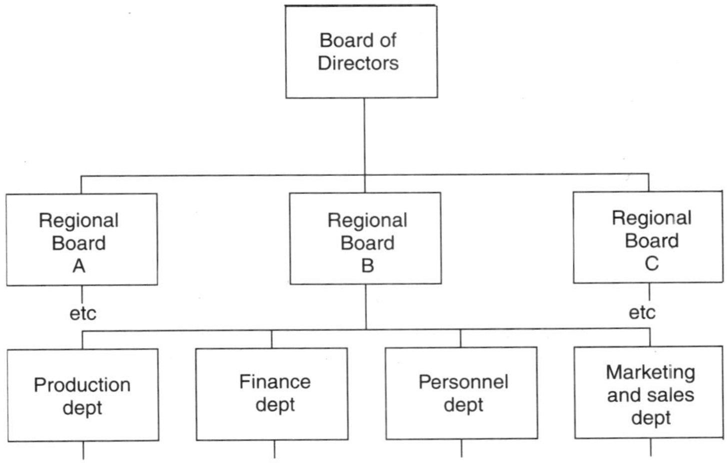

Figure 3.2 Geographic organisation

3.2 By function

Functional organisation involves grouping together people who perform similar tasks or use similar technology or materials. Primary functions in a manufacturing company might be production, sales, finance, and general administration. Sub-departments of marketing might be selling, distribution and warehousing (see Figure 3.3).

(a) *Advantages*

(i) **Expertise is pooled** and related technology/equipment/materials accessed more efficiently.

(ii) It **avoids duplication** (eg one management accounts department rather than several) and offers economies of scale.

(iii) It makes **easier** the **recruitment**, training, and motivation of professional specialists.

(b) *Disadvantages*

(i) It is organisation by inputs and **internal processes**, rather than by outputs and **customer demands**, which are what ultimately drive a business.

(ii) **Communication problems** may arise between different specialisms, with their own culture and language.

(iii) **Poor co-ordination**, may result, especially in a **tall** organisation structure. Frequent upward referrals, or inter-department meetings, need to be held.

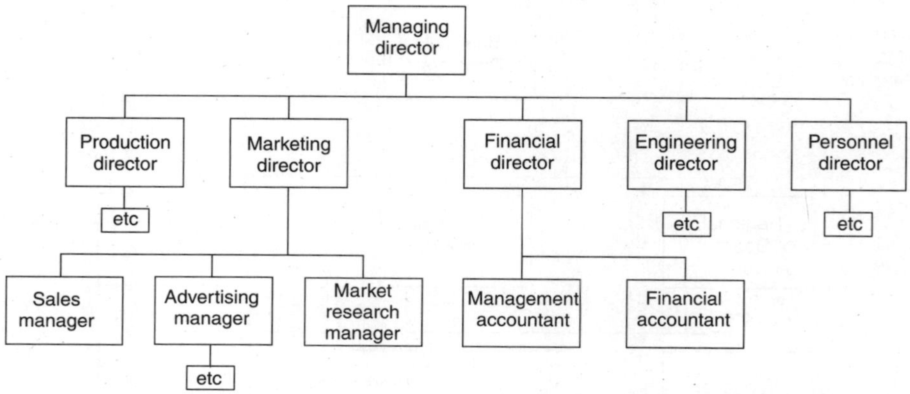

Figure 3.3 Functional organisation

3.3 By product/brand

Some organisations group activities on the basis of **products** or product lines. Some functional departmentation remains (eg manufacturing, distribution, marketing and sales) but a divisional manager is given responsibility for the product or product line, with authority over personnel of different functions. (see Figure 3.4)

(a) *Advantages*

   (i) **Accountability.** Individual managers can be held **accountable** for the **profitability** of individual products.

   (ii) **Specialisation**. For example, some salespeople will be trained to sell a specific product in which they may develop technical expertise and thereby offer a better sales service to customers.

   (iii) **Co-ordination.** The different functional activities and efforts required to make and sell each product can be co-ordinated and integrated by the divisional/product manager.

(b) *Disadvantages*

   (i) It **increases the overhead costs** and managerial complexity of the organisation.

   (ii) Different product divisions may **fail to share resources** and customers.

A brand is the name (eg 'Persil') or design which identifies the products or services of a manufacturer or provider and distinguishes them from those of competitors. (Large organisations may produce a number of different brands of the same basic product, such as washing powder or toothpaste.) Branding brings the product to the attention of buyers and creates **brand loyalty** – often the customers do not realise that two 'rival' brands are in fact produced by the same manufacturer. Brand managers may be appointed in the same way as product managers.

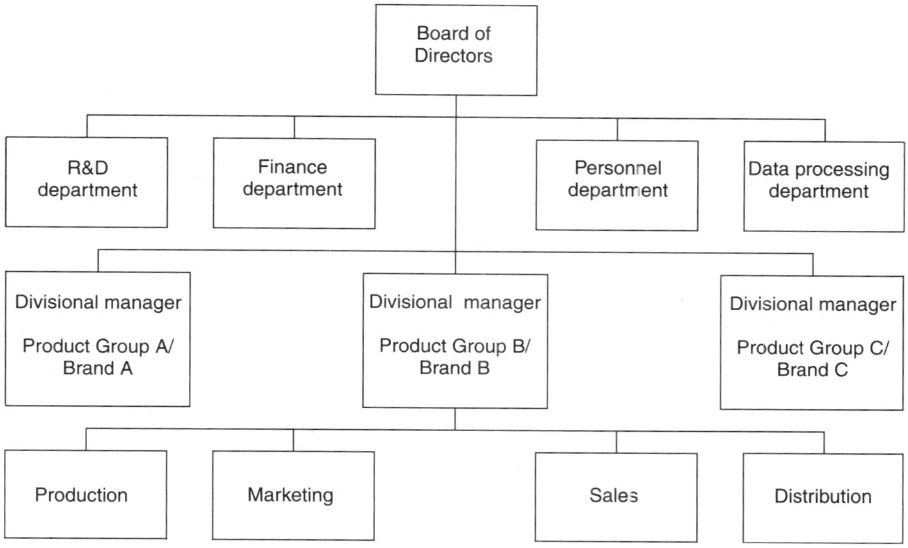

Figure 3.4 Product/brand organisation

Activity 3 **(10 minutes)**

What type of departmentation has:

(a) Central government?
(b) Independent television?
(c) Your college?

What if you could have the accountability and flexibility advantages of product/brand management, without the duplication and complexity of dividing up your functional departments? What if you could somehow share or 'cross' the two? That is where the Matrix comes in!

3.4 The Matrix

Matrix organisation 'crosses' **functional** and **product/customer/project** organisation, as shown in Figure 3.5.

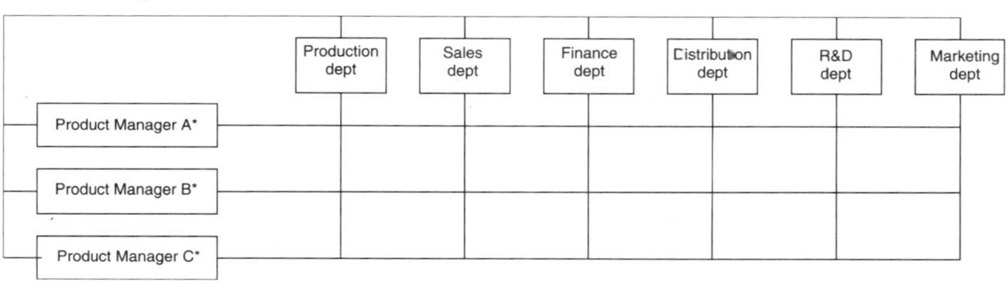

Figure 3.5 A matrix organisation

Authority is shared between the product managers (or area managers or project co-ordinators or whatever) and the heads of the functional departments. The functional department heads are responsible for the management of their own activities and staff, but the product managers are responsible for those activities and staff where they are involved in the production, selling, distributing (and so on) of their particular product. The product managers are thus co-ordinators of all the different functions towards their particular objectives.

A multi-disciplinary project team, members of which are drawn from different functions, is another simple example of a matrix structure.

You may have noticed that matrix management challenges classical ideas about organisation in two ways.

(a) It rejects the idea of 'one man, one boss'.

(b) It replaces the idea of authority based on hierarchy/status with the idea of influence based on expertise.

Activity 4 **(15 minutes)**

What do you think the advantages and disadvantages of a matrix structure might be? Give three points on each side.

3.5 Multifunctional teams and multidivisional structures

A multifunctional team is a group of individuals brought together from more than one functional area of a business to work on a problem or process that requires the knowledge, training and capabilities across the areas to successfully complete the work. This type of structure emphasises multi-skilling and multiple competencies and teaches people how to work in partnership with others.

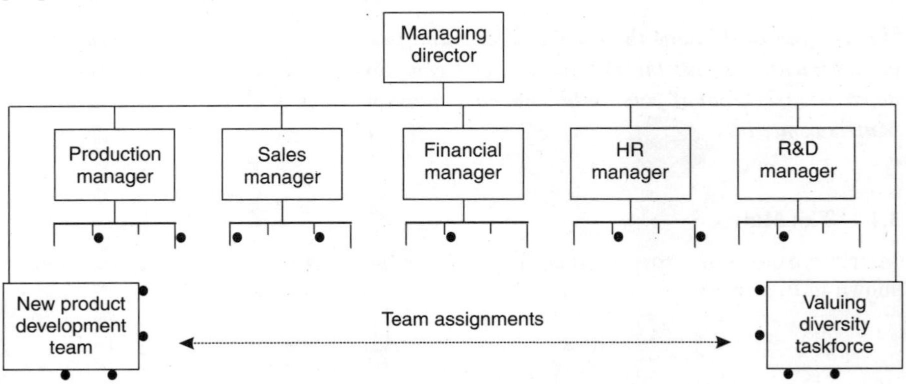

Figure 3.6 Multifunctional team

(a) *Advantages of team structures*

(i) Eliminates barriers between operating departments
(ii) Improved morale due to cross-functional interaction
(iii) Improved quality and speed of decision-making
(iv) Increased enthusiasm for work

(b) *Disadvantages*

(i) Conflicting loyalties among members.

(ii) Excessive time spent in meetings.

(iii) Effective use of time depends on quality of interpersonal relations, group dynamics, and team management.

A multidivisional structure is an organisational structure in which each distinct product line, market or business unit is placed in its own self-contained unit or division and each division has within it several functional sub-divisions for production, marketing and so on. The corporate headquarters' staff monitors divisional activities and exercises financial control over each of them. Figure 3.7 below shows a typical chemical company.

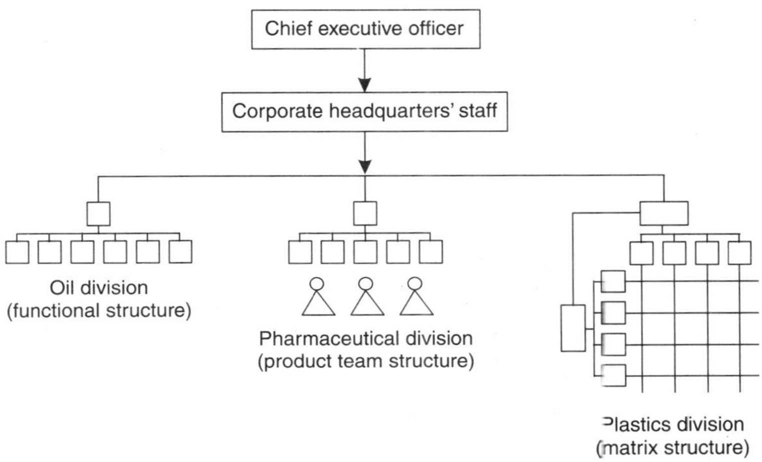

Figure 3.7 Multidivisional organisation

(a) *Advantages of multidivisional structures*

(i) Better financial and strategic control – decision-making responsibility is retained at the headquarters' level

(ii) Growth is easier – new units do not have to be integrated across organisation

(iii) Stronger pursuit of internal efficiency – performance of individual units is readily measurable.

(b) *Disadvantages*

(i) Bureaucratic costs
(ii) Difficulty establishing authority relationship
(iii) Communication problems
(iv) Competition for resources

4 ORGANISATIONAL NETWORKS AND LINKAGES

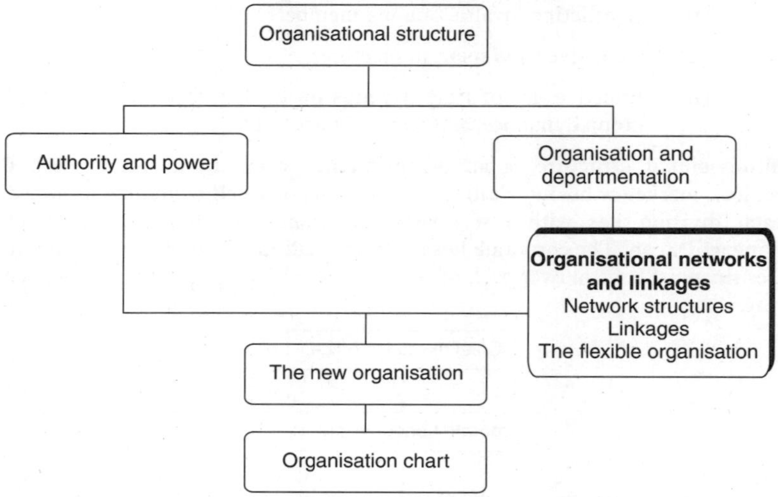

4.1 Network structures

Today's organisations are faced with a dynamic and turbulent environment that requires flexible and fast responses to changing business needs. The newest trend in structure is networks – almost non-organisation. The theory here is that the enterprise is at heart little more than a network of people with specialised skills. As opportunities arise, the organisation re-shapes itself into whatever form is necessary for it to prosper.

Definition

> A **network** is a contemporary organisational structure that is founded on a set of alliances with other organisations that serve a wide variety of functions.

All organisations have structures at three basic levels to connect their members in work related groups.

(a) The primary unit is a **cluster of individuals** in a team or department unit. Examples include the management team, problem-solving teams and project teams.

(b) The next level is the **connection of the teams** within the company. The matrix is the only well defined structure although other structures such as the fan and the web are being developed.

(c) The third level is the **connection of the company** with other companies.

Advances in communication technologies have enabled organisations to acquire and retain such distributed structures by supporting co-ordination among people working from different locations.

The main features of network organisations are:

(a) Separation of major functions into separate companies linked by a small core organisation

(b) Support functions subcontracted to create more flexible structures

(c) Focus on core competence

(d) Creates new managerial role as broker – acting as a facilitator and catalyst. Brokers help companies to form strategic partnerships, organise network activities and identify new business opportunities. Their task is to spread the network concepts, promote co-operation, organise groups of firms, and connect them to the product designers, marketing specialists, training providers, and industry services programmes they need to compete successfully.

There are three different types of network organisation: internal, vertical and dynamic.

Internal networks

Internal networks are traditional organisations in which divisions or units of the same firm are seen as separate profit centres and are given freedom to buy and sell from each other and also from others outside the firm. They attempt to own and control all the assets within the organisation and yet give each part freedom. This structure aims to inspire entrepreneurship internally without using outsourcing.

These networks are usually single firms that employ price-transferring mechanisms within their subsidiaries, each of which is still owned by the mother company. One reason for doing this is the belief that if units have to operate with prices set by the market, they have the incentive to improve performance and reduce prices.

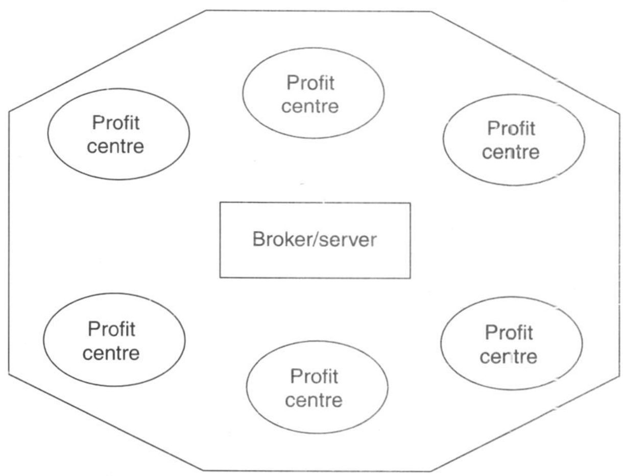

Figure 3.8 Internal network

In these organisations, corporate headquarters act like a broker, a bit like the role of government in business in Japan.

Vertical or stable networks

Vertical or stable networks consist of central organisations that outsource much of their operations to other companies. These structures include long-term relationships that often appear in mature industries with largely predictable market cycles. In high-tech industries (eg the automobile, telecommunication and manufacturing industries) where the product development cycle is relatively long and investments are high, a stable network is promoted in order to guarantee reliable product supply, close co-operation and quality requirements. For example, at BMW, they outsource about 65% of the total production cost of a car. This serves to spread the risk across a number of separate players and encourages the network to support product diversity and innovation.

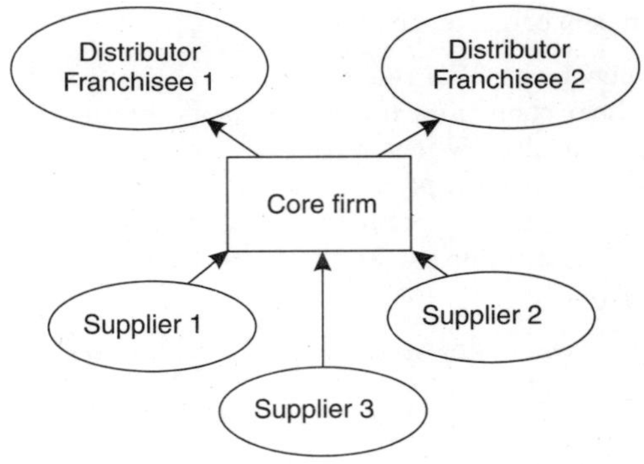

Figure 3.9 Vertical network

Dynamic networks

Dynamic networks – sometimes called 'virtual organisations' are the most flexible of the three. They are more temporary alliances of firms with key skills usually organised around a lead or brokering firm. Each of the units tends to be independent and collaborates on a specific project or opportunity and then disbands, later to connect again, perhaps with others, for another project. Such networks are more agile than stable networks, especially in creating new products.

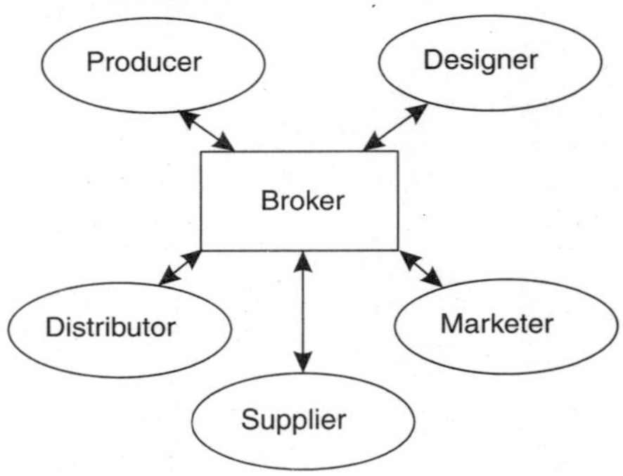

Figure 3.10 Dynamic network

This type of network structure prevails in the fashion, toys and publishing industries where competition is keen and the rate of change is fast. The co-operation exhibited between core firms and other participating firms is more opportunistic and short-term. For example, Nike is the centre of a dynamic network. It began as a U.S. distributor of athletic shoes made in Japan by Onitsuka Tiger and its only functions now are R&D and Marketing.

EXAMPLE

VISA

Imagine a large, successful, global organisation growing at 20 to 50 percent a year continuously for 25 years. It holds over 20,000 institutions in 200 countries and territories. There are more than 1.59 billion Visa cards worldwide and annual sales volume is more than $4.8 trillion. It is worth $150 billion on the stock market but it cannot be bought, sold, or raided. There is very little centralised control, and the portion of business created by each of the components of the organisation is theirs and theirs alone.

Visa is a networked organisation that functions well, even though none of its members – hundreds of thousands of merchants and financial institutions – knows the whole, nor does the whole know all the parts.

Advantages of network structures

- Maximises the effectiveness of the core unit
- Flexibility
- Firms can operate with fewer full-time employees and less complex internal systems
- Reduced overhead costs and increased operating efficiency
- Permits operations across great distances

Disadvantages of network structures

- Control and co-ordination problems may arise from network complexity
- Potential loss of control over outsourced activities
- Success is dependent on ability to locate sources
- Potential lack of loyalty among infrequently used contractors

---

FOR DISCUSSION

The following advantages for a network organisation have been cited.

(a) Increasing actual or perceived size
(b) Reaching new markets
(c) Sharing resources and risk

What do you think is meant by perceived size? How can the organisation reach markets that were previously unavailable to them? What sorts of resources are being shared?

4.2 Linkages

It is useful to think of structure as the linkage or network between the organisation's environment and the internal sub-systems – the technology used in the transformation process, the relationships among people performing various tasks and the managerial system of planning and control.

Network members collaborate, co-ordinate their activities and share data using information communications technology (ICT) as their main or only point of contact. They are supported by on-going developments in ICT that allow data sharing and synchronisation, interactive communication and virtual meetings across barriers of time and geographical distance. Historically, network organisations have used electronic mail (e-mail) to share information and co-ordinate their work. Use of e-mail allows these groups to call on expertise whenever needed regardless of where it resides. Nowadays, the Internet has enabled companies to form a virtual organisation where partners or workers located over a wide area are linked seamlessly.

One of the most significant changes for the existing industry structures is that critical new organisations such as transaction guarantors have been created to provide secure trade environment for electronic commerce.

4.3 The flexible organisation

One of the major advantages of the network organisation is the ability to adapt to turbulent market situations. Membership is diverse and structurally fluid enough to respond to equally diverse and changing customer/client requirements.

The flexibility is determined by the relationships between the individual parts, and the distance to the decision-making authority. Network structures allow organisations a high degree of flexibility:

Functional flexibility

- The physical dispersal of (and loose contractual relationship with) members offers cost savings for the parent organisation in areas such as employment (no redundancy obligations, benefits), overheads and logistics.
- Dynamic networks have fluid, organic structures, with indistinct boundaries (since members may also be suppliers, customers or competitors) and few barriers of geographical location or functional specialisation. They are particularly well suited to exploiting international markets, as they enable the parent firm to take advantage of local knowledge, indigenous language speakers, indigenous trading partnerships and so on.
- Virtual organisations focus on accessing core competencies (rather than recruiting people): members are selected for high-level expertise, across industry and geographical boundaries.
- Workers are required to undertake multiple duties (the end of demarcation)

Temporal and financial flexibility

- Network structures are particularly well suited to an increasingly 'portfolio' or 'skill vendor' labour market, in which long-term contractual employment relationships have been eroded.
- They allow a simplification of (bureaucratic) pay grades, and the practice of zero hour contracts.
- Pay flexibility includes flexitime, local pay bargaining, profit and performance related pay and flexible benefits – eliminating or reducing paid breaks.

Numerical flexibility

- They allow growth in agency, job-share, part-timers, etc, potential to vary numbers day-to-day. The result is the creation or two main groupings, core and peripheral employees.

5 THE NEW ORGANISATION

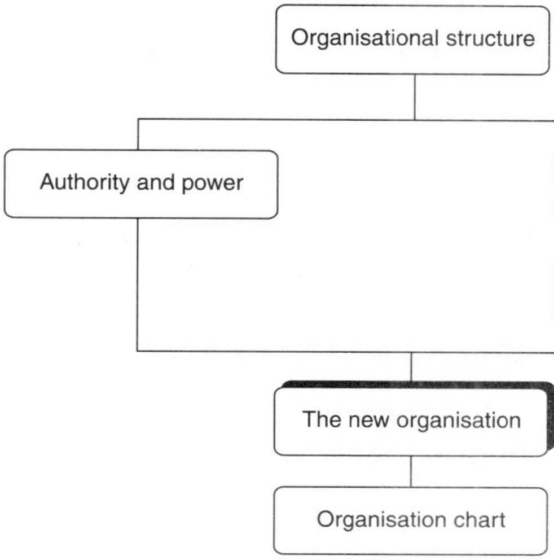

Some recent trends and ideas on organisation structure include the following.

(a) **Flat structures**. The flattening of hierarchies does away with levels of organisation which lengthened lines of communication and decision-making and encouraged ever-increasing specialisation. Flat structures are more responsive, because there is a more direct relationship between the organisation's strategic centre and the operational units serving the customer.

(b) '**Horizontal structures**'. What Tom Peters (1992) (in *Liberation Management)* calls 'going horizontal' is a recognition that functional versatility (through multi-functional project teams and multi-skilling, for example) is the key to flexibility. In the words (quoted by Peters) of a Motorola executive: 'The traditional job descriptions were barriers. We needed an organisation soft enough between the organisational disciplines so that ... people would run freely across functional barriers or organisational barriers with the common goal of getting the job done, rather than just making certain that their specific part of the job was completed.'

(c) '**Chunked' and 'unglued' structures**. So far, this has meant teamworking and decentralisation, or empowerment, creating smaller and more flexible units within the overall structure. Charles Handy's (1993) 'shamrock organisation' (with its three-leafed structured of core, subcontractor and flexible part-time labour) is gaining ground as a workable model for a leaner and more flexible workforce, within a controlled framework.

(d) **Output-focused structures**. The key to all the above trends is the focus on results, and on the customer, instead of internal processes and functions for their own sake. A **project management** orientation and structure, for example, is being applied to the supply of services within the organisation (to internal customers) as well as to the external market, in order to facilitate listening and responding to customer demands.

(e) '**Jobless' structures**. Meanwhile, the employee becomes not a job-holder but the vendor of a portfolio of demonstrated outputs and competencies. However daunting, this is a concrete expression of the concept of **employability**, which says that a person needs to have a portfolio of skills which are valuable on the open labour market: employees need to be mobile, moving between organisations rather than settling in to a particular job.

Activity 5 **(10 minutes)**

Give an example of your experience as a *customer* encountering a business reorganisation.

(a) Vertically: ie going from one *level* of the organisation to another

(b) Horizontally: ie going from one *function/department* of the organisation to another

Which do you think is more common, in your experience?

6 ORGANISATION CHART

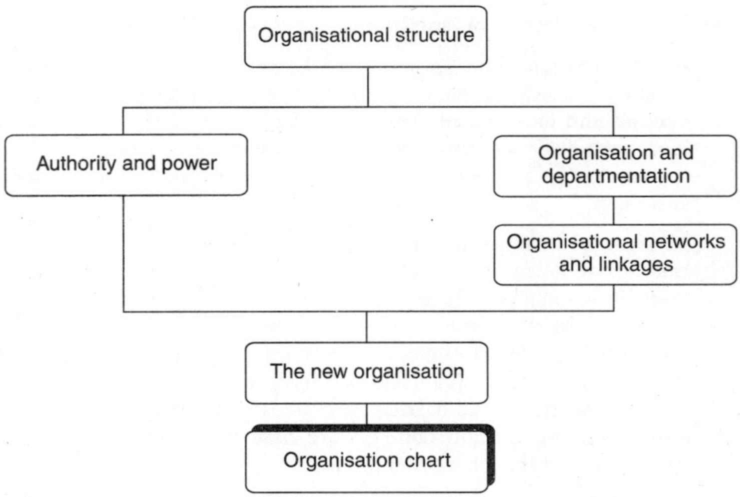

Organisation charts, such as those used to illustrate Section 3 above, are a traditional way of setting out in diagrammatic form:

(a) The **units** (departments etc) into which the organisation is divided and how they relate to each other

(b) The formal **communication** and reporting **channels** of the organisation

(c) The **structure** of **authority, responsibility and delegation** in the organisation including, for example, the extent of decentralisation and matrix authority relationships

(d) Any **problems** in the above: insufficient delegation, long lines of communication or unclear authority relationships.

So far we have seen the most common **vertical organisation chart**. There are alternatives.

(a) The **horizontal chart**. This may suggest a less hierarchical, more horizontal organisation style of culture, in which the superior-subordinate nature of relationships is played down.

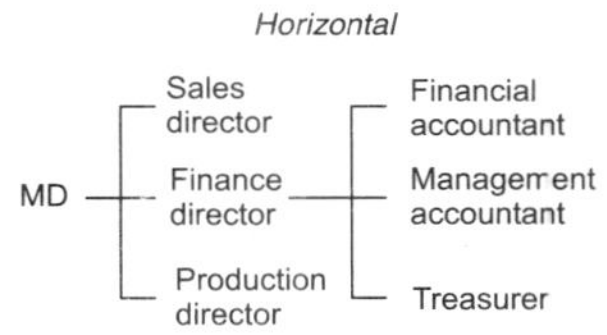

Figure 3.11 Horizontal chart

(b) The **concentric chart**, in which levels of the hierarchy are shown in circles spreading outwards from the centre.

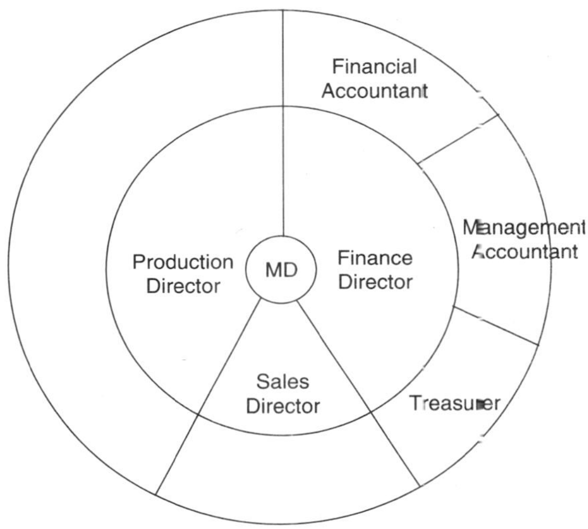

Figure 3.12 Concentric chart

(c) **Matrix charts,** as shown in Figure 3.11, which use both vertical and horizontal elements to show dual authority.

(d) '**Metaphors**', such as Charles Handy's (1993) 'cloverleaf' or 'shamrock' organisation structure, pyramids, network spider-webs – or any illustration the organisation finds helpful.

Note that organisation charts only give an **impression** of the structure and self-image of the organisation. They can aid managerial thinking and communication, but have limitations.

(a) They are a **static** model, while organisations are **dynamic**, constantly changing. It must be realised that charts are like snapshots of the organisation frozen in time. They go swiftly **out of date**.

(b) They show only the **formal structure** of authority and communication. As we saw earlier, there is a lot of **informal** influence and communication going on in an organisation that the average chart does not show.

(c) They describe the **structure** of the organisation – **not** the organisation itself, its **mission** and **values**, its people and activities.

Activity 6 **(15 minutes)**

Get hold of a copy of your organisation's chart. (Check the Office Manual, or ask the Human Resources Department.) What does it tell you about the organisation, the role of your department, and your position within it? If no chart is available, try drawing one!

Chapter roundup

- There are many types of organisation. They can be classified in various ways, for example by size, by volume of transactions, by type of business activities, by legal status, or according to whether they are profit-orientated or not profit-orientated.
- Many organisations are based on the principle of hierarchy. There is a line of decision making power from the top of the organisation to the bottom. In general, no employee reports to two bosses, whereas the boss may manage a number of different employees. This scalar chain is intimately connected to the concept of span of control, which is the number of individuals under the direct supervision of any one person.
- Centralisation and decentralisation refer to the extent to which authority is delegated in the organisation.
- Recent trends have been towards delayering organisations of levels of management. In other words, tall organisations (with many management levels, and narrow spans of control) are turning into flat organisations (with fewer management levels, wider spans of control) as a result of technological changes and the granting of more decision making power to front line employees.
- Organisations can be departmentalised on a functional basis (with separate departments for production, marketing, finance etc), a geographical basis (by region, or country), a product basis (eg world wide divisions for product X, Y etc), a brand basis, or a matrix basis (eg someone selling product X in country A would report to both a product X manager and a country A manager). Some organisations might feature a variety of these types.
- Modern management theory stresses flexibility as a key value, and organisational measures such as matrix and horizontal structures, teamworking, empowerment and output focused structures (such as project management) are being explored.
- Organisation charts provide a useful (but limited) snapshot of organisational structure.
- There are three different types of network organisations. Internal networks are usually single firms that employ price-transferring mechanisms within their subsidiaries. Vertical networks consist of central organisations that outsource much of their operations to other companies. Dynamic networks are more temporary alliances of firms with key skills. They tend to be independent – collaborating on a specific project or opportunity and then disbanding.

Quick quiz

1 What are the major differences between (a) a sole trader and a limited company and (b) a private sector organisation and a public sector organisation?

2 What is a contractor?

3 What objectives should an organisation's structure achieve?

4 What is span of control?

5 What is delayering?

6 What is functional organisation?

7 What is a matrix organisation?

Answers to quick quiz

1 (a) A sole trader is not legally distinguished from his business, and is liable to meet its debts from his personal resources. A limited company is a separate legal entity, distinguished from its owners.

(b) A private sector organisation is owned by shareholders or investors and is usually profit-oriented; a public sector organisation is owned by the state and its main reason for existing is not the generation of profit.

2 A contractor completes work for a client on the basis of a contract or agreement about the work to be done, its cost and timescale.

3 Linking in individuals in an established network of relationships; grouping together necessary tasks, and allocating them; allocating authority and ensuring accountability; co-ordinating separate units and facilitating co-operation and communication.

4 The number of subordinates immediately reporting to a given official.

5 The reduction in the number of management levels.

6 People are grouped together as they do similar work.

7 A matrix organisation crosses functional boundaries and involves overlapping chains of command.

Answers to activities

1 (Our suggestions only.)

(l) An airline

(m) A business which makes pop videos

(n) An orchestra

(o) Surrey Police

(p) A firm which does market research for its clients

(q) An art dealer

(r) A political party

(s) A radio station

(t) A football club

(u) A college or university which runs higher education and professional qualification courses

(v) A government department

(w) A local authority

(x) The Royal Air Force

(y) A pressure group promoting environmental awareness

(z) A private training provider and publisher of learning materials for a range of professional qualifications

2 Ways of distinguishing different types of organisation include:

(a) Size (eg by number of employees)

(b) Activity (eg retailing, manufacturing, service)

(c) Legal status (eg partnership or limited company)

(d) Profit orientated or non-profit orientated (eg charity)

(e) Public sector or private sector

(f) Geographical spread (eg limited to one region or country, or multinational)

The activity asked for five ways of distinguishing organisations. Six have been given here, and you can probably think of many more.

3 Functional; territorial; product.

4 *Advantages*

(a) Greater *flexibility*

(i) *People.* Employees develop an attitude geared to accepting change, and departmental monopolies are broken down.

(ii) *Tasks and structure.* The matrix structure may be readily amended.

(b) *Better inter-disciplinary co-operation* and a mixing of skills and expertise.

(c) *Motivation by providing employees* with greater participation in planning and control decisions.

Disadvantages

(a) Dual authority threatens a conflict between functional managers and product/ project area managers.

(b) An individual with two or more bosses is more likely to suffer stress at work.

(c) Matrix management can be more costly – product management posts are added, meetings have to be held, and so on.

5 (a) Vertical customer experience: If you had a complaint and the sales staff were unable or unwilling to deal with it; you would ask (or be asked) to talk to the supervisor or manager who has the authority to deal with the matter.

(b) Horizontal customer experience: You purchase an item (dealing with sales staff). You receive an invoice (accounts department). After a week, you receive a follow-up call from the customer service department. You say that you have a technical problem, and are referred to technical support. The argument against horizontal structures is that it is frustrating and time-consuming for the customer who may therefore be reluctant to make a repeat purchase and follow the circuitous loop through the organisation.

The argument for horizontal structures is that the horizontal experience is much more common, so organisations should be structured to make it smoother, quicker and easier (not: 'Sorry. That's not my department…').

6 The answer to this is specific to you and your organisation.

Chapter 4:
THE HUMAN RESOURCE FUNCTION

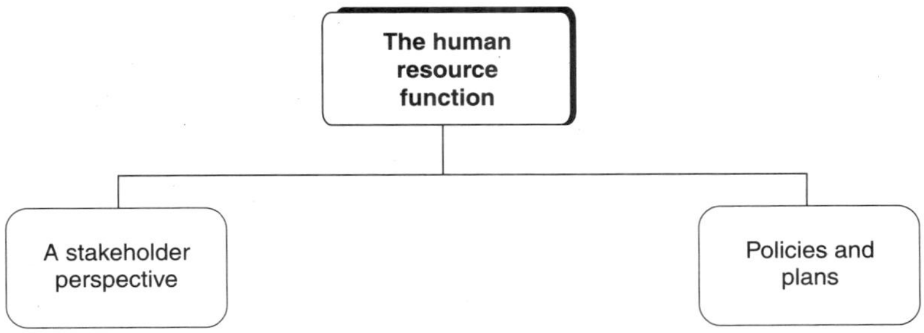

Introduction

The term Personnel Management can refer to the activities of specialist staff in a specialised section: the Personnel Department. It can also be viewed in broader terms as the management of people, which forms a part of every manager's job. In this chapter, we look at the personnel function, and consider the implications of the term 'Human Resource Management', which is now used in some organisations to describe its activity.

Your objectives

In this chapter you will learn about the following:

(a) The nature of personnel management and the various roles that the personnel function can play in an organisation

(b) The value and implications of the term 'Human Resource Management'

(c) Strategic goals for the personnel function, and evaluate them from a stakeholder perspective

(d) The basis and features of personnel policies and plans

1 THE HUMAN RESOURCE FUNCTION

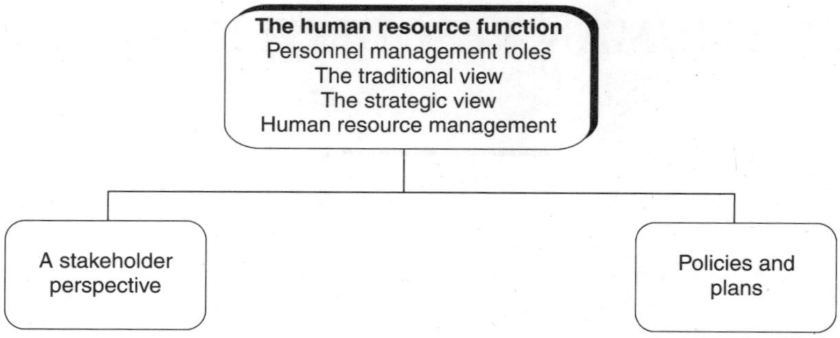

1.1 Personnel management roles

The main professional body for personnel managers is the Chartered Institute of Personnel and Development (CIPD), formerly known as the Institute of Personnel Management (IPM). The IPM said [our emphasis] that:

> 'Personnel management is that part of management concerned with people at work and with their relationships within an enterprise. It applies not only to industry and commerce but to all fields of employment. Personnel management aims to achieve both efficiency and justice, neither of which can be pursued effectively without the other.
>
> It seeks to bring together, and develop into an effective organisation, the men and women who make up an enterprise, enabling each to make his or her own best contribution to its success both as an individual and as a member of a working group. It seeks to provide fair terms and conditions of employment, and satisfying work for those employed... . Personnel management must also be concerned with the human and social implication of change in internal organisation, methods of working, and of economic and social changes in the community.'

Note that the emphasis is both on people/relationships/justice etc and on the development of an effective organisation and contribution to success. Personnel management has evolved at a significant pace since its early days of providing a welfare/counselling service, through the development of expertise in recruitment, training, reward systems, human resource planning and compliance with employment legislation to a new role in the management of change and changing employment

Activity 1 **(15 minutes)**

The following headings represent the main components of a personnel manager's job. Think of typical duties which may be placed under these headings.

Organisation	*Employee resourcing*	*Employee development*	*Reward*	*Employee relations*	*Health & Safety*	*Administration*
1 Job design	1 Recruitment	1 Training systems	1 Pay unions	1 Trade with law	1 Complying keeping	1 Record
2	2	2	2	2	2	2
3	3	3	3	3	3	3

1.2 The traditional view

The traditional view of personnel management has been essentially task-, activity- or technique-based. Dr Dale Yoder (1952) of the Graduate School of Business, Stanford University, defines the personnel management function as follows.

(a) Setting general and specific **management policy** for employment relationships, and establishing and maintaining a suitable organisation for leadership and co-operation.

(b) **Collective bargaining**: negotiating working terms and conditions with employee representatives.

(c) **Staffing and organisation**: finding, getting and holding prescribed types and numbers of workers.

(d) Aiding the **self-development** of employees at all levels, providing opportunities for personal development and growth as well as requisite skills and experience.

(e) Developing and maintaining employee **motivation**.

(f) **Reviewing** and **auditing manpower** and management in the organisation.

(g) **Industrial relations research**, carrying out studies designed to explain employment behaviour, and thereby improve manpower management.

Crichton (1968) complained that personnel management was often a matter of 'collecting together such odd jobs from management as they are prepared to give up.'

Other writers shared this view, notably Peter Drucker (1989), who – while recognising the importance of human resources in the organisation – saw the personnel function of the time as 'a collection of incidental techniques without much internal cohesion'. According to Drucker, the personnel manager saw the role as 'partly a file clerk's job, partly a housekeeping job, partly a social worker's job and partly "fire fighting" to head off union trouble or to settle it.'

Figure 4.1 shows a simple diagram illustrating the personnel function and its relationships, according to this traditional view.

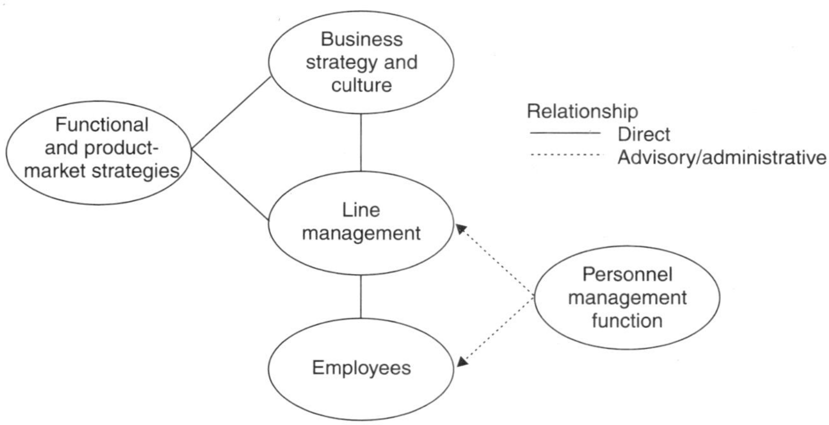

Figure 4.1 Personnel function and its relationships

In this model, you might have noticed that personnel management is not directly involved in the business strategy.

The status and contribution of the personnel function is still often limited by the image of 'fire-fighting', an essentially reactive and defensive role. The personnel manager is judged according to his or her effectiveness in avoiding or settling industrial disputes, preventing accidents and ill-health (and their associated costs), filling vacancies and so on.

FOR DISCUSSION

'People may be regarded as a vital resource – at least plenty of lip service is paid to this concept by company chairmen in their annual statements – but many managers find it difficult to appreciate where the personnel department fits in, except in the simplest terms as a procurement and fire-fighting function.'

Armstrong (1997)

Role play a discussion between the company chairperson and the personnel manager about the role of the personnel function.

This is a vicious circle. As long as personnel policy and practice are divorced from the strategy of the business, and fail to be proactive and constructive, personnel will be perceived by line management as having little to do with the 'real' world of business management, or the 'bottom line' (profitability). Personnel specialists therefore command scant respect as business managers, and their activities continue to be limited to areas of little strategic impact.

Clearly then, the concept of personnel management has not been without its critics. A new approach was called for.

1.3 The strategic view

Human assets

Andrew Mayo (1998) quotes Tom Watson, former president of IBM

> 'All the value of this company is in its people. If you burnt down all of our plants and we just kept our people and information files, we would soon be as strong as ever. Take away our people and we might never recover.'

Mayo sees this view of employees as major assets of the business, and therefore a key to adding value, as a challenge to the Human Resource function.

> 'Forever fretting over whether "serious" business people see the function as adding value, HR now has no excuse for failing to make a major contribution.'

It seems that research is beginning to bear this out. Research findings reported in *People Management* ('Profitable personnel, 8 January 1998) showed that:

> 'the acquisition and development of skills (via selection, induction, training and appraisal) and job design are significant predictors of changes in both profitability and productivity. More broadly, the study concludes that – compared with, say, research and development, quality, technology and strategy – far the most powerful indicators of future business performance are the HR practices.'

HR at a strategic level

Alongside this vital recognition of employees as a business asset, there have come a number of related perceptions.

(a) Personnel management has been changing in various ways in recent years. Many of its activities have become more complex and sophisticated and, particularly with the accelerating pace of change in the business environment, less narrowly concerned with areas previously thought of as personnel's sole preserve (hiring and firing, training, industrial relations and manpower planning). The personnel function has become centrally concerned with issues of broader relevance to the business and its objectives, such as change management, the introduction of technology, and the implications of falling birth-rates and skill shortages for the resourcing of the business.

(b) Personnel management can and should be integrated with the strategic planning of the business; that is, with management at the broadest and highest level. The objectives of the personnel function can and should be directly related to achieving the organisation's goals for growth, competitive gain and improvement of 'bottom line' performance.

(c) Personnel managers can and should be businessmen or women – even entrepreneurs, who mobilise resources for maximum added value.

It is this more strategic viewpoint that has been labelled 'Human Resource Management' or HRM. It can be illustrated in Figure 4.2, which should be compared with Figure 4.1.

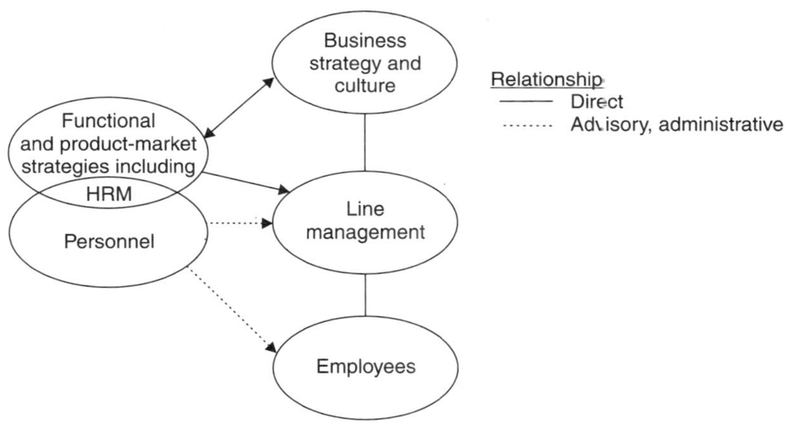

Figure 4.2 Strategic view of HRM

Activity 2 **(30 minutes)**

Ultraleisure plc is a rapidly growing company involved in the design, building and operation of theme parks and adventure centres. In the UK, the company runs theme parks in Liverpool, Birmingham, Dagenham (South East London) and Dover (expected to benefit hugely as a rival to Disney World from the opening of the Channel Tunnel). In Europe, the company operates large theme parks in Rotterdam, Hamburg and Copenhagen. The company is planning expansion into Eastern Europe, as it considers that land and labour are cheap, and that it will be well positioned to take advantage of the growing market for leisure. You have just had a chat with the Human Resources Manager, the person in charge of the firm's human resources. She is not a Board member but reports directly to the Chief Executive. 'In the past we've hired and fired on an ad hoc basis – there's always a pool of students wanting the job' she says. 'We obviously need skilled technicians to run the rides, so anybody with the right qualifications will do. The students are involved in the retail side, and in guiding customers around, helping them out. Our recruitment policies depend directly on the total number of visitors we expect. We expect a lot of visitors from Northern France to come over to Dover, but I don't really see the need to alter our recruitment policies – we'll just get local people as usual. We haven't quite decided what to do about Eastern Europe. Our research into the local labour market would indicate that many people want a career in theme parks – but it's the sort of business where there really aren't that many management positions available. We'll probably have to change our normal policies to cope with long-termers'.

Comment on Ultraleisure plc's approach to managing its human resources: to what extent has it embraced an HRM approach to its resourcing problems?

In Figure 4.2, we can see that HRM is part of a business's set of strategies. Its objectives are thus integrated with the strategy of the business.

1.4 Human resource management (HRM)

Definition

Human resource management is 'a strategic and coherent approach to the management of an organisation's most valued assets: the people working there who individually and collectively contribute to the achievement of its objectives for sustainable competitive advantage'. (Armstrong, 1997)

The term Human Resource Management (HRM) originated in the USA in the late 1970s as a label for the way certain blue-chip companies such as IBM, Xerox and Hewlett Packard were managing their people. In order to give themselves a competitive edge over their rivals, these companies managed their people according to what David Guest (2002) later defined as the four underlying principles of HRM.

(a) **Strategic integration** – people must be managed in a way that contributes to the organisation's goals and strategies, for example by creating a culture and agreeing performance targets which support what the organisation is trying to achieve.

(b) **Commitment** – people must be managed in a way that ensures their genuine commitment to the success of the organisation, for example by offering meaningful chances for development and by rewarding good performance.

(c) **Flexibility** – HRM policies must be structured to allow maximum flexibility for the organisation, so it can respond to ever-changing business needs; for example by adding new skills to employees' lists of duties and responsibilities and by employing people on flexible, fixed-term contracts.

(d) **Quality** – the notion of quality must run through everything the organisation does, for example by responding to customer needs and by reducing waste and error to a minimum.

The emergence of HRM has sparked a lively debate among academics and practitioners about its relevance, whether it is a fair and desirable way to manage people and whether it makes any difference to organisational performance.

Some commentators have noted a wholesale change of 'label' – from personnel to HR – with little difference in practice. However, where more than lip-service is paid to the concept, the following features might be observed.

(a) Believing that human assets are the key to business success, organisations will assign responsibility for HRM at the top level of management, with input to strategic decision-making.

(b) Responsibility for HRM will also percolate throughout the organisation. Within an HR strategy and policy framework, all managers and team leaders are involved in HRM.

(c) The HR function will be a leader and communicator of organisational culture and values.

(d) The orientation of HRM will be towards commitment and involvement of employees, not mere compliance with organisational directives: 'partnership' will be a key concept (whatever term is used).

(e) Employee relations will reflect the HR function's conviction that there need be no inherent conflict to interest between the goals of the organisation and those of its employees.

(f) The fit of people with organisational strategy will be reflected in all areas of HRM: recruitment and selection, employee development, reward for performance and so on.

Activity 3 **(20 minutes)**

In June 1993 *Personnel Management* magazine (subtitled 'The magazine for human resource professionals') published an article entitled 'The mystery of the missing human resource manager'. This reported on a survey whose results suggested amongst other things, that:

(a) only 17% of establishments in the UK employing more than 25 people have a personnel specialist;

(b) only 44 out of the 2,061 respondents used the 'HRM' title;

(c) however, there was some evidence to support the possibility that HRM is found at head offices, 'a strategic phenomenon at the strategic apex of the organisation'.

The article continues:

'Perhaps predictably, the title does not necessarily reflect practice. IBM, for example, has retained the personnel title despite being frequently held up in the past as an exemplar of human resource management. Even in the United States, where it has been estimated that over half of the top 50 corporations now use the human resource title, IBM has kept the personnel label. One explanation is that it only makes sense to change if it provides some competitive advantage. Maybe establishments in the UK have taken that message on board. Certainly, we can refute the “old wine in new bottles” argument that some of us promulgated. There may be some good wine around – some good human resource policy and practice – but it is still marketed in the old bottles.'

Do you think the name of the function matters? Why?

You may have noticed that there is some ambiguity in the role of HRM in the organisation. We have seen throughout this chapter so far its emphasis on both the interests of the employees (though ensuring fair, safe and satisfying terms and conditions at work) and the interests of the organisation (though ensuring enhanced business performance and added value). This is a natural reflection of a stakeholder view of organisations.

2 A STAKEHOLDER PERSPECTIVE

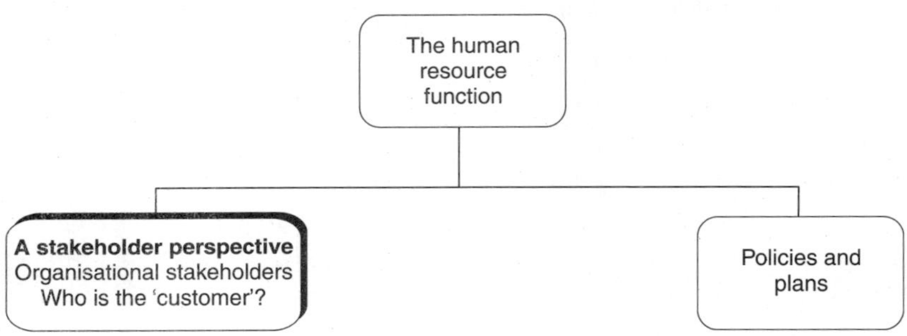

2.1 Organisational stakeholders

Definition

> **Stakeholders** are all those individuals, groups and institutions who have a legitimate interest or 'stake' in the organisation's activities and performance.

Stakeholders in a given organisation may include the following.

(a) Shareholders, the owners of the business

(b) Other investors and/or financers of the business or not-for-profit organisation (for example, financial lending institutions, charitable donors, government funding agencies)

(c) Suppliers (of goods, materials, services, information, labour and other resources) to the organisation

(d) Customers of the organisation

(e) Managers of the organisation

(f) Other employees of the organisation

(g) Trade unions and other occupational and professional groups representing the employees of the organisation

(h) Government and other agencies (such as the Inland Revenue, Customs and Excise, Commission for Racial Equality, Health and Safety Executive) whose objectives intersect with organisational activities

(i) Special interest and lobby groups (consumer protection groups, environmentalists and so on) whose objectives may intersect with organisational activities

(j) The wider community in which the organisation operates; from which it employs labour; through which it circulates information and so on.

> **Activity 4** **(30 minutes)**
>
> Brainstorm some examples of what 'stake' or interest you think the stakeholders listed above might or should have in the organisation. What are they entitled to demand or expect? What might they legitimately object to? What kind of influence would they have on organisational policy and practice?

At a strategic and operational level, human resource management may expect to impact on all the stakeholders listed above, through:

(a) Direct responsibility for areas such as health and safety, equal opportunity and compliance with a range of legislation and regulation, intersecting with the activities of external agencies

(b) The selection, training and motivation of managers and other employees, which are reflected in the quality of their service to customers and dealings with suppliers as well as the image and conduct of the organisation in the community at large

(c) Development and deployment of human resources in such a way as to support line management objectives, add value to the business (or achieve efficiency/service objectives, in the case of a not-for-profit organisation) and secure a return on investment for it owners and investors

(d) Offer fair and equitable treatment and, if possible, positive satisfaction to employees

So who is really the 'customer' of the HR function?

2.2 Who is the customer?

The internal customer concept is important to the personnel function.

Definition

> The **internal customer concept** suggests that any unit of an organisation whose task contributes to the work of other units can be regarded as a supplier of services, like any other supplier used by the organisation. The 'receiving' units are thus customers of that unit. The service unit's objective thus becomes the efficient and effective identification and satisfaction of customer needs – as much within the organisation as outside it.

According to the IPD's Code of Professional Practice in Personnel Management, the personnel manager has three principal areas of responsibility.

(a) '*A personnel manager's primary responsibility is to his employer*.'

In his book *Perfect Customer Care* (1994), Ted Johns makes the distinction between 'customers' as people who use a product or service and pay for it, as opposed to 'users' who benefit from a product or service without paying.

'Applying this framework to the personnel department... it turns out that they only have one customer in the strictest sense of the term: the Board – or, even more precisely, the CEO (Chief Executive Officer).'

(b) *The personnel manager must*

'resolve the conflict which must sometimes exist between his position as a member of the management team and his special relationships with the workforce in general and with individual employees.'

(c) The personnel manager must 'use his best endeavours to enhance the standing ... of his *profession*' in dealings within the organisation and with other bodies.

> **Activity 5** **(30 minutes)**
>
> Whose side is the personnel manager on? Give three examples of the 'conflict which must sometimes exist between his position as a member of the management team and his special relationship with the workforce', and discuss what you feel are the issues involves. Where would you stand on these issues?

Personnel managers may have to occupy the middle ground between employee and employer on some occasions. In a sense both employers/management and employees are their customers. Yet the personnel manager is not in any formal sense the 'representative' of the workforce, and is paid to be part of the organisation's management team, as both representative and adviser. The 'diplomatic' role of personnel may thus pose a dilemma of dual allegiance – particularly where there is conflict in the relationship between the personnel function and other (line) members of the management team.

3 POLICIES AND PLANS

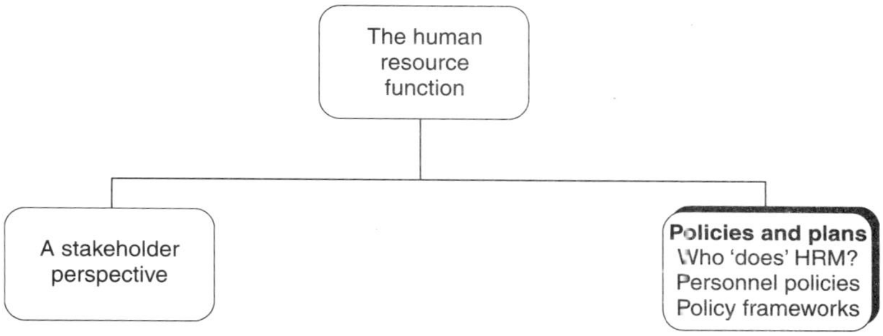

3.1 Who 'does' HRM?

The personnel 'function' **may** consist of a specialist department or departments under the control of a personnel manager (or director, where the function is represented on the Board) – but in a smaller organisation the owner, manager, company secretary or any designated individual may undertake the necessary tasks.

In any organisation, there is a need for:

- Specialist advice on personnel matters (whether from within the organisation or outside), and/or
- Well-defined personnel policies

because:

- Constant developments in personnel management require expertise – perhaps increasingly so (as discussed below), and
- Personnel management practice needs to be consistent, fair, efficient and in line with organisational goals.

Several factors have contributed to the perceived need for a specialised personnel function.

(a) The need to **comply with changing regulation and legislation** means that expert attention will have to be given to matters such as recruitment and selection (to avoid racial or sexual discrimination), termination of the employment contract (to avoid unfair dismissal), and health and safety at work.

(b) Constant **changes in the labour market** have required that policies be designed and implemented by individuals with current knowledge.

(c) There is continuing pressure for **social responsibility** towards employees, with new requirements for communication, involvement and working conditions – notably, from Europe.

(d) Behavioural sciences (psychology, sociology and social psychology) are increasingly used to explain and predict how individuals operate and co-operate (or not) at work. Up-to-date research on such matters as motivation, stress, resistance to change, industrial fatigue and response to leadership style need to be monitored.

(e) Trade unions, Industrial Tribunals, the Advisory, Conciliation and Arbitration Service (ACAS) and others have a continuing role in employee relations: familiarity with legislation, best practice, liaison and negotiation techniques and so on will be required.

FOR DISCUSSION

'Managers, if one listens to the psychologists, will have to have insights into all kinds of people. They will have to be in command of all kinds of psychological techniques. They will have to understand an infinity of individual personality structures, individual psychological needs, and individual psychological problems... But most managers find it hard enough to know all they need to know about their own immediate area of expertise, be it heat-treating or cost accounting or scheduling.' Drucker: Management

Do you think this is an argument for

- The irrelevance of all the 'psychological techniques' to day-to-day management

or

- The need for specialists who can explain to managers what lies behind people's behaviour at work?

However, it has been suggested that a separate personnel function need not exist at all: **every** manager needs to achieve results through the efforts of other people, and must therefore take an interest in personnel management tasks.

If you ask everyone to be aware of the need for constructive employee relations and the management of human resources towards efficient and effective task performance, how do you control the process? How do you ensure that people are treated fairly and consistently in all areas of the organisation? How do you ensure that the organisation's goals and values in managing people are upheld by individual managers? This is where personnel **policy** comes in.

3.2 Personnel policies

Definition

> A '**policy**' is a general statement or understanding which provides guidelines for management decision making.

Policies might be formulated for any of the activities of the personnel function, in order to ensure:

(a) That people are treated fairly and consistently

(b) That people are treated in the way the organisation had defined as important and desirable to secure a required level of performance and which is consistent with the image it wishes to convey to its employees and to the outside world

(c) That laws and regulations are complied with

Here are some examples.

EXAMPLES

- **A multiskilling policy**. Jobs are not 'owned' by particular groups: instead, the most appropriate individual to do a particular job should be trained in the skills to do it.
- **A single status policy**. Salary and benefit systems should be common to all employees, breaking down barriers of status/reward between different grades or specialisms.
- **An equal opportunities policy**. Selection for vacancies, promotions or training opportunities should not be based on any discrimination of sex, race, age, marital status, or disability.
- **A succession/promotion policy**. Where possible, the organisation will seek to promote skilled individuals from within the organisation, in preference to external recruitment.
- **An employee communication policy**. Employees or their representatives will be given all information necessary to perform their tasks and to appreciate their role in the organisation's performance, and all information that will affect their working terms and conditions.
- **A disciplinary policy**. All employees are to be given oral warnings prior to disciplinary proceedings. All employees are to be given a fair hearing, accompanied by a representative, prior to disciplinary measures being taken.
- **A recruitment policy**. All vacancies are to be advertised internally. No discrimination shall be shown in the placement or wording of advertisements. All applicants will be treated fairly and clearly, and informed of the progress of their application.
- **A safety policy**. Training in safe use of all equipment and machinery, and in safety and emergency procedures, will be provided.

We will encounter further examples later in the course book.

3.3 Policy frameworks

Personnel polices are based on:

(a) Employment legislation, and laws and regulations in work-related areas such as health and safety and discrimination

(b) The values and philosophies of the organisation about how people should be treated and what kind of treatment will enable them to work most effectively on the organisation's behalf

(c) The needs, wants and rights of employees to be treated fairly and with dignity

(d) The organisation's need to attract and retain the kind of employees it wants, by its reputation and practice as an employer

According to Cuming (1985), there are three main principles on which personnel policies in British industry, commerce, and public service are based.

(a) All employees should be treated with **justice**: that is, fairly, without discrimination, and consistently (from one case to another and over time).

(b) The **needs** of employees must be **recognised,** particularly 'their desires for job satisfaction, for knowledge of what is going on within the organisation, and for consultation before changes affecting them take place'.

(c) A business will **function better democratically** than autocratically; success is more likely with employee co-operation in achieving objects than with the use of coercion.

Chapter roundup

- The personnel function takes different forms in different organisations. Traditionally, it has been regarded as a primarily administrative, reactive, problem-handling function, concerned with hiring and firing, employee welfare and industrial relations.
- The personnel function takes different forms in different organisations. Traditionally, it has been regarded as a primarily administrative, reactive, problem-handling function, concerned with hiring and firing, employee welfare and industrial relations.
- Human Resource Management (HRM) is a concept which seeks to recognise employees as a vital asset of a business, and their sourcing and management as a key element of business strategy.
- HRM terminology is often used interchangeably with more traditional personnel management ideas, but the proactive and strategic approach is distinctively 'HRM'.
- The role of the personnel function is often ambiguous, as it carries responsibilities to both senior management (as prime customer) and employees (as prime users).

Quick quiz

1 Outline the main areas of expertise which developed in the emergence of personnel management.

2 According to Drucker, the personnel manager sees the role as 'partly a file clerk's job, partly a housekeeping job, partly a social worker's job and partly 'firefighting' to head off union trouble or to settle it'.

Explain what Drucker meant by each of these.

3 Why is it so important for personnel management to be linked with corporate strategy?

4 List four underlying principles of HRM.

5 Suggest three reasons why specialised expertise might be valuable in the area of personnel management.

6 Who are the customers and users of personnel management?

7 Why do organisations need personnel policies?

8 What are the three main principles on which personnel policies in Britain are based?

Answers to quick quiz

1 Welfare, recruitment, training, reward systems, human resource planning and employment legislation.

2 Administration and record-keeping, maintaining order in staffing issues, counselling and welfare, industrial relations.

3 So that it can make (and demonstrate) a contribution to the 'bottom line' or added value.

4 Strategic integration, commitment, flexibility, quality.

5 Changing regulation/legislation; changing labour market; changing expectations/ requirements for social responsibility; changing findings of behavioural research; the need for advanced communication/negotiation skills for employee relations.

6 The customers of personnel management are the CEO, Board of Directors, ultimately the shareholders who pay for the service. Other users include line managers, employees, people in the labour market.

7 For fairness, consistency; organisational image; compliance with laws and regulations.

8 Justice, the recognition of needs, democracy.

Answers to activities

1 Personnel managers' duties within the given components include:

Organisation: Job analysis, organisation design
Resourcing: HR planning, termination
Development: Appraisal, career management
Reward: Market surveys, benefits

Relations: Involvement, communication
Health and safety: Welfare, stress management
Administration: Management information, data protection

2 Ultraleisure plc is in a halfway house between personnel management and HRM.

(a) The 'hiring and firing on an *ad hoc* basis' and the fact that the manager is not considered as important as, say, the Marketing Director, would indicate that the firm has not really adopted HRM. This impression is further supported by the fact that the human resources needs of the Dover Theme Park (with its large number of French-speaking visitors) have not been assessed in any coherent way. No mention is made of recruiting people who are bi-lingual.

(b) However, the company is moving towards HRM in its dealing with Eastern Europe.

3 It clearly matters to some of the people who perform the functions what name is used, for their own sense of self-esteem. The change in name from 'Personnel' to 'HRM' may also be seen as an attempt to increase the status and influence of the function. An important consideration is whether the managers view their staff as 'resources' or not.

4 Your ideas may have included the following.

(a) Acceptable performance, dividends etc. Sufficient, accurate, truthful information for investment decisions, AGM participation etc

(b) Repayment of debt, interest as planned
Accurate reporting on performance
Value for money invested

(c) Fair, courteous dealings
Prompt payment of accounts
Continuing business?

(d) Safe products, courteous service
Goods/service supplied as advertised

(e) Development opportunities
Backing for authority
Fair pay and conditions

(f) Fair pay and conditions
Employment security
Safe working environment

(g) Communication and consultation in compliance with negotiated and regulated arrangements

Education/employment opportunities for members

Practices upholding reputation, standards, interests

(h) Compliance of members with law and regulation

Statistical returns, reports, payments (or whatever) required by the agency

(i) Policies and practices consistent with legitimate concerns

Hearing for legitimate concerns, provision of information where appropriate

(j) Socially responsible recruitment/employment practices
True and inoffensive marketing messages
Community investment/involvement where appropriate

5 Examples of conflicts of interest might include the following.

(a) The need for downsizing or delayering for organisational efficiency. The workforce may well see this as a betrayal, yet it is part of resource management to know when to liquidate assets: organisational survival may even depend on increased efficiency/flexibility or cost cutting.

(b) The negotiation of reward packages. As a member of management, you may wish to minimise increases in the cost of labour, or rationalise them in some way (eg through job evaluation). The workforce perceives pay rises as a 'right' or as an indication of the organisation's value of their services, and may be disappointed.

(c) Disciplinary procedures. The interests of management may be best served by 'clamping down' on absenteeism, poor time-keeping and so on in order to keep general discipline and efficiency – but the workforce, and particular individuals, will often feel that rules are unfair or unfairly applied.

Broadly, these are issues of the way power is used in the organisation. The personnel function can go a long way to minimising the potential hurt and conflict caused by applying and communicating the decisions of management fairly and sensitively.

Chapter 5:
ORGANISATIONAL CULTURE

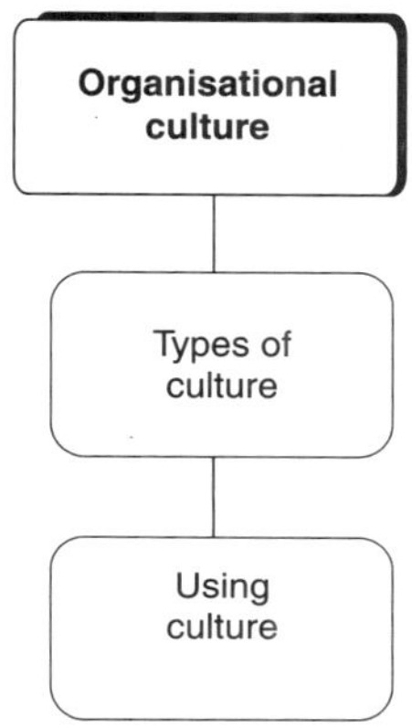

Introduction

This subject is about organisations as social arrangements – collections of people. We mentioned in Chapter 1 that organisational culture is, in a sense, the 'human' side of structure: that certain 'style' that the members of the organisation collectively bring to its operations. There's a lot talked about the 'strong' cultures of companies such as McDonald's, Disney, Marks & Spencer or IBM. In this chapter, we look at what makes culture, and why.

Your objectives

In this chapter you will learn about the following:

(a) Organisational culture

(b) The features of power, role, task and person cultures

(c) The development of culture and how it can be managed in the interests of organisational performance

1 ORGANISATIONAL CULTURE

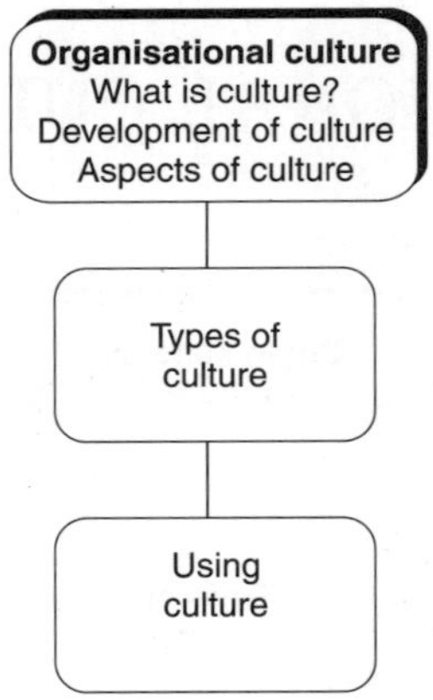

1.1 What is culture?

Definition

Culture (in the sense of organisational 'climate') is the collective self-image and style of the organisation; its shared values and beliefs, norms and symbols.

Charles Handy (1987) sums up 'culture' as 'that's the way we do things round here'. For Edgar Schein, it is 'the pattern of basic assumptions that a given group has invented, discovered, or developed, in learning to cope with its problems of external adaptation and internal integration, and that have worked well enough to be considered valid and, therefore, to be taught to new members as the correct way to perceive, think and feel in relation to these problems.'

Activity 1 **(15 minutes)**

What do you think would differentiate the culture of

- A regiment in the army
- An advertising agency?

1.2 Development of culture

There are many factors which influence the organisational culture, including the following.

(a) *Economic conditions*

In prosperous times organisations will either be complacent or adventurous, full of new ideas and initiatives. In recession they may be depressed, or challenged. The struggle against a main competitor may take on 'heroic' dimensions.

(b) *The nature of the business and its tasks*

The types of technology used in different forms of business create the pace and priorities associated with different forms of work, for example the hustle and frantic conditions for people dealing in the international money market compared with the studious life of a research officer. Task also influences work environment to an extent, and this is an important visual cultural indicator.

(c) *Leadership style*

The approach used in exercising authority will determine the extent to which subordinates feel alienated and uninterested or involved and important. Leaders are also the creators and 'sellers' of organisational culture: it is up to them to put across the vision.

(d) *Policies and practices*

The level of trust and understanding which exists between members of an organisation can often be seen in the way policies and objectives are achieved, for example the extent to which they are imposed by tight written rules and procedures or implied through custom and understanding.

(e) *Structure*

The way in which work is organised, authority exercised and people rewarded will reflect an emphasis on freedom or control, flexibility or rigidity.

(f) *Characteristics of the workforce*

Organisation culture will be affected by the demographic nature of the workforce, for example its typical manual/clerical division, age, sex and personality.

1.3 Aspects of culture

All organisations will generate their own cultures, whether spontaneously or under the guidance of positive managerial strategy. The culture will consist of the following aspects.

(a) The **basic, underlying assumptions** which guide the behaviour of the individuals and groups in the organisation: for example customer orientation, or belief in quality, trust in the organisation to provide rewards, freedom to make decisions, freedom to make mistakes, and the value of innovation and initiative at all levels. Assumptions will be reflected in the kind of people employed (their age, education or personality), the degree of delegation and communication, whether decisions are made by committees or individuals and so on.

(b) **Overt beliefs** expressed by the organisation and its members, which can be used to condition (a) above. These beliefs and values may emerge as sayings, slogans, mottos such as 'we're getting there', 'the customer is always right', or 'the winning team'. They may emerge in a richer mythology – in jokes and stories about past successes , heroic failures or breakthroughs, legends about the 'early days', or about 'the time the boss...'. Organisations with strong cultures often centre themselves around almost legendary figures in their history. Management can encourage this by 'selling' a sense of the corporate 'mission', or by promoting the company's 'image'; it can reward the 'right' attitudes and punish (or simply not employ) those who aren't prepared to commit themselves to the culture.

(c) **Visible artefacts** - the style of the offices or other premises, dress 'rules', display of 'trophies', the degree of informality between superiors and subordinates and so on.

(d) **Symbols** – like artefacts, are things that act as triggers to remind people in the culture of its rules, beliefs, etc. They act as a shorthand way to keep people aligned. Symbols can also be used to indicate status within a culture. This includes clothing, office decor and so on. Status symbols signal to others to help them use the correct behaviour with others in the hierarchy. They also lock in the users of the symbols into prescribed behaviours that are appropriate for their status and position.

(e) **Rules, norms, ethical codes and values** – the norms and values of a culture are effectively the rules by which its members must abide, or risk rejection from the culture (which is one of the most feared sanctions known). They are embedded in the artefacts, symbols, stories, attitudes, and so on.

(f) **Rituals, rites, ceremonies and celebrations** – rituals are processes or sets of actions that are repeated in specific circumstances and with specific meaning. They may be used in such as rites of passage, such as when someone is promoted or retires. They may be associated with company events such as the release of a new event. They may also be associated with everyday events such as Christmas. Whatever the circumstance, the predictability of the rituals and the seriousness of the meaning all combine to sustain the culture.

Activity 2 **(20 minutes)**

Choose an organisation of which you are a member, or which you know fairly well as a customer. List its particular cultural attributes, under the headings:

(a) Underlying assumptions/values
(b) Stated beliefs/slogans etc
(c) Visible signs and symbols

There have been many efforts to classify different cultural styles. One of the best known is the classification by Charles Handy. In 'Gods of Management' (1987) he suggested that organisation cultures can be grouped into four different 'ideal' types. To each type, Handy attached the name of a Greek deity. In Ancient Greece people followed a particular god, not out of contempt for all the others, but accepting that each god represented a particular **trait or set of values** ***(Mars for soldiers etc). Handy holds that this is true of organisations which do different things***

2 TYPES OF CULTURE

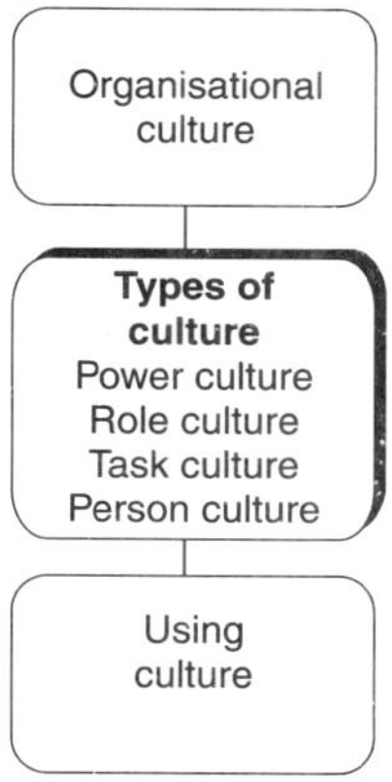

2.1 Power culture

Zeus, the ruler of the gods, is the god representing the **power culture** or **club culture.** The organisation is controlled by key, central figures – often the owners or founders of the organisation.

Characteristic	Comment
Based on personalities	Zeus is a dynamic entrepreneur who rules with snap decisions. Power and influence stem from a central source, perhaps the owner-directors or the founder of the business. Important decisions are made by key people. Employees will try to second guess what the boss thinks.
Adaptable and informal	The organisation is not rigidly structured, and is capable of adapting quickly to meet change. However, success in adapting will depend on the luck or judgement of the key individuals who make the rapid decisions.
Small size	Personal influence decreases as the size of an organisation gets bigger. The power culture is therefore best suited to smaller entrepreneurial organisations, where the leaders have direct communications with all employees.
Good personal relations	People have to get on well with each other for this culture to work. Staff have to empathise with each other. These organisations are like clubs of like-minded people ... working on empathetic initiative with personal contact rather than formal liaison.'

This may be expressed as a **web**. The boss sits in the centre, surrounded by ever widening circles of intimates and influence. The diagonal lines represent **business functions** (remember our concentric charts in Chapter 3) but these are less important than the concentric circles.

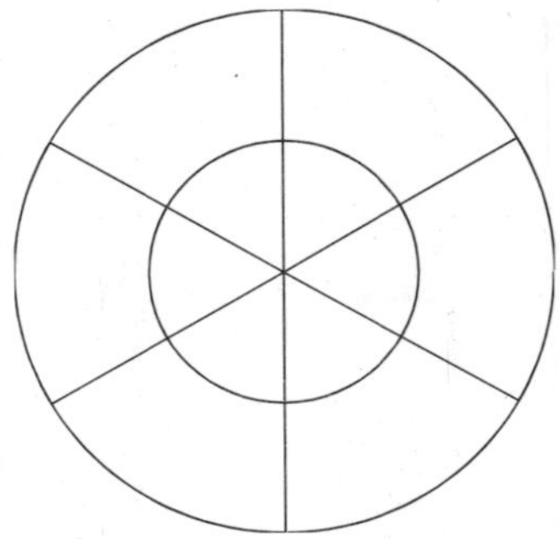

2.2 Role culture

Apollo is the god of the **role culture**. This is the classical, rational organisation or **bureaucracy**.

Characteristic	Comment
Roles, not personalities	The organisation structure defines the authority and responsibility of individual managers, who enact the **role** expected of their position. As many people are capable of doing the same job, the efficiency of this organisation depends on the structuring of jobs and the design of communications and formal relationships, rather than on individual personalities.
Not entrepreneurial	Individuals who work for such organisations tend to learn an expertise without experiencing risk; many do their job adequately, but are not over-ambitious.
Stability	The bureaucratic style can be very efficient in a stable environment when the organisation is large, where the work is predictable.
Slow to change	Unfortunately, bureaucracies are very slow to adapt to change and respond to change by doing more of the same (eg by generating cross functional liaison teams and a bureaucracy to support them).

This may be expressed as a Greek temple. A series of job boxes make up the functions (the pillars) which are then co-ordinated through the pediment at the top.

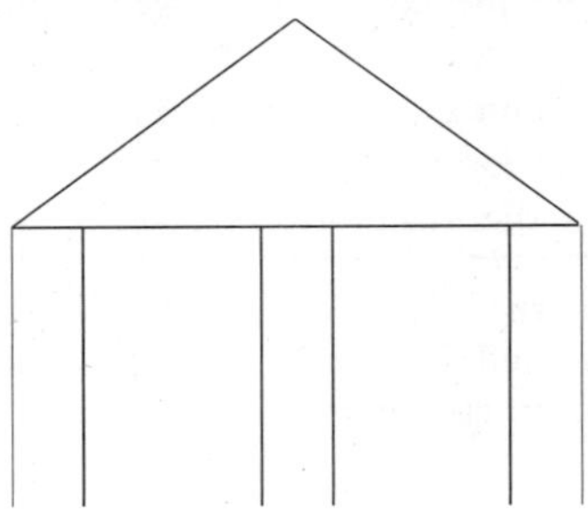

2.3 Task culture

Athena is the goddess of the **task culture**. Management is seen as completing a succession of **projects** or **solving problems,** often as **part of a team.**

Characteristic	Comment
Team based	The task culture is reflected in a matrix organisation or else in project teams and task forces. In such organisations, there is no dominant or clear leader
Get the job done	The principal concern in a task culture is to get the job done
Expertise	The individuals who are important are the experts with the ability to accomplish a particular aspect of the task. Each individual in the team considers he has more influence than he would have if the work were organised on a formal 'role culture' basis. Expertise and talent are more important than length of service.
Results-orientated	Performance is judged by results. Such organisations are flexible and constantly changing. For example, project teams are disbanded as soon as their task has been completed
Costly, because of variety	Task cultures are expensive. Experts demand a market price. Task cultures also depend on variety. To tap creativity requires a tolerance of perhaps costly mistakes. They are ideal when funds are available. Where cost is a worry, controls are necessary.
Job satisfaction	Job satisfaction tends to be high owing to the degree of individual participation and group identity. But this type of structure might only be successful if the nature of the work is suited to matrix project organisation or project work, and the employees of the organisation want the work organised in this way

A net which can pull its cords this way and that and can regroup at will illustrates this culture. This also means that resources are easy obtained from all parts of the organisation. These cultures are suited to organisations who are concerned with problem solving and short-term one-off exercises. Young, energetic people are attracted to this type of organisation.

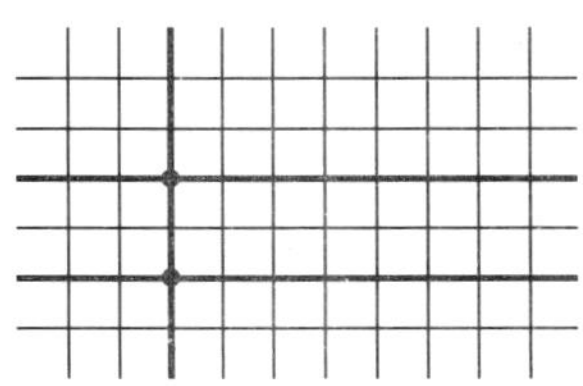

Figure 5.1 Task culture

2.4 Person culture

Dionysus is the god of the person or **existential culture**. In the other three cultures so far, the individual is subordinate to the organisation or task. An person culture is found in an organisation whose purpose is to **serve the interests of the individuals within it.** These organisations are rare, although individuals may operate this way within other cultures.

CASE EXAMPLES

(a) Studio artists, or cast of actors, look on their job as a means of expressing themselves artistically.

(b) University lecturers might use their official position as a springboard from which to launch a wider career in authorship, public speaking and so on.

(c) Barristers (in the UK) work through chambers. The clerk co-ordinates their work and hands out briefs, but does not control them.

The organisation depends on the talent of the individuals – a set of stars that operate independently. Management is derived from the consent of the managed, rather than the delegated authority of the owners. Indeed, the managers in these organisations are often lower in status than the professionals and are labelled secretaries, administrators, bursars, registrars or chief clerk.

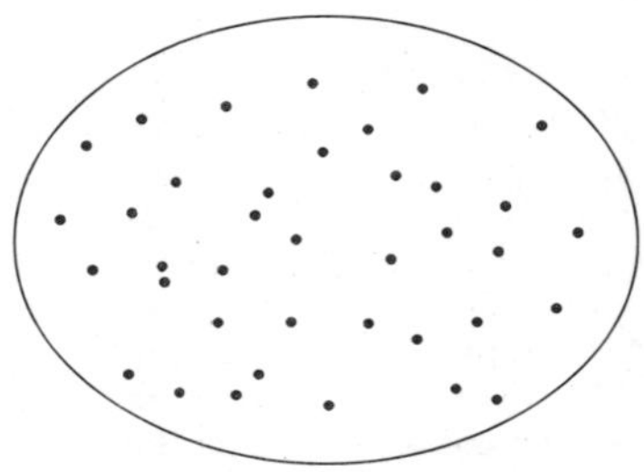

Figure 5.2 Person culture

Activity 3 **(15 minutes)**

Review the following statements. Ascribe each of them to one of Handy's four corporate cultures.

People are controlled and influenced by:

(a) The personal exercise of rewards, punishments or charisma

(b) Impersonal exercise of economic and political power to enforce procedures and standards of performance

(c) Communication and discussion of task requirements leading to appropriate action motivated by personal commitment to goal achievement

(d) Intrinsic interest and enjoyment in the activities to be done, and/or concern and caring for the needs of the other people involved

3 USING CULTURE

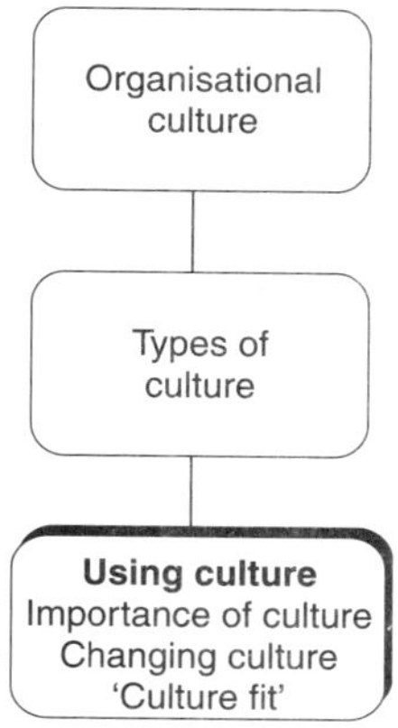

3.1 Importance of culture

Peters and Waterman (1982) found that the 'dominance and coherence of culture' was an essential feature of the 'excellent' companies they observed. A 'handful of guiding values' was more powerful than manuals, rule books, norms and controls formally imposed (and resisted). They commented: 'If companies do not have strong notions of themselves, as reflected in their values, stories, myths and legends, people's only security comes from where they live on the organisation chart.'

Organisational culture may be important in its influence on performance.

(a) It affects the **motivation and satisfaction of employees** (and possibly therefore their performance) by encouraging commitment to the organisation's values and objectives, making employees feel valued and trusted, fostering satisfying team relationships, and using 'guiding values' instead of rules and controls. A negative culture, however, can be equally influential.

(b) It can aid the **adaptability of the organisation,** by encouraging innovation, risk-taking, sensitivity to the environment, customer care, willingness to embrace new methods and technologies and so on. On the other hand, a strongly traditional safety-oriented culture may be powerful in resisting risk, change and innovation.

(c) It affects the **image of the organisation**. The cultural attributes of an organisation (attractive or unattractive) will affect its appeal to potential employees and customers. For example, the moves of banks to modernise and beautify branch design are meant to convey a 'style' that is up-to-date, welcoming, friendly but business-like, with open-plan welcome areas, helpful signposting and lots of light and plants.

FOR DISCUSSION

'I believe that the real difference between success and failure in a corporation can very often be traced to the question of how well the organisation brings out the great energies and talents of its people. What does it do to help these people find common cause with each other? And how can it sustain this common cause and sense of direction through the many changes which take place from one generation to another?...I think you will find that it owes its resiliency not to its form of organisation or administrative skills, but to the power of what we call *beliefs* and the appeal these beliefs have for its people.'

Watson (IBM), quoted by Peters and Waterman

Does this idea appeal to you? Or is it just nice-sounding, naïve (or perhaps manipulative?) lip-service on the part of a chief executive office.

3.2 Changing culture

Research suggests that it takes three to eight years to 'turn around' the culture of a large, well-established organisation.

It is, however, possible to 'turn round' a negative culture, or to change the culture into a new direction.

(a) The overt beliefs expressed by managers and staff can be used to 'condition' people, to sell a new culture to the organisation by promoting a new sense of **corporate mission**, or a new image. Slogans, mottos ('we're getting there'), myths and so on can be used to energise people and to promote particular values which the organisation wishes to instil in its members.

(b) **Leadership** provides an impetus for cultural change: attitudes to trust, control, formality or informality, participation, innovation and so on will have to come from the top – especially where changes in structure, authority relationships or work methods are also involved. The first step in deliberate cultural change will need to be a 'vision' and a sense of 'mission' on the part of a powerful individual or group in the organisation.

(c) The **reward system** can be used to encourage and reinforce new attitudes and behaviour, while those who do not commit themselves to the change miss out or are punished, or pressured to 'buy in or get out'.

(d) The **recruitment and selection policies** should reflect the qualities desired of employees in the new culture. To an extent these qualities may also be encouraged through induction and training.

(e) **Visible emblems of the culture** – for example design of the work place and public areas, dress code, status symbols – can be used to reflect the new 'style'.

Activity 4 **(20 minutes)**

(a) British Airways ran a series of corporate advertisements in the late 1980s based on the idea that their cabin staff possessed superhuman powers. Who do you think the advertising was aimed at - cabin staff or customers?

(b) Market research indicates that British Airways really is 'The World's Favourite Airline'. Which do you think came first, the slogan or the fact?

(c) Watch out in the press for other examples of organisations' attempts to change their culture. Local government should be a good source, as should organisations due for privatisation.

3.3 'Culture fit'

Recruitment, selection, training, corporate socialisation and reward systems are often used deliberately in order to attract, find, recognise and promote individuals who will 'fit in' with an organisation's desired cultural direction. Marks & Spencer, Mars and the vast majority of Japanese companies operating in the United Kingdom use such tactics to a greater or lesser extent.

Some companies go further and seek to fit their culture to the values, attitudes and practices of their customers establishing 'rapport' on a large scale.

'In order to gain competitive edge Heron Distribution looked at how well it served the needs of its customers. It drew up a diagram of each of its client companies' cultures, then looked at how closely its own attitudes and practices fitted in to the machine. Where there was a mismatch it geared up the recruitment and training of its own employees accordingly', a process it calls 'culture fit'.

(*Personnel Management*, March 1993)

Activity 5 **(20 minutes)**

You are the consultant to a large airline. As you walk through its offices, you notice that people's job titles are on their office doors, not their names. Late one evening as you leave you encounter one of the senior directors overlooking the airport. 'They're all here', he says, 'the whole fleet, apart from one which is due back from Switzerland in half an hour.' 'What if you wish to fly to Switzerland *tonight?'* you ask. 'Go by Helvetic Airways. None of this lot are leaving until tomorrow morning', he says.

What does the above tell you about the culture of the airline?

Chapter roundup

- Culture in an organisation is found in the formalisation of its structure, how decisions are taken, the degree to which authority and responsibility are delegated, and the degree to which initiative is allowed.
- Charles Handy notes four cultures, to which he gives the names of Greek deities. The club/power culture (Zeus) is run by one individual, who makes snap decisions, with people who share his or her outlook and values. The role culture (Apollo) describes a rule-driven specialised bureaucracy. A task culture (Athena) is one in which people group and regroup into teams to accomplish specific projects. An existential culture (Dionysus) is one in which management serves employees who are professionals or experts. Some companies or tasks require more than one of these cultures.
- The importance of corporate culture for organisation success has been highlighted by excellence theories. Cultures can be positive or negative in their influences.
- Cultures can be altered (gradually) through leadership, recruitment and selection, reward, training and culture 'selling'.

Quick quiz

1. What are the elements of culture?
2. What characterises a 'power' culture?
3. What type of culture is a classic bureaucracy?
4. What type of culture would you expect in a company set up to design and build a mass production factory? What culture would you expect to find in the factory once it is up and running?
5. What is 'culture fit'?
6. Give three examples of the negative effects of a strong culture.

Answers to quick quiz

1. Beliefs and values, customs, artefacts, rituals, symbols.
2. Based on personalities; adaptable and informal; small businesses.
3. Role culture (Apollo).
4. Task (Athena) for the design project: professionals, multi-disciplinary project etc. However, in the factory (mass production), probably role culture (Apollo). (Handy cites an example of this very thing: the design team tried to run the factory on task/democratic lines, but the workers resented being asked to help sort out management's problems.)
5. A company altering the culture of customer service or other units to 'match' that of customer organisations.
6. Negative attitudes influencing staff, strong traditional norms impeding change, negative image presented to the outside world.

Answers to activities

1. Here are some hints. The army is very disciplined. Decision-making is made by officers; behaviour between ranks (eg saluting) is sometimes very formal. Each regiment has its own history, of battles fought and honours won, and new recruits are expected to feel a continuity with the past.

   An advertising agency, with a different mission, is more fluid. Individual creativity, within the commercial needs of the firm, is expected. .

2. Hints only:
   (a) Look for the attitudes that come across in the organisation's service style and management style.
   (b) Look for slogans, mottos, advertising messages.
   (c) Look for uniforms, décor, emblems, body language.

3. (a) Zeus (Power)
   (b) Apollo (Role)
   (c) Athena (Task)
   (d) Dionysus (Person)

4 This activity is designed to make you think. Keep an eye out for cultural messages and their target audiences.

5 This is not so much a commercial airline, but a military airforce. Hence, the concentration on rank, and the 'I counted them all out, and I've counted them in' mentality. A corporate culture which delighted in, or was relieved by, assets not used and more importantly, potential customers not served, is hardly a business operation at all. (Note. This exercise was drawn from a case history described by Charles Hampden-Turner.)

Chapter 6:
INDIVIDUAL BEHAVIOUR AT WORK

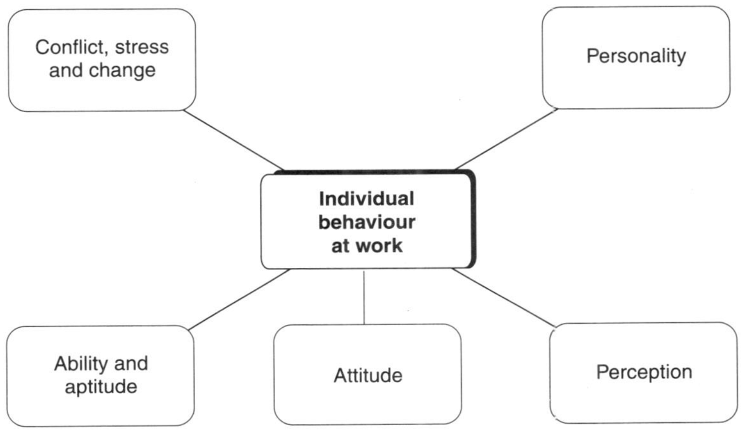

Introduction

In order to manage people, you need to understand people. If you understand why people behave as they do, you may be able to encourage – or change – their behaviour. If you know what types of behaviour make people effective as workers, you may be able to encourage or change their behaviour in such a way as to increase their contribution to organisational goals.

Unfortunately, human behaviour is not easy to describe, let alone to explain – let alone to predict! All individuals are different, and so behave differently. Each individual behaves differently over time, in different circumstances and with different people. Interpersonal behaviour (the interaction between two or more people) is different from individual behaviour. Groups of people behave rather differently than their individual members would if they were on their own. (In the following chapters, we will be looking at individual, interpersonal and group behaviour.)

In this chapter, we will be looking at what makes individuals tick and specifically what makes them behave in ways that work organisations might find helpful – or not.

Your objectives

In this chapter you will learn about the following:

(a) The nature of individual differences

(b) Basic theories of personality, perception, attitude

(c) Their significance for human behaviour at work

(d) Managerial strategies for the diagnosis and control of individual behavioural problems, such as stress and resistance to change

1 PERSONALITY

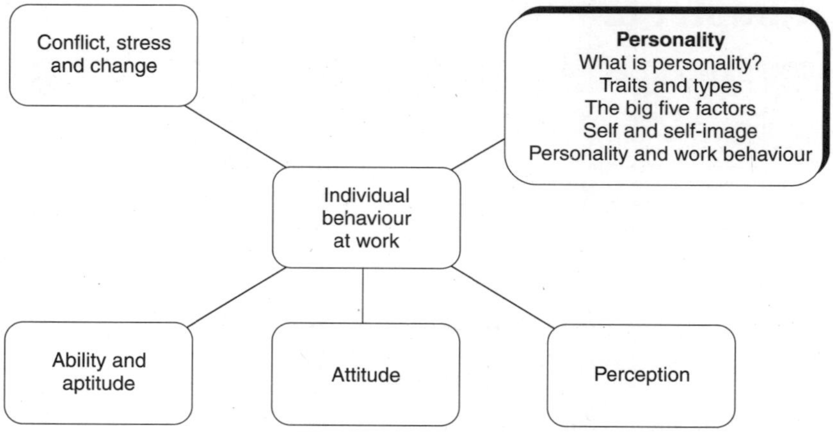

1.1 What is personality?

Individuals are unique. In order to identify, describe and explain the differences between people, psychologists use the concept of personality. Everyday use of the term tends to focus on a single characteristic of behaviour: someone is said to have an 'outgoing personality', for example. It also tends to get confused with charisma and social success, and adds the idea of quantity: TV 'personalities' by implication have 'lots of personality', while other individuals are said to 'lack personality'. Both these ideas are faulty, according to psychologists' more precise definition.

Definition

> **Personality** is the total pattern of characteristic ways of thinking, feeling and behaving that constitute the individual's distinctive method of relating to the environment.

There is a debate about whether or how far the factors of heredity (nature) and environment (nurture) influence personality. There are two main approaches.

- The **nomothetic ('law setting') approach** suggests that personality is more or less fixed, and that various elements of personality (called traits) are the same from individual to individual. Individuals possess a selection of these traits, which tend to go together in compatible trait clusters, effectively dividing people into personality types.
- The **idiographic approach** individualises. It suggests that personality develops through interaction with the environment (ie experience), and in accordance with how the individual sees himself. Personality can therefore be studied only as a picture of a particular individual at a particular time.

We will look briefly at each of these approaches, and see how they might be useful to a manager.

1.2 Traits and types

Traits are consistently observable properties, or the tendency for a person to behave in a particular way. If you say someone is generally sweet-tempered or undemonstrative, you are identifying traits in their personality.

Individual personality is simply a 'pick and mix' from a range of possible traits. People are different because individuals possess different traits, and different strengths of the same traits.

However, people who possess a particular trait are likely to possess certain other compatible or related traits: **trait clusters**. Thus a person who is sociable and expressive is (according to H J Eysenck, a leading exponent of this approach) also likely to be impulsive, risk-taking, active, irresponsible and practical. Taken as a whole the trait cluster forms an identifiable **personality type**: in this case, an 'extrovert' personality.

Trait/type theories of personality basically pigeon-hole people, putting them into categories defined by certain common behaviour patterns.

If you find yourself doing this at work, bear the following points in mind.

(a) The ability to make snap assessments of the personality of others, with very little to go on, is an essential part of social interaction: how else could you talk sensibly to a stranger? We treat people as types, on the basis of a few observable traits: a process called stereotyping. The accuracy of such assessments varies widely, according to peoples' powers of observation and judgement, and any prejudices they may have: at best, stereotypes are over-simplified (and at worst wildly inaccurate) – but at least they are a starting point for interpersonal contact.

(b) Such an approach is not, however, an accurate basis for predicting individual behaviour. In particular, the validity and effectiveness of personality trait tests in employee selection is hotly debated.

   (i) An individual may score highly on desirable traits in testing, but behave rather differently in practice: he may have given false answers in the test (based on what he thought the organisation would want to hear), or the test may have been irrelevant to the real job and work group.

   (ii) It is difficult for organisations to identify which traits are in fact desirable in employees: do you go for conformity to authority, or creative innovation, for example?

Organisations will inevitably make certain generalised assumptions about the personalities of the individuals they employ, about the type of individuals they would like to employ and to whom they would wish to allocate various tasks and responsibilities.

1.3 The big five factors

In the past 20 years, the views of many personality psychologists have converged regarding the structure and concepts of personality. Generally, researchers agree that there are five robust factors of personality, which can serve as a model for accurately classifying and describing personality. The five-factor model is comprised of five personality dimensions (OCEAN):

Openness to Experience vs. not open to experience

Conscientiousness vs undirectedness

Extraversion vs. introversion

Agreeableness vs. antagonism

Neuroticism vs. emotional stability

The five dimensions are held to be a complete description of personality.

Each of the five factors is made up of six facets and the facets that make up the five factors describe the distinctiveness and uniqueness of an individual in more detail.

The Big Five Factors	The facets that make up each factor	
Openness to Experience – describes an individual's pro-active seeking and appreciation of experience for its own sake.	• Imagination • Artistic interests • Emotions	• Adventurousness • Intellect • Liberalism
Conscientiousness – describes how organised, motivated and thorough an individual is in life and in pursuing goals.	• Resourcefulness • Achievement Striving • Sense of duty	• Self-discipline • Orderliness • Cautiousness
Extraversion – describes how energetic and enthusiastic a person is – especially when dealing with people.	• Friendliness • Gregariousness • Excitement seeking	• Activity level • Assertiveness • Cheerfulness
Agreeableness – describes a person's attitudes towards other people.	• Trust • Morality • Altruism	• Co-operation • Modesty • Sympathy
Neuroticism or natural reactions – measures the different ways people have of reacting emotionally to pressure and stressful circumstances.	• Anxiety • Self-consciousness • Anger	• Immoderation • Depression • Vulnerability

The Big Five represents a classification system of traits that some personality psychologists suggest captures the essence of individual differences in personality. These traits were arrived at through factor analysis studies. Factor analysis is a technique generally done with the use of computers to determine meaningful relationships and patterns in behavioural data. You begin with a large number of behavioural variables. The computer finds relationships or natural connections where variables are maximally correlated with one another and minimally correlated with other variables, and then groups the data accordingly. After this process has been done many times a pattern appears of relationships or certain factors that capture the essence of all of the data.

Strict trait personality psychologists go so far as to say our behaviour is really determined by these internal traits, giving the situation a small role in determining behaviour. In other words, these traits lead to an individual acting a certain way in a given situation.

FOR DISCUSSION

Do you think an assessment of personality should form part of an organisation's recruitment process? What traits might it think desirable?

If you completed the above discussion, you may appreciate the difficulty of selecting desirable traits, from the organisation's point of view. In fact, the question: 'What type of person – possessing what traits – will make a successful....?' is naive. As we will see, ability and experience, education and skill training, motivation, job design, sex, age, attitudes, opportunity and many other factors will influence job performance. Research has simply not been able to show significant correlation between any personality trait and successful performance.

We will now turn to the idiographic approach, which attempts to look at whole people, as they are, and as they change over time.

1.4 Self and self-image

According to the idiographic approach, personality is the complex product of a dynamic process whereby the individual interacts with his or her environment and other people, through experience.

Self

George Herbert Mead (1934) noted that despite the constraints of social values and norms, people still display originality and individuality. He argued that the 'self' has two components:

(a) 'I' – the unique, active, impulsive part of the individual, which rises above conformity; and

(b) 'Me' – the mental process which reflects objectively on the self and measures it against the social norms, values and expectations which the individual has taken on board as the result of experience in society.

A similar tension is the basis of Sigmund Freud's psychological constructs: the 'ego', 'id' and 'super-ego'.

Self-image

People have a subjective picture of what their own self is like: this is called a 'self-image'. Self-image is developed primarily through experience, and interaction with other people – particularly important people, such as our family through childhood, and our peers in adolescence. We evaluate ourselves according to the effect of our behaviour on other people, and how they respond to us. If people regularly praise your hard work, for example, you may have an image of yourself as a conscientious, successful worker. People tend to behave in accordance with their self-image, and how they expect to be treated.

Personality development

As well as an adjustment to the environment, personality development is an internal psychological process. According to most accepted theories, the personality is made up of various psychological forces or 'parts' which combine and interact to shape the behaviour of the whole person. The general trend as people mature is towards increasing diversity and complexity of these 'parts', and usually therefore an increasing sense of selfhood and the need to develop personal potential. They tend, as they mature, to become more actively independent, to take on more equal or superior relationships (moving from child-adult, to adult-adult and adult-child relationships) and to develop self control and self awareness.

These things do not inevitably happen alongside physical ageing. Individuals may remain psychologically immature in some aspects. Indeed, some psychologists consider that classical, efficiency-seeking organisations actively prevent people from maturing, by encouraging them to passive compliance with authority!

Whichever approach to personality we adopt, it is clear that the context in which individual and social behaviours emerge or develop is, for very many individuals, a work organisation. So how do you manage personality differences?

1.5 Personality and work behaviour

Obviously, personalities are complex and individual. Nonetheless, if we assume broad consistency in traits or types of personality, we can make some useful observations about individual behaviour at work – at least enough to be going on with in the real world. Adopting a contingency approach, managers will have to consider the following aspects.

(a) *The compatibility of an individual's personality with the task*

Different personality types suit different types of work. Without detailed psychological analysis, a manager should be aware that a person who appears unsociable and inhibited will find sales work, involving a lot of social interaction, intensely stressful – and will probably not be very good at it!

(b) *The compatibility of an individual's personality with the systems and management culture of the organisation*

Some people hate to be controlled, for example, but others (of an 'authoritarian' personality type) want to be controlled and dependent in a work situation, because they find responsibility threatening.

Some people (of a 'need to achieve' personality type) have a strong desire for success and a strong fear of failure. Such people tend to want personal responsibility, moderately difficult tasks and goals (which challenge them but do not present the risk of failure) and clear, frequent feedback on performance.

(c) *The compatibility of the individual's personality with that of others in the team*

Personality clashes are a prime source of conflict at work. An achievement-oriented personality, for example, tends to be a perfectionist, is impatient and unable to relax, and will be unsociable if people seem to be getting in the way of performance: such a person will clearly be frustrated and annoyed by laid-back, sociable types working (or not working) around him. Even attractive traits, like a sunny temper, can get on the nerves of people of a different type.

Where incompatibilities occur, the manager will have to:

(a) *Restore compatibility* – this may be achieved by reassigning an individual to tasks more suited to his personality type, for example, or changing management style to suit the personalities of the team

(b) *Achieve compromise* – individuals should be encouraged to:

(i) Understand the nature of their differences. Others have the right to be themselves (within the demands of the team); personal differences should not be 'taken personally', as if they were adopted deliberately to annoy

(ii) Modify their behaviour, if necessary; if personality develops according to feedback from interaction with others, then people can be encouraged and trained to adopt positive traits and overcome negative ones; you can train people to be more achievement oriented, for example, or to restrain 'natural' aggression or temper

(c) *Remove the incompatible personality* – in the last resort, obstinately difficult or disruptive people may simply have to be weeded out of the team. Team selection should as far as possible ensure that potentially incompatible people never become part of the team in the first place.

Activity 1 **(20 minutes)**

Look at the following list and number the qualities in priority order: 1 is very important, 2 is quite important, 3 is unimportant.

(a) Good appearance
(b) Ability to do the job
(c) Ability to answer questions clearly
(d) A pleasant speaking voice
(e) Being objective
(f) A pleasant personality
(g) The ability to reason
(h) Being interested in further training
(i) Being used to working in a team
(j) Being a good listener

2 PERCEPTION

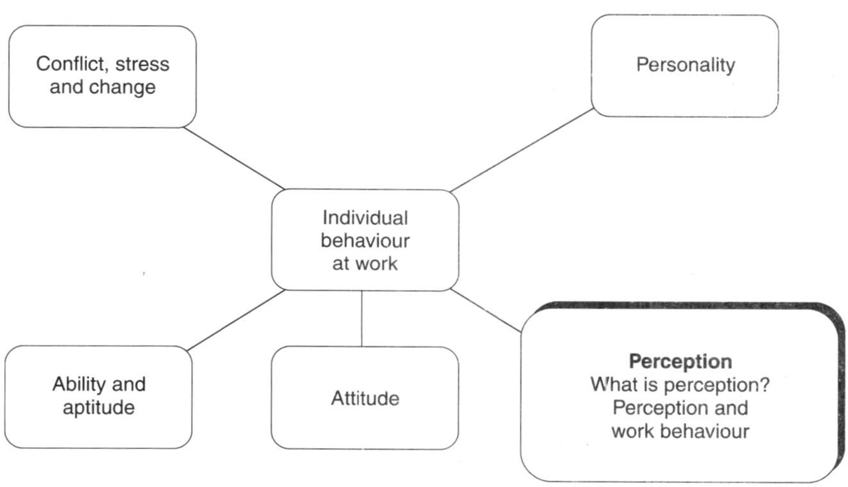

2.1 What is perception?

Different people 'see' things differently. And human beings behave in (and in response to) the world – not 'as it really is', but as they see it. That is why you need to understand perception.

Definition

> **Perception** is the psychological process by which stimuli or in-coming sensory data are selected and organised into patterns which are meaningful to the individual.

Perceptual selection

The sensory apparatus of humans (eyes, ears, skin and so on) has limitations, which filter out certain stimuli: certain pitches of sound, for example, (like a dog whistle) or types of light (infrared). Perception acts as a further screen. We are constantly bombarded by sensory data of all kinds, not all of which is interesting or useful to us. We would not be able to function if we had to deal with every sound, sight, smell and touch. (If you make a real effort to listen to all the sounds in the room where you are sitting now, you will realise that they were only 'background', or that you hadn't noticed them at all, while your attention was focused elsewhere – hopefully, on this Course Book...)

The filtering process is called **perceptual selectivity**. It means that the world picture that our brains actually hold is not a whole or accurate one. Selection may be determined by any or all of the following.

(a) The **context**. People 'see what they want to see': whatever is necessary or relevant in the situation in which they find themselves. You might notice articles on management in the newspapers, concerning motivation or wage negotiations while studying this module which normally you would not notice.

(b) The **nature of the stimuli**. Our attention tends to be drawn to large, bright, loud, unfamiliar, moving and repeated (not repetitive) stimuli. Advertisers know it...

(c) **Internal factors**. Our attention is drawn to stimuli that match our personality, needs, interests, expectations and so on. If you are hungry, for example, you will pick the smell of food out of a mix of aromas.

(d) **Fear or trauma**. People are able to avoid seeing things that they don't want to see: things that are threatening to their security or self-image, or things that are too painful for them.

Perceptual organisation

A complementary process of perceptual organisation deals with the interpretation of the data which has been gathered and filtered. The brain groups, separates and patterns stimuli to make them recognisable, intelligible and useful to the individual. Thus sound waves become music, black and white shapes become writing and so on.

The mind is remarkably resourceful in organising data to give it meaning. It tends to fill in gaps in partial or confusing information, according to its expectations or assumptions about what should be there. This is called closure. (It is partly why speed reading is possible: the mere shape of a familiar word, together with the context, which creates the expectation of what kind of word it must be, is enough for the mind to 'read' the word, without having focused on all the information available.)

FOR DISCUSSION

There is a famous story about a victorious (but unhealthy) French general who was heard to cry: 'Ma sacrée toux!' (My damn' cough!) by his aides. Unfortunately, they were on their way to ask him what he wanted done with all the prisoners taken in battle that day. They heard: 'Massacrez tous!' (Kill everyone!). And they did.

What does this suggest about the process of perceptual organisation?

Like personality, perception is highly complex and highly individual. It is not possible to draw up detailed prescriptions for how people's perceptions can be analysed and utilised by management. However, here are some general principles.

2.2 Perception and work behaviour

Remember that human beings do not respond to the world 'as it really is', but as they perceive it to be. If individuals act in ways that seem illogical or contrary to you, it is probably not because of stupidity or defiance, but because they simply do not see things in the same way you do.

(a) Consider whether **you** might be misinterpreting the situation. Is there any awkward information you are avoiding? Have you jumped to conclusions in your desire for closure? Does your view really fit the facts? What needs and biases colour your perception of things? What are you being sensitive about?

(b) Consider whether **others** might be misinterpreting the situation, or interpreting it differently from you. What might make them see things in a different light? Listen to people, and get to know what their blind spots and biases are. Try and see things through their eyes.

(c) When tackling a task or a problem, get the people involved to define the situation as they see it. Then everyone will know what they mean, and differences of perception can be cleared up before they can cause confusion. (It's the same when you write an essay: define your terms!)

(d) Be aware of the most common clashes of perception at work.

  (i) **Managers and staff.** The experience of work can be very different for managerial and non-managerial personnel, and this has tended to foster 'them and us' perceptions. Efforts to bridge the gap may be viewed with suspicion.

  (ii) **Work cultures**. Different functions in organisations may have very different time-scales and cultures of work, and will therefore perceive the work – and each other – in different ways Consider how a sales team might regard the importance of their work in relation to production workers – and *vice versa*.

(iii) **Race and gender**. A joke, comment or gesture that one person may see as a 'bit of a laugh' may be offensive – and construed as harassment under the law – to another. Minorities in the workplace are bound to be sensitive to implied discrimination, and may therefore perceive it even where none is intended. Managers should be aware of how their words and decisions may be construed.

Activity 2 **(30 minutes)**

Identify the perceptual problem(s) in the following cases.

(a) An autocratic manager tries to adopt a more participative style of management, in order to improve the morale of his staff. He tells them they will be given more responsibility, and will be 'judged and rewarded accordingly'. For some reason, morale seems to worsen, and several people ask to transfer to other departments.

(b) A woman has just been promoted to the management team. At the first management meeting, the chairman introduces her to her new colleagues – all male – and says: 'At least we'll get some decent tea in these meetings from now on, eh?' Almost everyone laughs. For some reason, the woman does not contribute much in the meeting, and the chairman later tells one of his colleagues: 'I hope we haven't made a mistake. She doesn't seem to be a team player at all.'

(c) A new employee wanders into the office canteen, and is offered a cup of coffee by a youngster in jeans and a T-shirt, who has been chatting to the canteen supervisor. The youngster joins the man at his table (to his surprise) and asks how he likes working there so far. After a while, glancing uneasily at the man behind the serving counter, the new employee asks: 'Is it OK for you to be sitting here talking to me? I mean, won't the boss mind?' The youngster replies: 'I am the boss. Actually, I'm the boss of the whole company. Biscuit?'

We will discuss perception further in Chapter 7.

3 ATTITUDE

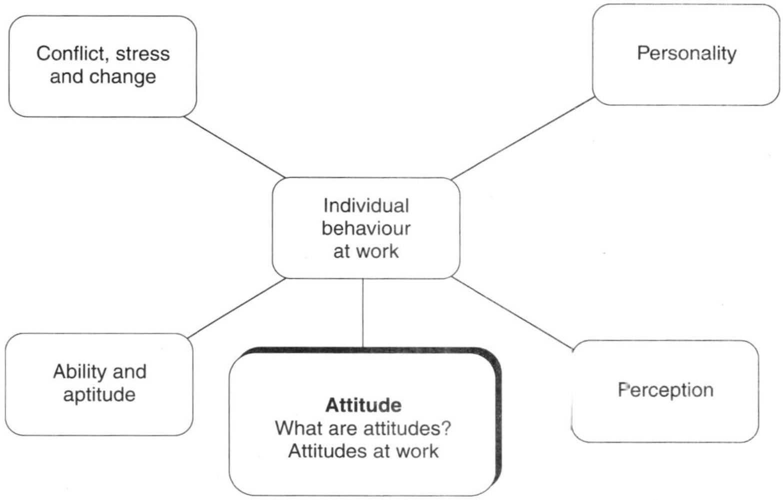

3.1 What are attitudes?

Attitudes are our general standpoint on things: the positions we have adopted in regard to particular issues, things and people, as we perceive them.

Definition

> Technically speaking, an **attitude** is 'a mental and neural state of readiness... exerting a directive or dynamic influence upon the individual's response to all objects and situations with which it is related.'

Attitudes are thought to contain three basic components:

- Knowledge, beliefs or disbeliefs, perceptions
- Feelings and desires (positive or negative)
- Volition, will or the intention to perform an action

So our attitude towards something includes what we think and feel about it – and also predisposes us to behave in a certain way in response to it. This will be of particular interest to a manager, because it suggests that if you can identify people's attitudes to things, you may be able to anticipate how they will behave.

3.2 Attitudes at work

Behaviour **in a work context** will be influenced by:

(a) Attitudes **to** work: the individual's standpoint on working, work conditions, colleagues, the task, the organisation and management

(b) Attitudes **at** work: all sorts of attitudes which individuals may have about other people, politics, education, religion among other things, and which they bring with them into the work place – to act on, agree, disagree or discuss

Positive, negative or neutral attitudes to other workers, or groups of workers, to the various systems and operations of the organisation, to learning – or particular training initiatives – to communication or to the task itself will obviously influence performance at work. In particular they may result in:

(a) Varying degrees of co-operation or conflict between individuals and groups, or between departments

(b) Varying degrees of co-operation with or resistance to management

(c) Varying degrees of success in communication – interpersonal and organisation wide

(d) Varying degrees of commitment and contribution to the work

Activity 3 **(15 minutes)**

Suggest four elements which would make up a positive attitude to work. An example might be the belief that you get a fair day's pay for a fair day's work.

Non-work factors that might influence attitudes to work, or affecting work, include the following.

(a) **Class and class consciousness**: attitudes about the superiority or inferiority of others, according to birth, wealth and education; attitudes to money and work (necessity or career?).

(b) **Age**. Attitudes to sexual equality, family and morality (for example) vary widely from one generation to the next. Attitudes in general tend to become less flexible with age.

(c) **Race, culture or religion**. Attitudes about these areas will affect the way people regard each other and their willingness to co-operate in work situations. Culture and religion are also strong influences on attitudes to work: for example, the 'Protestant work ethic', or Japanese concepts of the organisation 'family'.

(d) **Lifestyle and interests**. Attitudes to these areas affect interpersonal relations and self-image, as well as the relative importance of work and leisure to the individual.

(e) **Sex**. Attitudes to the equality of the sexes and their various roles at work and in society may be influential in:

   (i) **Interpersonal relations at work** (especially where women are in positions of authority over men: sexist attitudes may come into painful conflict with imposed power structures)

   (ii) **The self concept of the individual**: women at work may be made to feel inferior, incompetent or simply unwelcome, while men working for female managers might feel threatened

   (iii) **Attitudes to work**. Stereotypical role profiles ('a woman's place is in the home', 'the man has to support the family') may be held by both sexes and may create feelings of guilt, resentment or resignation about wanting or having to work

4 ABILITY AND APTITUDE

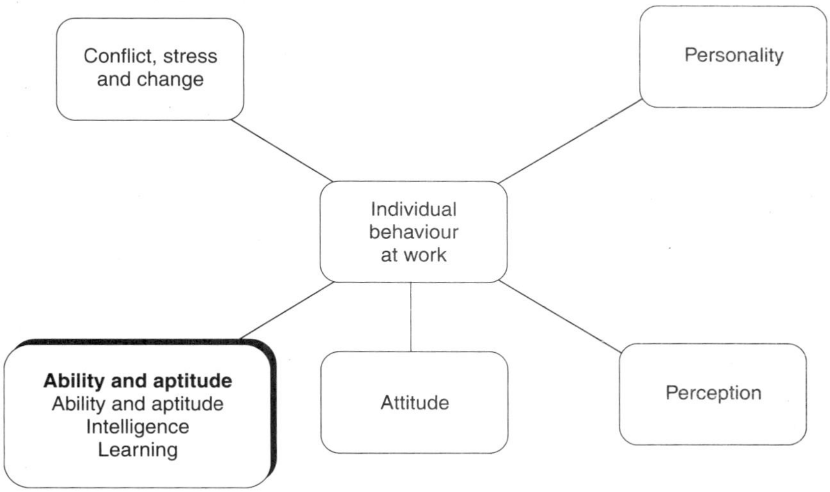

4.1 Ability and aptitude

There have been many attempts to make a useful distinction between:

(a) **Abilities** – things that people can do, or are good at – largely believed to be inherited

(b) **Aptitudes** – the capacity to learn and develop abilities or skill

There is not always a clear dividing line between the two concepts, however.

Organisations such as schools, colleges and businesses attempt to assess the sphere of individuals' abilities, and the level of required abilities which different individuals possess. It seems obvious that people are 'naturals' at music, drawing or football; some people have 'the gift of the gab', while others are good with numbers; some people are thinkers, while others are 'good with their hands'.

If a certain ability or aptitude is required for an individual to perform his job, or to perform it better, then it would be useful to test for and measure that ability or aptitude. That way the right person can be selected and/or trained for the job – or the task allocated to the person with the right ability or aptitude. However, ability is only one factor of performance in a work context. It may be essential to successful performance in a particular job – but it is unlikely to be sufficient, by itself. Willingness to perform the task, and suitable task design and working conditions, for example, will also be required.

The terms 'ability' and 'intelligence' have often been used interchangeably, and have been rather narrowly defined to denote such things as 'mental dexterity', 'logic' or 'verbal fluency'. Analytical intelligence (the kind measured by IQ tests) is still most frequently used as a measure of 'ability' in children and adults alike. However, there is more to intelligence than this.

4.2 Intelligence

Intelligence is a wide and complex concept. The more scientists explore the idea of creating 'Artificial Intelligence', the more they realise just how complex the nature and processes of human intelligence really are.

Recent work appears to confirm the commonsense observation that intelligence/ability takes many forms, including:

(a) Analytic intelligence – measured by IQ tests

(b) Spatial intelligence – the ability to see patterns and connections, most obvious in the creative artist or scientist

(c) Musical intelligence – the 'good ear' of musicians, mimics and linguists

(d) Physical intelligence – obvious in athletes and dancers

(e) Practical intelligence – some people can make and fix things without theoretical knowledge

(f) Intra-personal intelligence – the ability to know, be sensitive to and express oneself, observable in poets, artists and mystics

(g) Inter-personal intelligence – the ability to relate to and work through others; essential in leaders

The concept of intelligence has been further complicated by research into the processes of the brain. It has been suggested that the logical, analytical, intellectual functions of the brain – those commonly thought of as intelligence (IQ) – are performed in the left-hand half (hemisphere). The right-hand hemisphere was found to be the seat of less rational processes: intuition, hunches, vision, flair, imagination, emotion and creativity.

FOR DISCUSSION

Do you think management is a left-brain or right-brain activity? Give examples of management functions to support your view. Do more 'intelligent' people make better managers?

Whatever people's abilities and intelligence, their performance can be improved by extra knowledge, practice and experience – in other words, by learning. We will be covering the organisational aspects of education and training in Chapter 8, but here we will look briefly at how people learn.

4.3 Learning

Learning is how we come to know and do things.

Definition

> **Learning** is the process of acquiring, through experience, knowledge which leads to changed behaviour.

Learning changes behaviour: the test of whether you have learned how to do something is whether you can perform an action, when you could not do so before. This is important because it enables us to define what we want the outcome of learning to be (for example, in designing training programmes) and to measure what people have learned.

There are two main approaches to learning, based on very different theories about how people know things and whether scientists are entitled to make inferences about the internal, unobservable workings of the human mind.

The **behaviourist** or **stimulus-response** approach suggests that we behave in response to sensory stimuli or influences from the environment. Depending whether our experience is positive or negative, we will repeat or modify that response next time. In other words, the result of our responses may be rewarding (**positive reinforcement**) or punishing (**negative reinforcement**) and act as an incentive or a deterrent to similar behaviour in the future. This shaping of behaviour through reinforcement is called **conditioning**. Trial-and-error learning and 'carrot-and-stick' motivation are based on this idea.

Activity 4 **(20 minutes)**

Give examples of how a manager might use:

(a) Positive reinforcement
(b) Negative reinforcement

to condition team members' behaviour. Which do you think would be most successful?

The **cognitive or information processing** approach to learning suggests that the human mind actively interprets sensory information, analyses experience and takes it into account in making decisions about how to behave in future. Reinforcements do not merely create habits (as conditioning theories suggest): they are one of many factors in our choice of how we will need to behave in order to fulfil our needs and purposes. **Feedback** on the results of our actions is essential so that we can continually adjust our plans and behaviour to fit the situation. In other words, learning is a control process.

The learning cycle

Learning as an information-processing and control activity is modelled in the 'learning cycle', Figure 6.1.

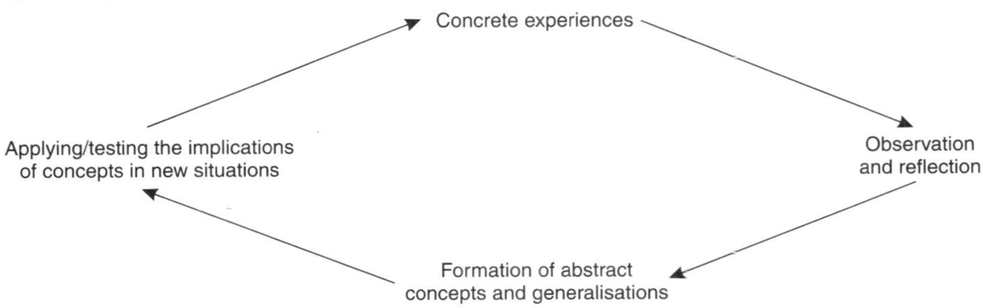

Figure 6.1 The learning cycle (Kolb, 1984)

Say a team member interviews a customer for the first time (concrete experience). He observes his performance and the dynamics of the situation (observation) and afterwards, having failed to convince the customer to buy the product, he analyses what he did right and wrong (reflection). He comes to the conclusion that he had failed to listen to what the customer really wanted and feared, underneath her general reluctance: he realises that the key to communication is listening (abstraction/generalisation). In his next interview he applies his strategy to the new set of circumstances (application/ testing). This provides him with a new experience with which to start the cycle over again.

5 CONFLICT, STRESS AND CHANGE

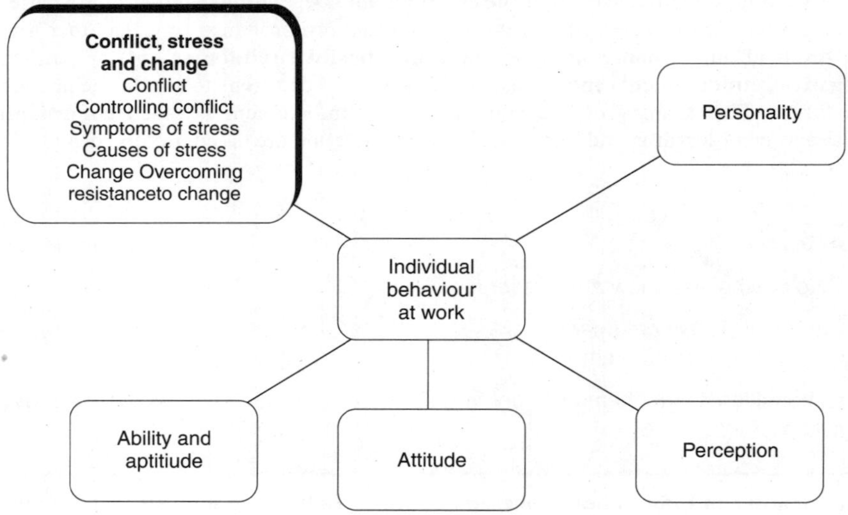

5.1 Conflict

Definition

> **Conflict** is any personal divergence of interests between groups or individuals.

The major sources of conflict arise from:

- the need to share scarce resources
- differences in goals between organisational units
- differences in values, attitudes or perceptions among members of different units

You might assume that, as the opposite of co-operation, conflict is a bad thing. Indeed, conflict can be destructive, or negative. It may:

(a) Distract attention from the group's task (to personal objectives, like scoring points off other group members)

(b) Polarise views and fragment – or even destroy – the group

(c) Encourage defensive or 'spoiling' behaviour

(d) Stimulate emotional, win-lose arguments and hostility

However, conflict can also clarify issues and revitalise relationships – as you may know if you 'enjoy a good argument'! Conflict can be helpful or constructive when its effect is to:

(a) Introduce new solutions to problems, as people 'spark' ideas off each other

(b) Define relationships more clearly

(c) Encourage the testing of ideas to see whether they are valid

(d) Focus attention on individual contribution and responsibility rather than allowing people to hide behind group decisions

(e) Provide opportunity for the release of hostile feelings and attitudes that have been, or may be, repressed otherwise.

Sometimes, what appears to be a rather painful argument can have very positive outcomes: a strike, for example, may normally be seen as destructive and hostile. In fact it can provide an impetus to problem-solving, and a way of clearing the air. Too much co-operation and agreement may conversely produce a 'love-in', where task objectives become secondary to the group's enjoyment of its interpersonal relationships.

So how is a manager to get the best out of conflict in his team – and not the worst?

5.2 Controlling conflict

Argument means resolving differences by discussion. This can encourage the integration of a number of viewpoints into a better solution. Charles Handy (1987) suggests that in order for argument to be effective:

(a) The arguing group must have leadership, mutual trust, and a challenging task to focus on

(b) The logic of the argument must be preserved: the issues under discussion must be clear, the discussion must concentrate on available information (not guesswork or fantasy), and all views must be heard and taken into account

If such argument is frustrated, or if the argument itself is merely the symptom of underlying, unexpressed hostility, then conflict will be the result.

Competition can:

(a) Set standards, by pointing to the 'best' performance achieved by one of the competing parties

(b) Motivate individuals to better effort

(c) 'Sort out the men from the boys'

In order to be fruitful, competition must be seen to be **open**, rather than **closed**. 'Closed' competition is a win-lose (or 'zero-sum') situation, where one party's gain will be another party's loss: one party can only do well at the expense of another, in competition for resources, recognition and so on. 'Open' competition exists where all participants can increase their gains together: for example, if bonuses are available to **all** teams which produce more or better output, not just the 'best' team.

If competition is perceived to be open, the rules are seen to be fair, and the competitors feel that the factors leading to success are within their control, then competition can be extremely fruitful.

Activity 5 **(10 minutes)**

What symptoms might indicate to you that conflict was becoming a problem in a team?

Charles Handy (1987) suggests two types of strategy that may be used to turn harmful conflict into constructive competition or argument, or to manage it in some other acceptable way.

(a) **Environmental ('ecological') strategies** involve creating conditions in which individuals may be better able to work co-operatively with each other. Such strategies include:

   (i) Agreement of common objectives
   (ii) Reinforcing the group or 'team' nature of organisational life
   (iii) Providing feedback information on progress
   (iv) Providing adequate co-ordination and communication mechanisms
   (v) Sorting out territorial/role conflicts in the organisational structure

(b) **Regulation strategies** are directed to the **control of conflict** when it arises. Possible methods include:

   (i) The provision of arbitration to settle disputes
   (ii) The establishment of detailed rules and procedures for conduct by employees
   (iii) Using confrontational inter-group meetings to hammer out differences, especially where territorial conflicts occur
   (iv) Separating the conflicting individuals
   (v) Ignoring the problem, if it is genuinely likely to go away, and there is no point in opening fresh wounds

Activity 6 **(20 minutes)**

In the light of the above, consider how conflict could arise and how it might be resolved in the following situations.

(a) Two managers who share a secretary have documents to be typed at the same time.

(b) A company's electricians find out that a group of engineers have been receiving training in electrical work.

(c) Department A stops for lunch at 12.30 while Department B stops at 1 o'clock. Occasionally the canteen runs out of puddings for Department B workers.

(d) The Northern Region and Southern Region sales teams are continually trying to better each other's results, and the capacity of production to cope with the increase in sales is becoming overstretched.

5.3 Symptoms of stress

Stress is a term which is often loosely used to describe feelings of tension or exhaustion – usually associated with too much, or overly demanding, work. In fact, stress is simply the product of demands made on an individual's physical and mental energies: boredom can be just as stressful as pressure. Demands on an individual's energies may be stimulating, as well as harmful, and most people require some form of stress to bring out their best performance. Executive stress, however, can be damaging. This is why we talk about the control or management of stress, not its elimination: it is a question of keeping stress to helpful proportions.

Harmful stress or 'strain' can be identified by its effects on the individual and his or her performance. Symptoms usually include:

(a) **Nervous tension** – this may manifest itself in various ways: irritability and increased sensitivity, preoccupation with details, a polarised ('black and white') view of issues, or sleeplessness; various physical symptoms, such as skin and digestive orders, are also believed to be stress-related

(b) **Withdrawal** – this is essentially a defence mechanism, which may show itself in unusual quietness and reluctance to communicate, abuse of drugs or alcohol, or physical withdrawal by absenteeism, poor time-keeping or even leaving the organisation

(c) **Low morale** – low confidence, dissatisfaction, poor discipline, frustration amongst other symptoms

5.4 Causes of stress

Stress may be caused by a number of work and non-work factors.

(a) **Too many demands on the individual**: overwork, or pressure, too much responsibility or too little time.

(b) **Too few demands on the individual**: monotony (or 'sameness'), boredom – in short, frustration.

(c) **Uncertainty and therefore insecurity**, especially where the outcome is important to the individual, or his responsibility. (This is why career change, redundancy, retirement, innovations at work, moving house and change of family circumstances are highly stressful.)

(d) **Personality factors**. People who are naturally 'laid back' are simply better able to handle stress than those who are dynamic and competitive. The amount of stress people of either type will be able to cope with depends on factors such as:

   (i) Emotional sensitivity (can you shrug off unpleasantness?)

   (ii) Flexibility (do you bend – or snap – under pressure?)

   (iii) Inter-personal competence (do you draw strength from others in a crisis?)

   (iv) Sense of responsibility (do you have an 'easy come, easy go' attitude, or do you fear letting people down?)

Activity 7 **(20 minutes)**

See if you can suggest ways of controlling stress that arises from each of the causes listed in section 5.4. (Look for the logical solution. There's no great 'mystique' to stress management...)

5.5 Change

Change affects individuals in all sorts of ways. A change in shift-work patterns or work conditions, for example, may affect workers' bodies. Office relocation will affect their circumstances. Changes in office layout or work organisation may change their network of relationships.

Most importantly, change affects individuals psychologically.

(a) It may create feelings of disorientation or 'lostness' before new circumstances have been absorbed.

(b) This may threaten the individual's self-concept, because (s)he may no longer feel competent to cope in the new circumstances: most people feel guilty and inadequate as 'beginners'.

(c) Change involves uncertainty, which creates insecurity – especially at work, where there are great pressures for continuity (of employment, and of performance).

(d) The support offered by established relationships is likely to have been disrupted, and the need to start all over again with a new group of people can be daunting.

(e) Change can be particularly threatening if it is perceived as an outside force against which the individual is powerless.

Resisting change means attempting to preserve the existing state of affairs – the *status quo* – against pressure to alter it. Despite the possibly traumatic effects of change *per se*, most people do not in fact resist it on these grounds alone. Where people do resist change itself, it may be partly because of inflexibility (which may or may not be related to age) or strong needs for security and structure.

Activity 8 **(30 minutes)**

Resistance to particular proposed changes will depend on the circumstances. Read through some newspapers and give examples of resistance based on:

(a) Attitudes or beliefs
(b) Habit or custom
(c) Loyalty to a group
(d) Politics or holding onto power

So what do managers do about resistance to change? Here are a few ideas.

5.6 Overcoming resistance to change

The pace of change

Changes ought if possible to be introduced slowly. The more gradual the change, the more time is available for questions to be asked and answered, relationships to be adjusted, old ways unlearned, new ways learned and got used to, and individuals reassured that they will be able to cope. Timing will also be important: those responsible for change should be sensitive to incidents and attitudes that might indicate that 'now is not the time'.

The scope of change

Total transformation will create greater insecurity than moderate change – but also greater excitement, if the organisation has the kind of innovative culture that can stand it. Management should be aware of how many aspects of their employees' lives they are proposing to alter – and therefore on how many fronts they are likely to encounter resistance. There may be 'hidden' changes to take into account: a change in technology may necessitate changes in work methods, which may in turn result in the breaking up of work groups.

The manner of change

The manner in which a change is put across is vital: if possible the individuals concerned should be positively encouraged to adopt the changes as their own.

(a) Resistance should be welcomed and confronted, not denied or swept under the carpet. Talking through areas of conflict may give useful insights.

(b) There should be free circulation of information about the reasons for the change, its consequences and expected results. This information should appear sensible, consistent, realistic and trustworthy – not an attempt to 'pull the wool over the eyes' of people, or to 'blind them with science'.

(c) The change must be sold to the people as important, necessary or desirable – for them, if possible. (Changes in a crisis often face less resistance than changes of a routine nature.)

(d) People must be reassured that they have or will be given the skills and resources to implement the change successfully.

(e) The effects of insecurity may be lessened if people can be consulted or involved in the planning and implementation of the change. Successful change will usually be **initiated** from the top (otherwise the politics are too complicated), but will harness the knowledge and experience of those affected in the 'nitty gritty' of the change programme.

Chapter roundup

- Personality is the total pattern of an individual's thoughts, feelings and behaviours. It is shaped by a variety of factors, both inherited and environmental.
- Perception is the process by which the brain selects and organises information in order to make sense of it. People behave according to what they perceive – not according to what 'really is'.
- People develop attitudes about things, based on what they think, what they feel and what they want to do about it. Attitudes are formed by perception, experience and personality, which in turn are shaped by wider social influences.
- Ability is the capacity to do something. It is often equated with intelligence. It is now recognised that there are many types of ability/intelligence, not all of which are based about mental dexterity or verbal fluency.
- Stress is the product of mental and physical demands on the individual. It becomes 'strain' if excessive or uncontrolled.
- Conflict may be either destructive or constructive. Differences should be encouraged and channelled into argument or competition, not destructive conflict.
- Change poses a threat to individuals in many areas of their lives, and is often resisted. The change must be carefully managed to overcome this resistance.

Quick quiz

1 What is a trait cluster, and why might it be useful in everyday social interaction?

2 List three factors for a manager to consider in managing 'personality' at work.

3 Give three examples of areas where people's perceptions commonly conflict.

4 What are the three components of an 'attitude'?

5 Give three examples of non-work factors that might influence attitudes to work.

6 Indicate the difference between 'abilities' and 'aptitudes'.

7 Give four examples of non-analytical or non-intellectual intelligence.

8 What is (a) 'positive reinforcement' and (b) self actualisation?

9 Draw the 'learning cycle'.

10 List some symptoms of stress.

11 Outline a five-point plan for introducing change.

Answers to quick quiz

1 A number of related or compatible traits which form a personality type.

2 The compatibility of an individual's personality with the task, with the systems and culture of the organisation and with other members of the team.

3 Managers and staff, work culture, race and gender.

4 Knowledge, feelings and desires, volition.

5 Class, age, race, culture or religion, interests and sex.

6 Abilities are things people can do or are good at. Aptitude is the capacity to learn and develop abilities and skills.

7 Spatial, musical, physical, practical, inter-personal, intra-personal.

8 (a) Encouraging a certain type of behaviour by rewarding it.
(b) Personal growth and fulfilment of potential.

9

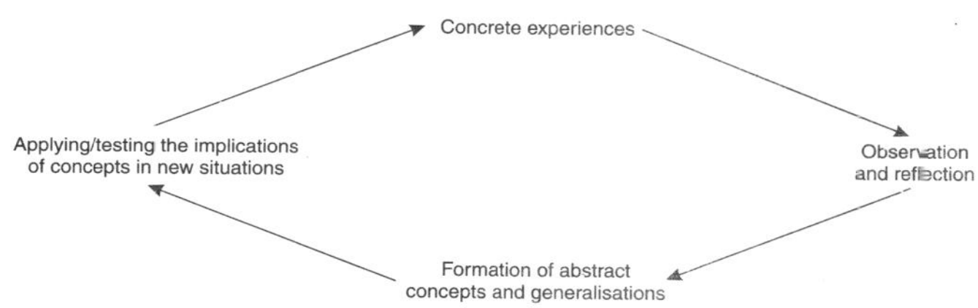

10 Nervous tension, physical symptoms, withdrawal, drink/drugs, low morale.

11 Sell change, give information and reasons, reassure, consult, deal with resistance.

Answers to activities

1 You probably felt as we did that none of the qualities listed were unimportant. You probably had similar priorities to ours, as follows:

1 = b, c, e, g, j. 2 = a, d, f, h, i.

2 The perceptual problems in the situations given are as follows.

(a) The manager perceives himself as 'enlightened', and his style as an opportunity and gift to his staff. He clearly thinks that assessment and reward on the basis of more responsibility is a positive thing, probably offering greater rewards to staff. He does not perceive his use of the word 'judged' as potentially threatening: he uses it as another word for 'assessed'. His staff obviously see things differently. 'More responsibility' means their competence – maybe their jobs – are on the line. Feeling this way, and with the expectations they have of their boss (based on past experience of his autocratic style), they are bound to perceive the word 'judged' as threatening.

(b) The chairman thinks he is being funny. Maybe he is only joking about the woman making the tea – but he may really perceive her role that way. He lacks the perception that his new colleague may find his remark offensive. From the woman's point of view, she is bound to be sensitive and insecure in her first meeting and with all male colleagues: small wonder that, joke or not, she perceives the chairman's comment as a slap in the face. The chairman later fails to perceive the effect his joke has had on her, assuming that her silence is a sign of poor co-operation or inability to communicate.

(c) This is a case of closure leading to misinterpretation. The new employee sees the informal dress, the position behind the counter, and the offer of coffee: his brain fills in the gaps, and offers the perception that the youngster must be the tea-boy. Perceptual selectivity also plays a part, filtering out awkward information that does not fit his expectations (like the fact that the 'tea-boy' comes to chat with him).

3 Elements of a positive attitude to work may include a willingness to:

(a) Commit oneself to the objectives of the organisation, or adopt personal objectives that are compatible with those of the organisation

(b) Accept the right of the organisation to set standards of acceptable behaviour for its members

(c) Contribute to the development and improvement of work practices and performance

(d) Take advantages of opportunities for personal development at work

4 Managers may use positive and negative reinforcement;

(a) Positive reinforcement: praise; pay (or extra pay, such as a bonus); promotion; prizes.

b) Negative reinforcement: warnings; loss of pay; threat of dismissal; the cold shoulder.

A person who has been punished may simply learn how to avoid punishment! Positive reinforcement is generally thought to be more effective, as well as more pleasant. However, if we take a contingency approach, we must recognise that negative reinforcement can be effective in certain situations – for example, if the punished person himself feels that the punishment was deserved.

5 Symptoms of conflict in a team might include:

(a) Poor communications

(b) Interpersonal friction

(c) Inter-group rivalry and jealousy

(d) Low morale and frustration

(e) Proliferation of rules and norms; especially widespread use of arbitration, appeals to higher authority, and inflexible attitudes towards change

6 The situations described might lead to the following kinds of conflict, each resolved as shown.

(a) Competition for scarce resources. There would need to be negotiated compromise (someone's documents would wait), borrowing of resources from elsewhere (an extra typist), or a decision on priorities by the two managers' joint boss.

(b) Inter-group rivalry, and dispute about power/job security/territory. The electricians will fight against the 'invasion' of their specialist area, and the implied threat to their jobs. Not easy to resolve -especially since the electricians have 'found out' rather than 'been informed'. Confrontation with management (if not the engineers) will bring fears and anger to the surface: reassurance, negotiation (eg cross-training for electricians too) and other conciliation methods will have to be tried. Meanwhile, the conflict may challenge the electricians to better performance – or cause a walkout! One to watch ...

(c) Similar to (a), but less important. It might not be worth stirring up resentment – unless Department B staff already feel very strongly about the issue.

(d) Excessive competition or rivalry. Managers will need to re-emphasise the common objectives (and capacity) of the organisation. Meetings of sales and production team representatives might help clarify the issues: production capacity might be increased! The causes of rivalry should be looked at (North/South attitudes?), as should pay incentives, which may be competitive (win-lose) rather than generally motivating.

7 (a) Overload and underload could both be addressed by management, in consultation with the individual. Tasks and responsibilities could be reallocated, or clarified. Training in delegation, planning and assertiveness (eg learning to say 'no') may help those who have problems tackling excessive workloads. Jobs may have to be redesigned, if the issue of stress is important enough and the workers are too valuable to be allowed to leave.

(b) Uncertainty can be alleviated to an extent by the provision of relevant information and counselling. Management style will be important in offering accessibility in the event of problems (an 'open door' policy, for example) and in showing confidence in the individual, to counteract the effects of insecurity.

(c) There is little you can do about personality, but inter-personal competence and flexibility, for example, might be improved by training. In addition, greater awareness of stress may be helpful. Stress management techniques such as rest breaks, relaxation techniques (breathing exercises, meditation), physical exercise and so on may be helpful.

8 Resistance to changes of attitudes, habit, loyalty and retaining power, include the following examples.

(a) Resistance to changes in the law on Sunday trading, or the ordination of women priests in the Church of England.

(b) 'You can't teach an old dog new tricks' (especially on computers!).

(c) Resisting merger with another team or company.

(d) Resisting multi-skilling in what has been a specialist area.

Chapter 7:

DIAGNOSING BEHAVIOURAL PROBLEMS

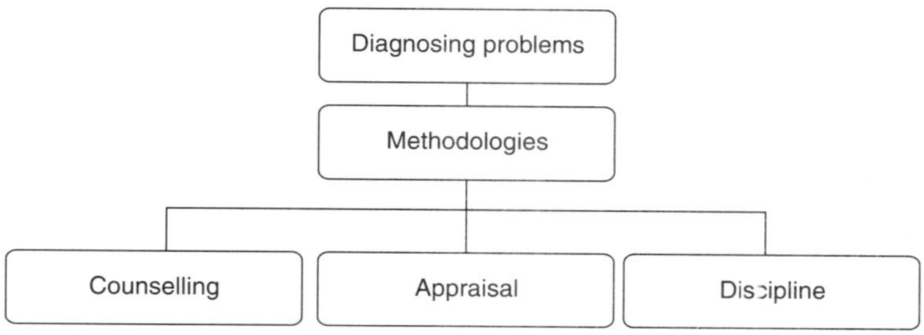

Introduction

We have already encountered the diagnosis of behavioural problems, in particular contexts: the symptoms and causes of stress, resistance to change, conflict, negative organisation culture and so on. It would clearly be useful for a manager to be able to identify behaviours that might have a negative influence on team members' work performance: you yourself might find it helpful to identify when and why, you weren't coping at work. However, there are a number of issues to consider. For example, what is a 'problem'? Are all problems the organisation's 'business'? We will discuss some of these points in this chapter.

We will also look at some of the procedural contexts within which managers often facilitate behavioural problem-solving: employee appraisal, disciplinary action and employee counselling.

Your objectives

In this chapter you will learn about the following:

(a) The concepts, principles and perspectives of behavioural problem-solving

(b) Available methodologies for problem diagnosis

(c) The processes of employee counselling, performance appraisal and disciplinary action with an awareness of behavioural issues

1 DIAGNOSING PROBLEMS

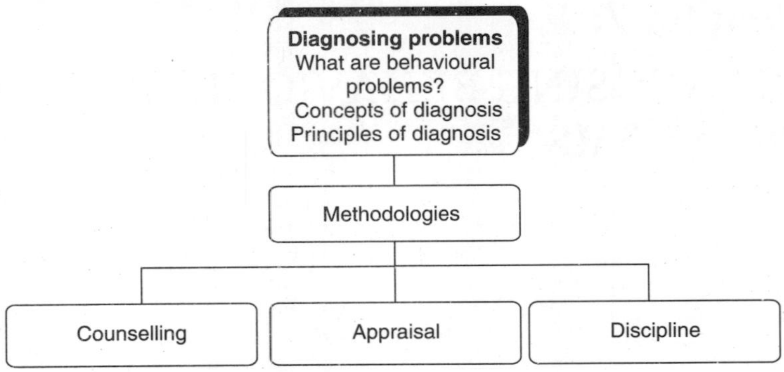

1.1 What are behavioural problems?

Broadly, we can say that a behavioural problem is anything in the behaviour of people – individual, interpersonal or group – that causes dysfunction or prevents them from fulfilling their personal or work objectives.

Definition

Dysfunction is any disturbance in a person (or system) which prevents it from functioning or fulfilling its intended role of purpose

Activity 1 **(10 minutes)**

Before we go on, can you immediately think of some behavioural dysfunctions:

(a) In the personal sphere?
(b) That would particularly affect your work life?

Brainstorm two sets of problem/dysfunctions, listing them inside two overlapping circles, as follows. If you think a problem is both personal and work-related, put it in the overlap area.

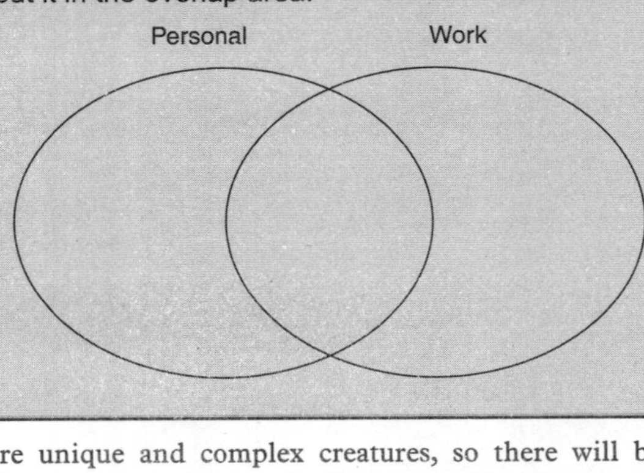

Human beings are unique and complex creatures, so there will be almost as many behavioural problems as there are people. Just as an idea, however, the following are some of the problems that may be relevant at work.

Problem behaviours that may affect work	*Problematic work behaviours*
Forgetfulness/inattention	Absenteeism
Apathy/depression/anxiety	Poor timekeeping (lateness etc)
Lack of anger management	Low morale/motivation
Addiction/substance abuse	Insubordination/resistance to authority
Poor interpersonal skills	Work-related stress
Poor self-management/discipline	Resistance to work change/learning
Poor goal setting	Theft/dishonesty
Lack of assertiveness	Inability to work with others
Over-controlling/compulsive behaviour	Inability to communicate effectively
Victim thinking/lack of responsibility	Conflict with colleagues/customers
Learning difficulties	Lack of organisation
Psychological disorders	Persistent work mistakes

Would you be happy putting the label of 'behavioural problem on the listed behaviours? There are a few reasons why you might hesitate.

(a) What if the behaviour (say, absenteeism) was only a *symptom* of a problem (say, substance abuse or work-related stress) and not the problem itself?

(b) What if the problem behaviour (say aggression, competitiveness or dishonesty) was only a 'problem' in some contexts (say, a charity or funeral service) but positive or functional behaviour in others (say, organised crime!)?

(c) What if the problem behaviour (say alcohol abuse or stealing) only manifested itself outside the workplace: would it still be relevant to the individual's manager?

We will look at these issues as we define some of the concepts of diagnosis.

1.2 Concepts of diagnosis

Definition

> **Diagnosis** is the thorough analysis of facts or problems in order to gain understanding. (A diagnosis is the opinion reached as a result of such analysis.) In medical terms, diagnosis is the identification of diseases through the examination of symptoms.

In the above definition, certain concepts emerge.

Symptoms

A symptom is an outward sign indicator, phenomenon or circumstance which suggests the existence of a problem or disease. It accompanies and points to the problem/disease: it is not the thing itself.

This is a very important point. You could correctly identify absenteeism as a work problem, but trying to change absentee behaviour is likely to be ineffective in the long term, because absenteeism is only a symptom, not a cause: not the 'real' problem. The real problem may be poor morale or stress, say. You might train or punish the individual out of the absenteeism, but the morale/stress problem would remain and would probably emerge in some other work behaviour, such as errors or withdrawal.

Causes

Causes are the underlying factors or events which produce an effect (say, a symptom). Does this mean that the 'cause' and the 'problem' are the same thing? Not necessarily. The symptom absenteeism, for example, may indicate the problem stress. But stress doesn't *cause* absenteeism: some people *thrive* on stress; others experience negative stress but do not respond with absentee behaviour.

When we speak of 'causes', we need to be aware how complex human behaviour is. We cannot really say, for example, that overwork and a tyrannical management style *caused* a person's stress: we would need to include influences such as the person's lack of assertiveness, poor prioritising and time management, personality type, attitudes towards authority and responsibility, self image, perhaps a tyrannical father-figure in the person's past, and so on.

Behavioural learning and patterns accumulate over time. They are like a journey – not like a mechanical device where if button x is pushed, behaviour y results. In human terms, if 'button x is pushed' (a event happens), behaviour y is influenced by the complex web of thoughts, feelings, beliefs, attitudes and perceptions that we have *about x*.

EXAMPLE

'The boss's abruptness really makes me stressed.'

Event x → *Behaviour y*
(Boss is abrupt) → *(stressed)*

Thoughts, feelings, perceptions etc
('I must have done something bad'
'He doesn't like me'
'Nobody likes me'
'It's unfair'
'My life is a misery'
'There's nothing I can do about this'
'I can't say no')

Activity 2 **(10 minutes)**

(a) Complete the following sentences, using the first thing that comes to mind.

1 ____________ makes me really angry.

2 I put off doing study activities because ________________

(b) Now complete the following diagrams, inserting your 'causes' from sentences 1 and 2, and then considering what are the underlying thoughts/beliefs/perceptions about those 'causes' that *actually* lead you to act the way you do. What are you *telling yourself* about x that leads to y?

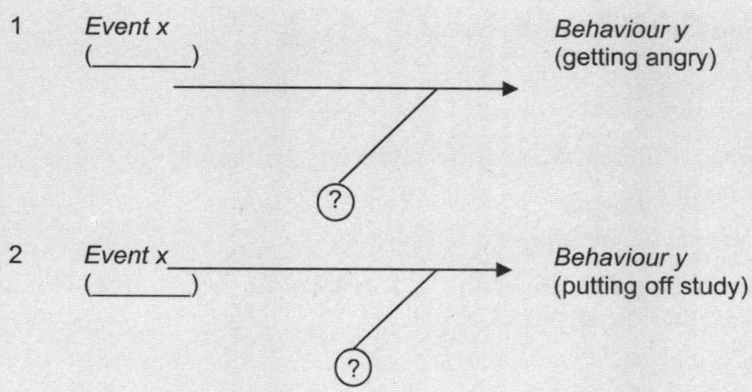

(c) Now, see if you can find a logical argument against each of your statements/thoughts/beliefs. Argue each one. (For example, if you thought: 'I need time with my friends', say: 'Well, you can get that time later, can't you?'. Of if you thought : 'I always do badly', say: '*Always?* That's just not true, is it?')

This is in fact one of the major approaches to counselling and psychotherapy (very much simplified). It is called the cognitive behavioural approach.

Problems

Remember our definition of 'dysfunction'. What may be a problem to one person may be a perfectly harmless characteristic, or indeed rational and positive choice, to another person. It only becomes a problem when it prevents a person from doing what (s)he needs and wants and intends to do.

In organisation and management terms, it also becomes a problem when it prevents a person from doing what his or her manager (or the rules, or whatever) requires him or her to do. However, non-conformity is a problem for the organisation – not necessarily for the non-conformist!

You should be aware that organisations may try to label and 'fix' as problems behaviours which are perfectly neutral or even positive for the individual, in order to create a particular organisation culture, impose uniformity or pursue particular objects. However, it is the choice of the individual whether to adapt his or her behaviour, or to resist, or to leave the organisation. Organisations buy people's time, knowledge and labour; they do not own people!

As we will see later in this chapter, the problematic nature of 'problems' makes it important for behavioural diagnosis to be handled sensitively and collaboratively.

Activity 3 **(5 minutes)**

'Too fussy' *or* 'pays attention to detail'?

'Can't focus in meetings' *or* 'dislikes wasting time; thinks creatively'?

'Lacks drive and aggression' *or* 'good at reconciliation/compromise; quiet achiever'?

See if you can brainstorm a set of behavioural problems and then 'reframe' them as neutral or positive behaviours or attributes.

Having covered some of the basic concepts, we will now put together some basic principles of diagnosing behavioural problems.

1.3 Principles of diagnosis

From our definition of diagnosis and the following discussion, we can formulate the following basic principles.

1 *Distinguish the symptom from the problem*

Don't confuse the behaviour – often, a 'cry for help' – from the underlying disease (literally, dis-ease).

2 *Look at the facts*

Diagnosis requires thorough examination of symptoms and analysis of facts. Tackling a problem which does not really exist is a waste of time. Don't assume. Don't generalise. Investigate.

3 *Don't be simplistic about causes*

Behaviour needs to be tackled at the level of its underlying influences if lasting change is to be achieved. Tackling the wrong causes is a waste of time, Again, don't assume. Don't generalise. Be aware that causes are *always* more complex than they appear to you, and to the individual with the problem: often, they are not within conscious awareness. Collaborative discussion (and perhaps professional counselling) is required to avoid prescriptive 'off the shelf' diagnoses which may not fit the problem.

4 *Focus on the problem, not the person*

Diagnosis is about helping a person to overcome a dysfunction which is harming or hampering him or her. It is not about 'fixing' or changing a 'bad' or 'inadequate' person. A person is not a problem: a *person* has a problem. Keep the two separate. Do not label the person: (s)he is not necessarily 'a forgetful person' because (s)he has forgotten things or behaved in a forgetful manner. Labelling the person can reinforce the problem: it is much harder to change 'who you are' than 'what you do'. Focus on positive goals and outcomes for change.

5 *Don't impose your own judgements*

You may feel that people who are addicted to drugs or gambling, say, are 'bad' or 'irresponsible' or 'weak' – or whatever. That is not relevant to your diagnosis of the problem. Beware your own prejudices and assumptions. If you find yourself getting emotional (impatient, angry, sad) about someone else's problem, it is a good sign that *you* may have a problem with something. Whatever your beliefs, values and interpretations of the problem, other than your own, it is not helpful (nor do you usually have the right or permission) to impose it: it is only your perspective. Ask how the other person sees it, feels about it, understands it: strive for empathy (if not sympathy) and respect.

6 *Respect privacy and confidentiality*

You don't have a right to information that a person does not wish to give (other than in very restricted legal circumstances). Still less do you have a right to share that information, however innocuous or anonymous it may seem, with third parties. Confidentiality is absolutely essential to establish trust, which in turn is absolutely essential in getting to the bottom of behavioural problems.

It may be worth adding that unless an employee requests, or willingly accepts, help with outside-work problems that do not affect his or her work performance it is not strictly speaking the employer's concern. Managers are not employed to help their employees be happier and healthier, unless in the process it helps them become more efficient and effective adders of value to the business.

FOR DISCUSSION

How might the above-listed principles of diagnosis apply to you, if you think you yourself might have a problem with some aspect of your behaviour? How might *self-diagnosis* work?

We will now look briefly at some of the tools and techniques used in monitoring and diagnosing behavioural problems. We'll encounter some of them in practice in Sections 3 – 5 below.

2 METHODOLOGIES

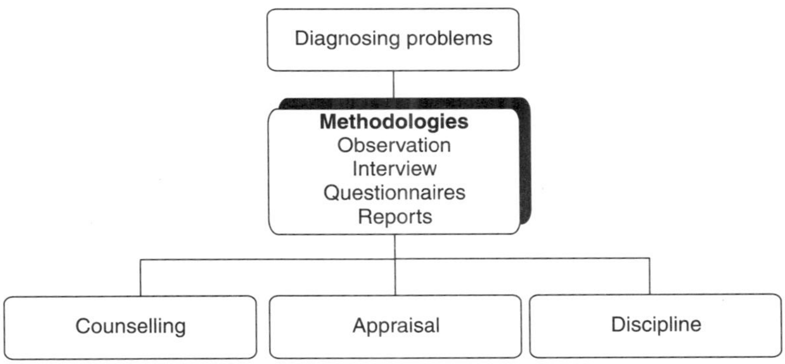

2.1 Observation

'Management by Wandering Around (MBWA) is actually a technique! Keeping an eye on people is a useful tool of behavioural monitoring – if you keep the eye open.

(a) **Critical incidents** (such as a fight in the office, or an employee bursting into tears) are useful indicators, and should be carefully noted and discussed with those involved ('debriefed') if possible, once things have cooled off.

(b) **Patterns** of behaviour (such as persistent conflict or absenteeism) may become noticeable over time. These 'habits' may be helpful or unhelpful.

(c) **Trends** in behaviour (such as escalating conflict, or increasing moodiness) may also become apparent. Negative trends will need to be monitored.

As well as informal observation, which may not be easily maintained (especially in a large team or department), there may be structured, intentional opportunities for observation, such as:

(a) Group training exercises, designed to highlight group interaction and communication skills

(b) Appraisal exercises, such as case studies and role plays, team games and so on

2.2 Interview

Observation may identify possible symptoms, but in order to investigate further, discussion is required.

Face-to-face interviews allow the manager or counsellor to explore problems verbally, and often also to observe the behaviour first-hand in the course of the interaction (especially problems in communication and relating behaviours). Interviews are ideally highly interactive and collaborative, and allow rapport and empathy to develop between the individuals involved. This is particularly suited to the gathering and exploration of personal information (if well handled).

We won't say more about interviews here, as we will look at different types of interview in practice in following sections.

2.3 Questionnaires

The 'scientific' testing of personality types and traits, emotional intelligence (and so on) was discussed in Chapter 6. Despite their objective appearance, the interpretation of such tests remains highly subjective and subject to bias. (See our answer to Assignment 6, if you have not already done so, for some reasons why.) Nevertheless, they are a popular tool in employee selection, assessment, training and development. Although their ability to predict job performance is severely limited, they can offer useful areas for investigation, and some appealing frameworks for discussing behaviour: 'types' and 'traits', for example.

Questionnaire-based personality profiles, such as the Myers-Briggs indicator or 16PF analysis, can suggest areas in which individuals are particularly strong or weak, although they usually place no value judgement on results. (In Myers-Briggs (1993), for example, you may be an introvert rather than an extravert, or a judger rather than a perceiver, but this is neither 'good' nor 'bad'. If your job required outgoing behaviour and a very flexible outlook, however, you might anticipate some difficulty or discomfort.)

2.4 Reports

Behavioural problems may come to light via the following reports.

(a) **Complaints** from colleagues, customers, suppliers or other parties who deal with the individual. All external complaints and internal complaints ('grievances') should be carefully considered and queried with the person concerned, bearing in mind the need to hear all sides of the story.

(b) The **appraisal system** of the organisation (discussed below), which is designed to provide regular reporting on employee behaviour and performance. This is not necessarily only from the employee's superior: 360° feedback, for example, seeks reports from colleagues, subordinates, customers, suppliers and so on.

(c) **Routine performance reports and forms**, such as time-sheets, output/sales records, error/wastage analyses, health and safety reports and so on. Relevant behavioural problems should show up in work performance: hours of work missed, poor record-keeping, reduced output, increased errors or accidents etc.

(d) **Employment records**, showing disciplinary incidents, accident reports, counselling received and so on.

> **Activity 4** **(10 minutes)**
>
> Think back through your education and/or work experiences. When or if you had behavioural/disciplinary/learning difficulties, how (if at all) did these come to light? How were they 'handled'?

We will now look at some of the organisational contexts of behavioural diagnosis.

3 COUNSELLING

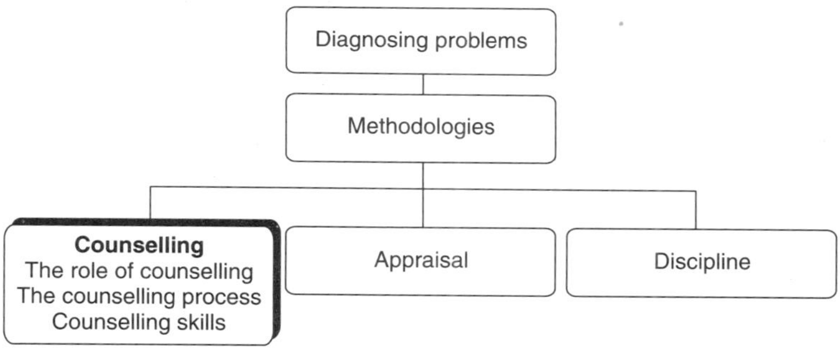

Definition

> '**Counselling** can be defined as a purposeful relationship in which one person helps another to help himself. It is a way of relating and responding to another person so that that person is helped to explore his thoughts, feelings and behaviour with the aim of reaching a clearer understanding. The clearer understanding may be of himself or of a problem, or of the one in relation to the other.' (Rees).

3.1 The role of counselling

The Institute of Personnel Development's 1992 *Statement on Counselling in the Workplace* makes it clear that effective counselling is not merely a matter of 'pastoral' care for individuals, but is very much in the organisation's interests.

(a) Appropriate use of counselling can prevent under-performance and reduce labour turnover and absenteeism.

(b) Effective counselling demonstrates an organisation's commitment to and concern for its employees and so is liable to improve loyalty and enthusiasm among the workforce.

(c) The development of employees is of value to the organisation, and counselling can give employees the confidence and encouragement necessary to take responsibility for self development.

(d) Workplace counselling recognises that the organisation may be contributing to its employees' problems and therefore provides an opportunity to reassess organisational policy and practice.

FOR DISCUSSION

'Staff spend at least half their waking time at work or in getting to it or leaving it. They know they contribute to the organisation when they are reasonably free from worry, and they feel, perhaps inarticulately, that when they are in trouble they are due to get something back from the organisation. People are entitled to be treated as full human beings with personal needs, hopes and anxieties; they are employed as people; they bring themselves to work, not just their hands, and they cannot readily leave their troubles at home.' (Martin).

Do you agree? Or do you think the non-work interests and affairs of employees are none of their employers' business?

Activity 5 **(10 minutes)**

The need for workplace counselling can arise in many different situations. Try and think of at least four examples.

EXAMPLE

The Body Shop runs an education and counselling programme on the Human Immuno-deficiency Virus (HIV) and Acquired Immune Deficiency Syndrome (AIDS). Its purpose is to give support to HIV-positive employees and employees with HIV-positive partners, and to prevent fear and discrimination by other employees, while promoting safe practices.

3.2 The counselling process

The counselling process is basically about empowering employees: enabling them to recognise, express and take responsibility for their own problem or situation. (This is not the same as giving advice or instruction.) The counsellor may offer guidance in identifying the problem and its causes, and resources for managing it (information, education, financial and non-financial assistance and so on), but this is still essentially a supportive and enabling role. No solution can be imposed on the individual.

Confidentiality

There will be situations when an employee cannot be completely open unless (s)he is sure that all comments will be treated confidentially. However, certain information, once obtained by the organisation (for example about fraud or sexual harassment) calls for action. In spite of the drawbacks, therefore, employees must be told when their comments will be passed on to the relevant authority, and when they will be treated completely confidentially.

The counselling session

The IPD statement includes a helpful checklist for counsellors, which we reproduce overleaf.

3.3 Counselling skills

Counsellors need to be:

(a) Observant enough to note behaviour which may be symptomatic of a problem

(b) Sensitive to beliefs and values which may be different from their own (for example religious beliefs)

(c) Empathetic (putting themselves into other people's shoes), to the extent that they appreciate that the problem may seem overwhelming to the individual

(d) Impartial

(e) Non-directive, willing to refrain from giving advice

(f) Skilled in questioning and active listening

Counsellors must have the belief that individuals have the resources to solve their own problems, albeit with passive or active help.

Counselling checklist

Preparation

- Choose a place to talk which is quiet, free from interruption and not open to view.
- Research as much as you can before the meeting and have any necessary papers readily available.
- Make sure you know whether the need for counselling has been properly identified or whether you will have to carefully probe to establish if a problem exists.
- Allow sufficient time for the session. If you know you must end at a particular time, inform the individual of this at the beginning of the meeting.
- Decide if it is necessary for the individual's department head to be aware of the counselling and its purpose.
- Give the individual the option of being accompanied by a supportive colleague.
- If you are approaching the individual following information received from a colleague, decide in advance the extent to which you can reveal your source.
- Consider how you are going to introduce and discuss your perceptions of the situation.
- Be prepared for the individual to have different expectations of the discussion, eg the individual may expect you to solve the problem – rather than come to terms with it himself/herself.
- Understand that the individual's view of the facts of the situation will be more important than the facts themselves and that their behaviour may not reflect their true feelings.

Format of discussion

- Welcome the individual and clarify the general purpose of the meeting.
- Assure the individual that matters of confidentiality will be treated as such.
- The individual may be reticent through fear of being considered somewhat of a risk in future and you will need to give appropriate reassurances in this regard.
- Be ready to prompt or encourage the individual to move into areas he/she might be hesitant about.
- Encourage the individual to look more deeply into statements.
- Ask the individual to clarify statements you do not quite understand.
- Try to take the initiative in probing important areas which may be embarrassing/emotional to the individual and which you both might prefer to avoid.
- Recognise that some issues may be so important to the individual that they will have to be discussed over and over again, even though this may seem repetitious to you.
- If you sense that the individual is becoming defensive, try to identify the reason and relax the pressure by changing your approach.
- Occasionally summarise the conversation as it goes along, reflecting back in your own words what you understand the individual to say.
- Sometimes emotions may be more important than the words being spoken, so it may be necessary to reflect back what you see the individual feeling.
- At the close of the meeting, clarify any decisions reached and agree what follow-up support would be helpful.

Overcoming dangers

- If you take notes at an inappropriate moment, you may set up a barrier between yourself and the individual.
- Realise you may not like the individual and be on guard against this.
- Recognise that repeating problems does not solve them.
- Be careful to avoid taking sides
- Overcome internal and external distractions. Concentrate on the individual and try to understand the situation with him/her.
- The greater the perceived level of listening, the more likely the individual will be accept comments and contributions from you.
- Resist the temptation to talk about your own problems, even though these may seem similar to those of the individual.

Source: IPD Statement on Counselling the Workplace

Activity 6 **(45 minutes)**

This is a role-play exercise, to be done with another person. One of you should take the role of the manager, and the other the role of the team member, Javed, in the following scenario, and actually attempt a counselling session. If possible, get others to observe you, and give you feedback in the specific areas covered by the checklist given above. The person playing Javed should also feed back how the manager's counselling style made him feel.

Javed is a member of the section which you lead. His work is normally well above average and he knows it. You find him mildly arrogant and have difficulty in liking him, although he seems to have a great deal of respect for you. Frankly, you think he is a bit of a crawler.

Of late you have noticed that Javed's work is slipping and he seems to keep himself to himself more than usual. One day he comes to you with a problem that he would normally deal with himself, and he is obviously distressed when you send him away to solve the problem on his own. On your guard, now, you observe that none of the other team members are co-operating with Javed and one or two rather catty remarks are being made behind his back.

You decide to have a counselling session with Javed. Go for it ...

4 APPRAISAL

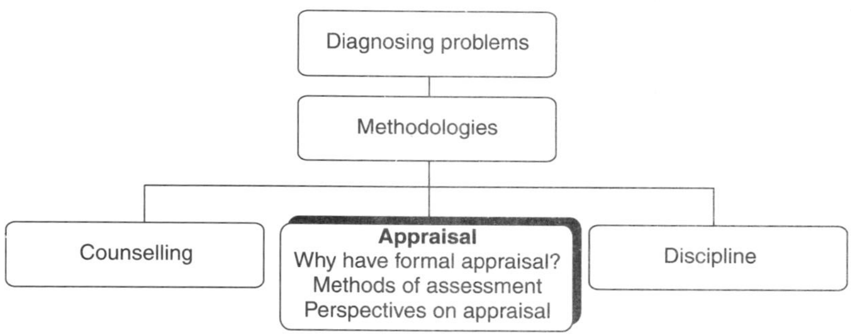

4.1 Why have a formal appraisal?

It must be recognised that, if no system of formal appraisal is in place, problems can arise.

(a) Managers may obtain random impressions of subordinates' performance (perhaps from their more noticeable successes and failures), but not a coherent, complete and objective picture.

(b) Managers may have a fair idea of their subordinates' shortcomings – but may not have devoted time and attention to the matter of improvement and development.

(c) Judgements are easy to make, but less easy to justify in detail, in writing, or to the subject's face.

(d) Different managers may be applying a different set of criteria, and varying standards of objectivity and judgement, which undermines the value of appraisal for comparison, as well as its credibility in the eyes of employees.

(e) Managers rarely give their subordinates adequate feedback on their performance. Most people dislike giving criticism as much as receiving it.

Activity 7 **(10 minutes)**

List four disadvantages to the individual of not having an appraisal system.

A typical system

A typical system would therefore involve:

(a) Identification of **criteria** for assessment

(b) The preparation of an **appraisal report**

(c) An **appraisal interview**, for an exchange of views about the results of the assessment, targets for improvement, solutions to problems and so on

(d) The preparation and implementation of **action plans** to achieve improvements and changes agreed, and

(e) **Follow-up**: monitoring the progress of the action plan.

Definition

A **criterion** (plural: criteria) is a factor or standard by which something can be judged or decided. For example, 'meeting output targets' is one criterion for judging work performance.

4.2 Methods of assessment

Overall assessment

This is much like a school report. The manager simply writes narrative judgements about the appraisee. The method is simple – but not always effective, since there is no guaranteed consistency of the criteria and areas of assessment from manager to manager (or appraisal to appraisal). In addition, managers may not be able to convey clear, precise or effective judgements in writing.

Guided assessment

Assessors are required to comment on a number of specified characteristics and performance elements, with guidelines as to how terms such as 'application', 'integrity' and 'adaptability' are to be interpreted in the work context. This is a more precise, but still rather vague method.

Grading

Grading adds a comparative frame of reference to the general guidelines. Managers are asked to select one of a number of levels or degrees (Grades 1–5 say) which describe the extent to which an individual displays a given characteristic. These are also known as rating scales, and have been much used in standard appraisal forms (for example, see Figure 7.1 on the following page). Their effectiveness depends to a large extent on two things.

(a) The **relevance of the factors chosen for assessment**. These may be nebulous personality traits, for example, or clearly-defined work-related factors such as job knowledge, performance against targets, or decision-making.

Date of review	Time on Position Yrs Mths	S.G.	Age Yrs	Name
Period of Review	Position Title			Area

Important: Read guide notes carefully before proceeding with the following sections

Section One	Performance Factors						Section Two	Personal Characteristics				
	N/A	U	M	SP	E	O		1	2	3	4	5
Administrative skills												
Communications -Written												
Communications - Oral												
Problem Analysis												
Decision Making												
Delegation												
Quantity of work												
Development of Personnel												
Development of Quality Improvements												

Section Three Highlight Performance Factors and particular strengths / weaknesses of employee which significantly affect Job Performance

Overall Performance Rating (taking into account ratings given)

Prepared by: Signature ______ Date ______ Position Title ______

Section 4 Comments by Reviewing Authority | I R Review Inital | Date

Signature ______ Date ______ Position Title ______

Section 5 Supervisor's Notes on Counselling Interview

Signature ______ Date ______ Position Title ______

Section Six Employee's Reactions and Comment

Signature ______ Date ______

Performance Classification

Outstanding performance is characterised by high ability which leaves little or nothing to by desired.
Personnel rated at such are those who regularly make significant contributions to the organisation which are above the requirements of their position. Unusual and challenging assignments are consistently well handled.

Excellent performance is marked by above-average ability, with little supervision required. These employees may display some of the attributes present in '**outstanding**', but not on a sufficiently consistent basis to warrant that rating. Unusual and challenging assignments are normally well handled.

Satisfactory Plus performance indicates fully adequate ability, without the need for excessive supervision.
Personnel with this rating are able to give proper consideration to normal assignments, which are generally well handled. They will meet the requirements of the position. '**Satisfactory plus**' performers may include those who lack the experience at their current level to demonstrate above average ability.

Marginal performance is in instances where the ability demonstrated does not fully meet the requirements of the position, with excessive supervision and direction normally required.
Employees rated as such will show specific deficiencies in their performance which prevent them from performing at an acceptable level.

Unsatisfactory performance indicates an ability which falls clearly below the minimum requirements of the position.

'**Unsatisfactory**' performers will demonstrate marked deficiencies in most of the major aspects of their responsibilities, and considerable improvement is required to permit retention of the employee in his current position.

Personal Characteristics Ratings

1 - Needs considerable improvement - substantial improvement required to meet acceptable standards.
2 - Needs improvement - some improvement required to meet acceptable standards.
3 - Normal - meets acceptable standards
4 - Above normal - exceeds normally acceptable standards in most instances.
5 - Exceptional - displays rare and unusual personal characteristics.

Figure 7.1 Personnel appraisal form

(b) The **definition of the agreed standards or grades**. Grades A-D might simply be labelled 'Outstanding – Satisfactory – Fair – Poor', in which case assessments will be rather subjective and inconsistent. They may, on the other hand, be more closely related to work priorities and standards, using definitions such as 'Performance is good overall, and superior to that expected in some important areas', or 'Performance is broadly acceptable, but the employee needs training in several major areas and motivation is lacking'.

Results-orientated schemes

All the above techniques may be used with more or less results-orientated criteria. A wholly results-orientated approach sets out to review performance against specific targets and standards of performance, which are agreed – or even set – in advance by a manager and subordinate together. This is known as performance management.

Activity 8 **(20 minutes)**

Peter Ward, who introduced 360-degree feedback at Tesco, gives an example of the kinds of questionnaire that might be used as the instrument of 360-degree feedback. 'A skill area like "communicating", for example, might be defined as "the ability to express oneself clearly and to listen effectively to others". Typical comments would include "Presents ideas or information in a well-organised manner" (followed by rating scale); or: "Allows you to finish what you have to say".'

Rate yourself on the two comments mentioned here, on a scale of 1–10. Get a group of friends, fellow-students, even a tutor or parent, to write down, anonymously, on a piece of paper their rating for you on the same two comments. Keep them in an envelope, unseen, until you have a few.

Compare them with your self-rating. If you dare... What drawbacks did you (and your respondents) find to such an approach?

4.3 Perspectives on appraisal

There are basically three ways of approaching appraisal interviews.

(a) The **tell and sell** method. The manager tells the subordinate how (s)he has been assessed, and then tries to 'sell' (gain acceptance of) the evaluation and any improvement plans.

(b) The **tell and listen** method. The manager tells the subordinate how (s)he has been assessed, and then invites comments. The manager therefore no longer dominates the interview throughout, and there is greater opportunity for counselling as opposed to pure direction. The employee is encouraged to participate in the assessment and the working out of improvement targets and methods; change in the employee may not be the sole key to improvement, and the manager may receive helpful feedback about job design, methods, environment or supervision.

(c) The **problem-solving** approach. The manager abandons the role of critic altogether, and becomes a counsellor and helper. The discussion is centred not on assessment of past performance, but on future solutions of the employee's work problems. The employee is encouraged to recognise the problems, think solutions through, and commit himself to improvement. This approach is more involving and satisfying to the employee and may also stimulate creative problem-solving.

EXAMPLE

A survey of appraisal interviews given to 252 officers in a UK government department found that:

(a) Interviewers have difficulty with negative performance feedback (criticism), and tend to avoid it if possible

(b) Negative performance feedback (criticism) is, however, more likely to bring forth positive post-appraisal action, and is favourably received by appraisees, who feel it is the most useful function of the whole process, if handled frankly and constructively

(c) The most common fault of interviewers is talking too much

The survey recorded the preference of appraisees for a 'problem-solving' style of participative interview, over a one-sided 'tell and sell' style.

Many organisations waste the opportunity represented by appraisal for **upward communication**. If an organisation is working towards empowerment, it should harness the aspirations and abilities of its employees by asking positive and thought-provoking questions.

(a) Do you fully understand your job? Are there any aspects you wish to be made clearer?

(b) What parts of your job do you do best?

(c) Could any changes be made in your job which might result in improved performance?

(d) Have you any skills, knowledge, or aptitudes which could be made better use of in the organisation?

(e) What are your career plans? How do you propose achieving your ambitions in terms of further training and broader experience?

5 DISCIPLINE

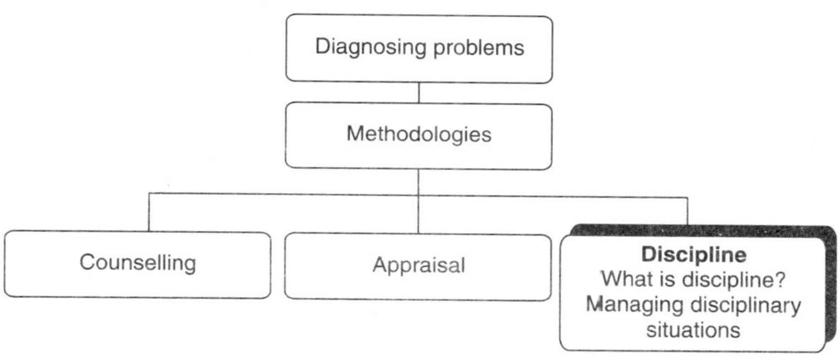

5.1 What is discipline?

The word discipline brings to mind the use of authority or force, and to many people it primarily carries the disagreeable meaning of punishment. However, there is another way of thinking about discipline.

Definition

> **Discipline** can be considered as: 'a condition in an enterprise in which there is orderliness in which the members of the enterprise behave sensibly and conduct themselves according to the standards of acceptable behaviour as related to the goals of the organisation'.

'Negative' discipline is the threat of sanctions designed to make employees choose to behave in a desirable way, although this need not be a wholly negative matter. Disciplinary action may be **punitive** (punishing an offence), **deterrent** (warning people not to behave in that way) or **reformative** (calling attention to the nature of the offence so that it will not happen again).

The best discipline is **self-discipline**. Most mature people accept that following instructions and fair rules of conduct are part of any job. They believe in performing their work properly, coming to work on time, following their leader's instructions, and so on. If employees know what is expected of them and feel that the rules are reasonable, self-disciplined behaviour becomes a part of group norms.

Types of disciplinary situations

There are many types of disciplinary situations which require attention by the manager. The most frequently occurring are:

(a) Excessive absenteeism (not coming to work, perhaps giving the excuse of ill health)

(b) Excessive lateness in arriving at work

(c) Defective and/or inadequate work performance

(d) Poor attitudes which influence the work of others or which reflect on the public image of the firm

In addition, managers might be confronted with disciplinary problems stemming from employee behaviour off the job: abuse of alcohol or drugs, or involvement in some form of law-breaking activity. If off-the-job conduct has an impact upon performance on the job, the manager must be prepared to deal with it.

Disciplinary action

Any disciplinary action must be undertaken with sensitivity and sound judgement: its purpose is not punishment, or retribution, but improvement of the future behaviour of the employee and other members of the organisation, or the avoidance of similar occurrences in the future.

ACAS guidelines for disciplinary action suggest that an employee should not be dismissed from his or her job for a first offence, except in the case of gross misconduct (such as serious theft, or violence against another employee). Many enterprises have accepted the idea of **progressive discipline**, which provides for increasing severity of the penalty with each repeated offence: a bit like the yellow card (warning), red card (sent off) system used in football.

FOR DISCUSSION

How (a) accessible and (b) clear are the rules and policies of your college: do people really know what they are and are not supposed to do? Have a look at the student regulations. How easy is it to see them – or were you referred elsewhere? Are they well-indexed and cross-referenced, and in language that all students will understand?

How (a) accessible and (b) clear are the disciplinary procedures? Who is responsible for discipline?

In addition to formal procedures, discipline raises a number of interpersonal issues.

5.2 Managing disciplinary situations

The following guidelines may help managers reduce the resentment that will be inevitable, to an extent, in all disciplinary actions.

(a) *Immediacy*

The manager should take disciplinary action as speedily as possible. However, (s)he should allow a brief 'cooling off' period in circumstances where on-the-spot emotion might lead to hasty judgements, and the ACAS Code of Practice requires investigation to be made, where possible, before action is taken.

(b) *Advance warning*

In order to encourage self-discipline, and ensure that disciplinary action is (and is seen to be) fair, it is essential that all employees know in advance what is expected of them and what the rules and regulations are. Policy provisions may be included in employee handbooks, recruitment literature or employment contracts.

(c) *Consistency*

Rules and penalties should apply equally to everyone and on every occasion. Inconsistency in application of discipline only creates uncertainty, and loss of respect. (Consistency does not mean imposing a standard penalty every time for a particular offence: there may be mitigating circumstances which partly excuse the offender's behaviour.)

(d) *Impersonality*

'Punishment' should be connected with the 'crime': based on clear rules and standards, not personalities. Once disciplinary action has been taken, the manager should not bear grudges or nurse suspicions. Impersonality is sometimes called the 'hot stove' rule (if you touch the stove, you get burnt – nothing personal ...).

(e) *Privacy*

As a general rule (unless the manager's authority is challenged directly and in public) disciplinary action should be taken in private, to avoid the spread of conflict and the humiliation – or martyrdom – of the employee concerned.

Chapter roundup

- Diagnosis is the thorough analysis of facts or problems in order to gain understanding.
- The principles of effective diagnosis are:
  - Distinguish the symptom from the problem
  - Look at the facts
  - Don't be simplistic about causes
  - Focus on the problem, not the person
  - Don't impose your judgements
  - Respect privacy and confidentiality
- Methods include observation, interviews, questionnaires and other tests and various reports and records.
- Counselling is an interpersonal process by which one person helps another to help himself.
- Performance appraisal is designed to monitor and measure employee performance against agreed criteria. It is most constructively viewed as a joint problem-solving exercise.
- Discipline has the same end as motivation: to secure desired behaviours from **members of the organisation.**

Quick quiz

1 What is 'dysfunctional' behaviour?

2 What are 'symptoms'?

3 Why are:

(a) Confidentiality, and

(b) Not labelling people,

important to the effective diagnosis of behavioural problems?

4 What three aspects of behaviour may attract the attention of a manager concerned to identify potential problems?

5 Give four examples of situations in which counselling might be offered to employees.

6 List three qualities required by counsellors.

7 What is the difference between performance appraisal and performance management?

8 What factors should a manager bear in mind in trying to control the disciplinary situation?

9 Which organisation gives advice on disciplinary matters?

Answers to quick quiz

1 Behaviour which prevents a person (or system) from functioning, or fulfilling its intended role and purpose.

2 Symptoms are signs or indicators, associated with a problem or disease, the presence of which suggests that the problem or disease may also be present.

3 Confidentiality builds and protects trust, which is necessary for open communication. Labelling can cause resistance, or can reinforce the problem behaviour.

4 Critical incidents, patterns of behaviour, trends in behaviour.

5 Disciplinary situations, where there are personal problems and cases of redundancy or harassment.

6 They should be observant, sensitive, empathetic and impartial.

7 Appraisal is a backward-looking performance review. Performance management is a forward-looking results-orientated scheme.

8 Immediacy, advance warning, consistency, impersonality, privacy.

9 ACAS

Answers to activities

1 Personal to you. For hints, see Section 1.1. If you had trouble deciding whether a problem was personal, work-related or both – good! It was meant to be complicated.

2 Again, personal to you. The example given immediately above the activity is a good model to follow if you get stuck.

3 There are lots you may have come up with. Some more examples include:

'Risk averse/stick in the mud' →'cautious, sensible'.
'Wastes time socialising' → 'has a gift for networking'.
'Is pushy' → 'is assertive'.

and so on.

4 You may have remembered: school reports or parent-teacher meetings; being 'caught' by a teacher; being complained about by peers to teachers; being rejected by employers after interview or testing; appraisal reports; accidents or other incidents at work, and so on.

5 Workplace counselling could be needed: during appraisal (for problem solving); in disciplinary situations; following change such as promotion or relocation, redundancy, dismissal or approaching retirement; as a result of personal difficulties such as bereavement, sickness, depression, divorce or similar problems; in cases of sexual harassment or violence at work.

6 There are no right answers to this problem: it depends how each pair decided to play their roles. You should now appreciate how difficult managing people can be.

7 The individual is not aware of progress or shortcomings, is unable to judge whether s/he would be considered for promotion, is unable to identify or correct weaknesses by training and there is a lack of communication with the manager.

8 Drawbacks to 360-degree appraisal include:

(a) Respondents' reluctance to give negative feedback to a boss – or friend

(b) The suspicion that management is passing the buck for negative feedback, getting people to 'rat' on their friends

(c) The feeling that the appraisee is being picked on, if positive feedback is not carefully balanced with the negative

Part C

Motivational Theories

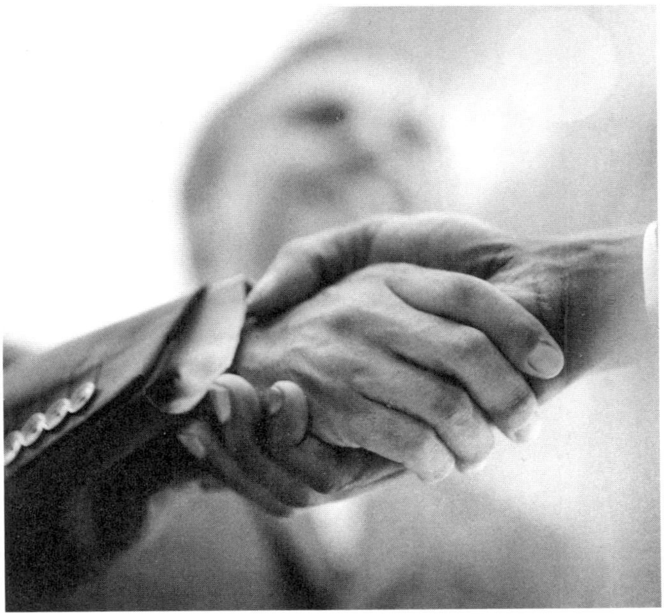

Chapter 8:
LEADERSHIP

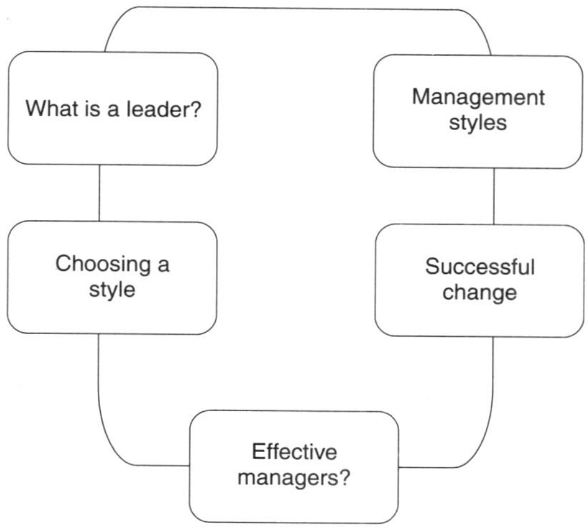

Introduction

Having looked at the nature of management in general in Part A, we can now turn to managing people. This corresponds to the function of management we have called 'commanding', 'directing' or 'leading'. As these varying terms suggest, there are different ways for managers to go about securing the co-operation and controlled performance of their staff. Some managers order people about; others try to persuade them; others encourage them to make their own decisions. So are these different types of manager, or different approaches or 'styles' that any manager can adopt? Is there a right or wrong way to handle people at work? And how does a manager decide which is the best way to go about it in his or her own situation? We will be answering such questions in this chapter.

Your objectives

In this chapter you will learn about the following:

(a) The difference between a manager and a leader

(b) Some of the major classifications of management style

(c) The contingency approach, and factors which will determine the appropriate management style

(d) The effectiveness of a given management style in a given situation

(e) How successful change in organisations may depend on leadership skills

1 WHAT IS A LEADER?

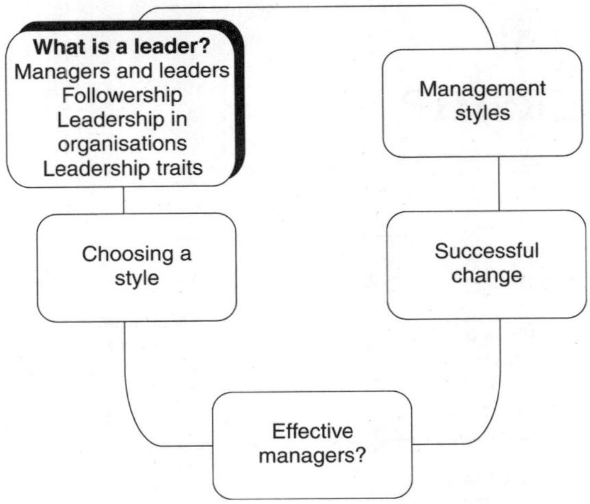

1.1 Managers and leaders

The terms 'management' and 'leadership' are often used interchangeably, and it will not matter much whether you refer to 'management style' or 'leadership style', for example. However, it is worth noting that it is possible to distinguish between the two ideas.

(a) The functions of management, as we discussed in Chapter 1, include planning, organising, co-ordinating and controlling. Management is primarily concerned with logic, structure and control. If done well, it produces predictable results, on time.

(b) Leadership, properly considered, involves a different kind of function, and – it may be argued – a rather different mind set. It involves essentially people-centred activities, with effects potentially beyond the scope of controlled performance. A leader's special function is to:

   (i) **Create a vision** of something different to the current status quo

   (ii) **Communicate the vision**. This will be particularly powerful if it meets the needs – conscious or unconscious – of other people, and if the leader can give it credibility in their eyes

   (iii) **Energise, inspire and motivate** others to translate the vision into achievement

   (iv) **Create the culture** that will support the achievement, through shared language, rituals, myths, beliefs and so on

In other words, while managers have authority by virtue of their position in the organisation to secure the obedience or compliance of their subordinates, leaders direct the efforts of others through vision, inspiration and motivation – forms of influence.

Definition

Influence is the process by which an individual or group exercises power to determine or modify the behaviour of others.

For routine work, mere compliance with directives may be sufficient for the organisation's needs. However, if it wishes to secure extra input from its employees – in terms of co-operation, effort and creativity – it may strive for the inspirational quality of leadership, over and above efficient management.

Activity 1 **(10 minutes)**

We often say that managers (as leaders) should motivate people to put forth extra effort. Above, we also use the word energy. As it happens, there are lots of words – all beginning with 'E' – which express the kinds of things managers would like to elicit from their staff. Charles Handy called them 'E Factors'. See if you can think of at least five more.

It should be clear that leadership is not merely a function that leaders themselves perform, or a set of techniques that they follow. Like beauty, leadership is largely in the eyes of the beholder: managers can only be called leaders if and when they have an inspiring, energising and motivating influence on their subordinates. A leader must have followers.

1.2 Followership

Some well-known writers on management have suggested that: 'The essence of leadership is followership. In other words, it is the willingness of people to follow that makes a person a leader.'

Leadership requires a conscious intention on the part of the leader to influence others. If you yawn, for example, and others around you feel an urge to do the same, it would more properly be called 'behavioural contagion' than leadership.

Activity 2 **(10 minutes)**

Suppose you were in a cinema and smelt smoke. How would you categorise the following possible actions on your part? Your options are behavioural contagion, management, and leadership.

(a) You rush to the door screaming 'Fire!' and everyone follows you.

(b) You rush to the door, switch on the lights, hit the fire alarm, and, grabbing a fire extinguisher, start looking for the source of the fire. People start moving towards the exits when they hear the fire alarm.

(c) You rush to the door, switch on the lights, shout for people not to panic but to move towards the exits (which they do) and ask for help to locate the fire and get the fire extinguishers (which you get).

(d) You do any or all of the above, but nobody takes any notice.

It is possible for an isolated individual to be a manager – but a leader requires people to influence: he or she will always be involved with people and groups, sensitive to their needs and behaviour, part of their networks of communication and influence. People tend to follow those whom they see as a means of satisfying their own personal goals. For managers to become effective leaders, they need to understand what motivates their subordinates, and what 'makes them tick'. (We will be looking at several aspects in the following chapters.)

Followership implies – as you may realise from your own experience – that leaders, unlike managers, are not always formally appointed to positions of delegated authority. Leaders *may* be appointed 'heads' – say military officers or business managers. They may, however, *emerge* out of the situations, activities and interrelationships of groups: think of gang leaders, or ringleaders in political protests. All leaders are, in a sense, elected, or at least recognised, by their followers.

FOR DISCUSSION

Select a number of historical (or fictional) figures whom you would identify as 'leaders'.

(a) Why do you think of them as 'leaders' (as opposed to 'heads')?

(b) What qualities in them and/or their context (the task that needed doing, tradition, hereditary 'headship' and so on) attracted followership?

(c) Were they viewed in the same light by everyone – in their own context, and in your discussion group?

It is often said of an influential person that (s)he is (or was) a 'born leader'. But is leadership something you've either got or not? The fact that you are studying management suggests that people can learn to be leaders – and we have already noted that situations can create leaders. On the other hand, your examples of leaders (if you did the discussion exercise above) may have appeared to have certain traits – such as charisma – in common.

1.3 Leadership in organisations

Most definitions of leadership reflect the assumptions that it is a relationship through which one person influences the behaviour or actions of other people in an organisational context. It is a dynamic two-way process of leading and following that can affect both individual and organisational performance. For example, a leader can influence the interpretation of events, the choice of objectives and strategies, the organisation of work activities, the motivation of people to achieve the objectives, the maintenance of co-operative relationships, the development of skills and confidence by members and the enlistment of support and co-operation from people outside the group or organisation.

Interest in leadership or management style within organisations was stimulated by the human relations movement and became a focus for research. In Chapter 2 Section 3 we discussed the Hawthorne experiment, which demonstrated that if managers took an interest in their employees and involved them in decisions affecting their work they would work harder. Those studies claimed to have identified the type of supervision/leader most likely to obtain a happy and motivated workforce.

1.4 Leadership traits

Early theorists suggested that the capacity to get others to do what you want them to do was an innate characteristic: you either had it, or you didn't. Studies on leadership focused on qualities, personality characteristics or 'traits' which were thought to make a good leader.

It seemed possible to show a significant correlation between leadership effectiveness and the traits of intelligence, initiative, self assurance and individuality – as you might expect.

Other supposed leadership traits included personal magnetism or charisma, (literally, 'gift from God'), interpersonal skills, analytical thinking, imagination, decisiveness, trustworthiness, persuasiveness, self-motivation, flexibility and vision. This list is by no means exhaustive, and various writers attempted to show that their selected list of traits were the ones that provided the key to leadership.

There are, however, several difficulties with the idea of leadership as a bundle of 'traits' or personal characteristics.

(a) The full list of traits is so long that it appears to call for a person of superhuman gifts. Nor, at best, does it help organisations to make better managers or leaders: it merely helps them recognise a leader when they see one.

(b) No two authorities agree on exactly which traits make an effective leader.

(c) Most of the traits listed are positive or desirable characteristics for human beings. Seldom is there any recognition of the possibility that leaders could be flawed individuals, or that their flaws may be the very features which enable them to succeed as leaders: ruthlessness, for example.

(e) Observation of actual successful leaders furnishes unreliable conclusions about leadership traits. If a leader takes risks and succeeds, then he is labelled 'courageous' and 'visionary'; if he takes risks and fails, he is merely 'foolhardy'.

(f) The trait approach does not take into account the individuality of followers, nor other factors in the leadership situation.

Though superficially attractive, and still entrenched in popular thinking, the trait or 'great man' approach to leadership is now largely discredited. Later approaches concentrate on the idea that leadership is a 'style' of relating to people and tasks, and that appropriate styles could be learned and adopted to suit different leadership situations. We will now look at a well-known classification of management style.

2 MANAGEMENT STYLES

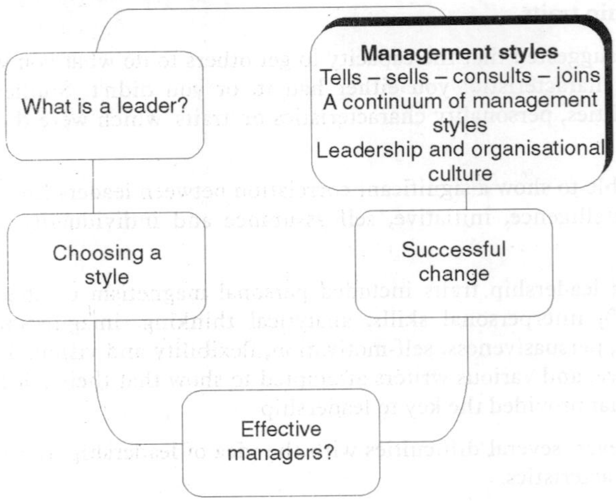

2.1 Tells – sells – consults – joins

Ashridge Management College carried out research in several industries in the UK to develop a classification of management styles. The Ashridge Studies (as the research came to be known) found four broad styles in use.

Style	Tells *(autocratic)*
Characteristics	The manager makes all the decisions, and issues instructions which must be obeyed without question
Strengths	(1) Quick decisions can be made when speed is required. (2) It is the most efficient type of leadership for highly-programmed, routine work.
Weaknesses	(1) Communication between the manager and subordinate will be one-way. There may be lack of helpful feedback. (2) It does not encourage contribution or initiative from subordinates.

Style	Sells *(persuasive)*
Characteristics	The manager still makes all the decisions, but explains them to subordinates, and attempts to motivate subordinates to carry them out willingly.
Strengths	(1) Selling decisions to staff might make them more willing. (2) Staff will have a better idea of what to do when unforeseen events arise in their work, because the manager will have explained his intentions.
Weaknesses	(1) Subordinates will not necessarily be committed to decisions in which they have not been involved. (2) It may be felt to be a 'tells' style dressed up with pretended concern for employees' views.

Style	Consults *(participative)*
Characteristics	The manager confers with subordinates and takes their views and feelings into account, but retains the right to make the final decision.
Strengths	(1) Employees are involved in decisions. This encourages motivation through greater interest and involvement. (2) Employees can contribute knowledge and experience, to help in solving problems related to their work.

Weaknesses	(1) It might take longer to reach decisions. (2) Subordinates might be limited in their viewpoint on organisational issues. (3) If the manager does not take employees' advice, they might perceive the process to be meaningless.
Style	**Joins** *(democratic)*
Characteristics	Leader and followers make the decision together, on the basis of consensus, or compromise and agreement.
Strengths	(1) It can provide high commitment to the decision reached. (2) It takes advantage of the knowledge and expertise of individuals in different areas, for high quality, flexible decision-making.
Weaknesses	(1) The authority of the manager might be undermined. (2) Decision-making might become a very long process. (3) Clear-cut decisions might be difficult to reach.

Activity 3 **(10 minutes)**

Which of the four Ashridge classifications would you expect:

(a) to be most popular with subordinates?
(b) to be perceived by subordinates as the most common style?
(c) to create most favourable attitudes towards work?

The four-style classification should not be seen as pigeon-holes into which a particular manager's style must fit. In fact, they are points along a 'continuum' or range of styles.

2.2 A continuum of management styles

Looking at management styles as a continuum or 'range' helps us to remember that they are highly flexible, and adaptable according to circumstances. Figure 8.1 shows one model which addresses a range of situations, albeit only in one dimension: the extent to which the manager retains and exercises control.

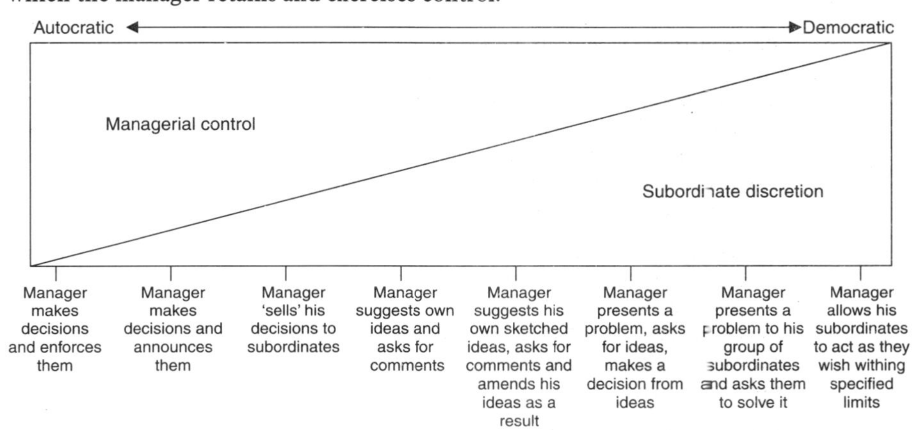

Figure 8.1 Management style continuum

So which style is the 'right' one? Which works best? A contingency approach to management suggests that a style which is appropriate and effective in one situation will not necessarily work in another. 'It all depends' on a number of variables in the leader's situation. In the following section, we will consider what some of those variables might be.

2.3 Leadership and organisational culture

Every organisation has its own unique culture, based in history and developing over time as groups establish patterns of behaviour and belief that seem effective in helping them to interpret and interact with the world in which they find themselves.

This culture then influences the decision-making processes, it affects styles of management and what everyone determines as success.

Goleman's (2000) research published in the *Harvard Business Review* investigated how each of six distinctive leadership styles correlated with specific components of an organisation's culture.

These cultural components are:

- **flexibility** – employees' ability to innovate without excessive rules and regulations
- **responsibility** – how responsible employees feel towards the organisation
- **standards** – the level of standards expected in the organisation
- **rewards** – the accuracy of performance feedback and rewards
- **clarity** – how clear employees are about the mission, vision and core values
- **commitment** – employees' commitment to a common purpose.

Goleman (2000) suggests that effective leaders choose from six distinctive leadership styles.

(a) **Coercive** (Do what I tell you) – this describes a leader that demands immediate compliance. This style can destroy an organisational culture and should only be used with extreme caution. It is useful in an emergency, and may work in a crisis or as a last resort with a problem employee. This leadership style has the most negative impact on the overall organisational culture.

(b) **Pacesetting** (Do as I do, now*)* – describes a leader who sets extremely high standards for performance. This style can also destroy a good culture and only works with a highly motivated and competent team who are able to 'read' the leader's mind. Others will feel overwhelmed and give up because they cannot see themselves reaching unrealistic standards. This style also has a negative impact on the overall organisational culture, especially on rewards and commitment.

(c) **Coaching** (Try this) – describes a leader who is focused on developing people for the future. These leaders are good at delegating, and are willing to put up with short-term failures, provided they lead to long-term development. This style works best when wanting to help employees improve their performance or develop their long-term strengths and has a positive impact on the overall organisational culture.

(d) **Democratic** (What do you think?) – describes a leader who achieves consensus thorough participation. This style builds trust, respect and commitment, and works best when wanting to receive input or get employees to 'buy-in' or achieve consensus. If handled correctly, this style has a positive impact on the overall organisational culture.

(e) **Affiliative** (People come first) – this describes a leader who is interested in creating harmony and building emotional bonds with employees. This style works best when motivating employees, building team harmony, improving communication, increasing morale or repairing broken trust and has a positive impact on the overall organisational culture. Because this style has virtually no downside, it is often described as the best overall approach.

(f) **Authoritative** (Come with me) – describes a visionary leader who gives people lots of scope to innovate and take calculated risks, provided that they move in the direction of the stated vision. This style works best when change requires a new vision or when employees are looking for a new direction but fails when employees are more knowledgeable or experienced than the leader, or if the authoritative style becomes overbearing. Provided that it is used subtly, this style has the most positive impact on the overall organisational culture

3 CHOOSING A STYLE

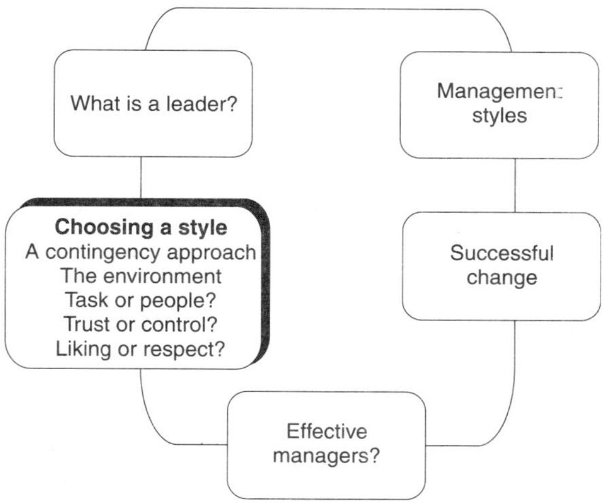

3.1 A contingency approach

Handy (1987) suggested a contingency approach to leadership.

According to Handy, the factors in any situation which influence the effectiveness of a particular management style are as follows.

(a) The **leader** (his or her personality, character and preferred style of operating).

(b) The **subordinates** (their individual and collective personalities, and their preference for a style of leadership).

(c) The **task** (the objectives of the job, the technology of the job, methods of working and so on).

(d) The **environment of management** (which we will discuss below).

Handy (1987) placed each of his three main variables on a version of the autocratic-democratic continuum, which he called a spectrum, ranging from 'tight' to 'loose' management control. Note that this spectrum (Figure 8.2) does not describe tight and loose styles of management themselves: you can think of them as 'tells' and 'joins' respectively. Instead, it describes the conditions in which a tight or loose style would be appropriate.

	Leader	*Subordinates*	*Task*
Tight control	• Preference for autocratic style	• Low opinion of own abilities	• Requires no initiative
	• High estimation of own capabilities	• Do not like uncertainty in work	• Routine and repetitive
	• Low estimation of subordinates	• Like to receive clear instruction	• Predictable outcome
	• Dislikes uncertainty	• Regard work as trivial	• Short time scale for completion
		• Inclined, through culture or expectation (based on past experience), to accept authority	• Trivial
		• High opinion of own abilities	
		• Like challenge	
		• Regard work as important	• Complex and non-routine
	• Preference for democratic style	• Prepared to accept uncertainty and longer time scales for results	• Involving problem-solving or decision-making
	• Confidence in subordinates		
	• Dislikes stress	• Inclined, through culture or past experience, to value independence	• Long time scales
Loose control	• Accepts reasonable risk and uncertainty		• Important

Figure 8.2 Choosing a management style

Handy argues that leadership style should be tight or loose according to the conditions in each of these areas, reflecting their position on the spectrum. Management will be most effective where there is a 'best fit' between the three variables: when they are on the same point of the spectrum. When 'best fit' occurs, the appropriately tight or loose style will suit the leader, subordinates and task at the same time, and the manager will therefore be successful in all areas: effective performance and team satisfaction.

In practice, there is likely to be a lack of fit, and the leader must decide which factor(s) should be changed to bring all three into line as far as possible. His or her own behaviour and style are easiest to address, in the short term, because they are most within the leader's control: hence the great emphasis on leadership in management literature, Handy argues. However, longer-term benefit might be achieved from tackling the other variables. If a manager wanted to create fit further towards the loose end of the spectrum, for example, (s)he could consult more, or could try to develop the confidence and abilities of the subordinates, or redefine the task to create more complex, integrated jobs with greater responsibility.

Activity 4 **(30 minutes**

Suggest an appropriate style of management for each of the following situations. Think about your reasons for choosing each style in terms of the results you are trying to achieve, the need to secure commitment from others, and potential difficulties with both.

(a) Due to outside factors, the personnel budget has been reduced for your department and one-quarter of your staff must be made redundant. Records of each employee's performance are available.

(b) There is a recurring administrative problem which is minor, but irritating to everyone in your department. Several solutions have been tried in the past, but without success. You think you have a remedy which will work, but unknown problems may arise, depending on the decision made.

(c) A decision needs to be made about working hours. The organisation wishes to stagger arrival and departure times in order to relieve traffic congestion. Each department can make its own decisions. It doesn't really matter what the times are, so long as department members conform to them.

(d) Even though they are experienced, members in your department don't seem to want to take on responsibility. Their attitude seems to be: 'You are paid to manage, we are paid to work: you make the decisions'. Now a decision has come up which will personally affect every person in your department.

3.2 The environment

However appropriate a particular style may be to the leader, subordinates and task, its effectiveness in practice may be constrained by other factors in the organisational context or 'environment' of leadership.

(a) **The position of power held by the leader in the organisation and work group**. A comparatively powerless leader may simply not be allowed to control the variables to achieve best fit, however clear the need to do so.

(b) **Organisational norms, structure and technology**. If the organisation has a tradition of autocratic leadership, for example, it will be difficult to introduce a participative style. If routine and repetitive work is 'built in' to the technology (eg an assembly line), challenging tasks will be difficult to create, and creative, flexible staff difficult to retain.

(c) **The variety of tasks and subordinates**. Placing the nature of the task on the loose-tight spectrum is difficult, if a group's activity varies from routine and simple to complex one-off problem-solving. Similarly, individuals within the work group are likely to be different (and changing, as members leave and arrive through labour turnover): some may require loose control and other tight control. (This is one reason why team building is so important.)

Activity 5 **(20 minutes)**

List four ways in which an organisation, by dealing with 'environmental constraints' can help its managers to adopt an appropriate management style.

We have already mentioned that managers have a dual responsibility for task achievement and for the satisfaction (or at least co-operative action) of people. Management often seems to involve a compromise, juggling or 'best fit' of these two aims. We will now look more closely at this and other managerial dilemmas: some of the tough choices managers face as they select and adopt a management style.

3.3 Task or people?

Our contingency approach assumes that management effectiveness can be measured according to:

(a) Task achievement, or
(b) The fulfilment of individual and group needs, or
(c) Both.

In order to adopt an appropriate leadership style, a manager has to ask: *what do I want to achieve?*

Research at Michigan and Harvard appeared to show that there were two distinct types of leader: 'task leaders', who were concerned with results and the structuring of activities, and 'socio-emotional' leaders, who were concerned with supportive and satisfying group practices and relationships.

However, another set of leadership studies (at Ohio State) suggested that, while concern for production/task structures and concern for people were two distinct dimensions, they were not mutually exclusive: a manager could have both concerns at the same time.

Blake's Managerial Grid

Blake and Mouton (1964) devised a 'grid' model showing how concern for people and concern for production could be combined in varying proportions, and what kind of management style would result, see Figure 8.3.

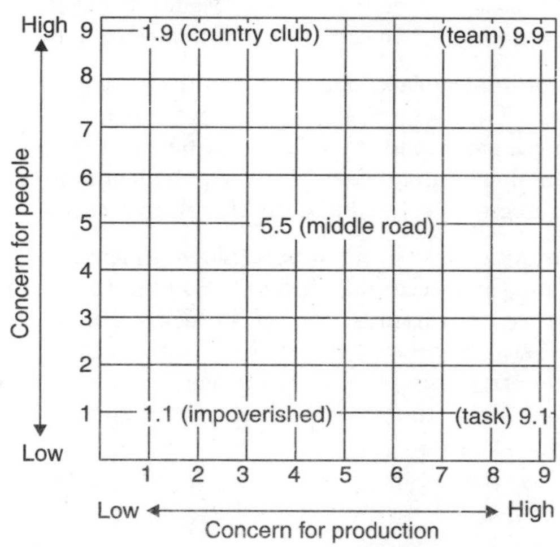

Figure 8.3 Blake and Mouton's managerial grid

Blake defined the extreme cases shown on the grid as follows.

(a) *1.1: impoverished*. The manager is lazy, showing little effort or concern for either staff or work targets.

(b) *1.9: country club*. The manager is attentive to staff needs and has developed satisfying relationships. However, he pays correspondingly little attention to achieving results.

(c) *9.1: task management*. Almost total concentration on achieving results. People's needs are virtually ignored and conditions of work are so arranged that people cannot interfere to any significant extent.

(d) *5.5: middle of the road*. The manager achieves adequate performance through balancing the necessity to meet work targets with maintaining the unity and morale of the group. (There is also a 'statistical 5.5', where the manager averages out at 5.5 by constantly veering between extremes.)

(e) *9.9: team*. The manager achieves high performance by leading people, who are committed to, and satisfied by, fulfilling task objectives.

Clearly, the most efficient manager combines high concern for the task with high concern for people: a 9.9.

The main value of the Managerial Grid is in the appraisal of managers' performance. Individual managers can be placed on the grid, usually using a questionnaire in which they have to choose between statements which represent different points on the grid. (See the Activity below.) A manager should then be able to see in which area his or her performance could be improved: a manager rated 3.8 for decision-making, for example, has further to go in improving the quality of his or her decisions than in involving subordinates in the decision-making process.

Activity 6 **(15 minutes)**

Here are some statements about a manager's approach to meetings. Which position on Blake's Grid do you think each might represent?

(a) I attend because it is expected. I either go along with the majority position or avoid expressing my views.

(b) I try to come up with good ideas and push for a decision as soon as I can get a majority behind me. I don't mind stepping on people if it helps a sound decision.

(c) I like to be able to support what my boss wants and to recognise the merits of individual effort. When conflict arises, I do a good job of restoring harmony.

Reddin's 3-D management grid

Professor Reddin (1997) argued that a simple task-people model is limited in its usefulness, compared to more thorough contingency approaches which allow for other variables. We may assume that a 1.1 manager is ineffective, because he simply follows rules, with little concern for people or task achievement, but in fact he may be *effective* in certain circumstances: for example, in a bureaucratic organisation, which functions steadily within its framework of rules and procedures.

Reddin therefore added a third dimension to Blake's grid: effectiveness (or ineffectiveness) according to the situation. For each of the combinations of task/people concern, there are two possible management styles. A 1.1 manager in an appropriate situation would be called a 'bureaucrat' and may well be effective: in an inappropriate situation, the same manager would be called a 'deserter', and would be ineffective. A 9.9 manager in an appropriate situation would be called an 'executive' (effective), but in an inappropriate situation he could be viewed merely as a 'compromiser' (ineffective).

You may already have picked up on another managerial dilemma, as we've talked about the range of management styles from autocratic to democratic, or from 'tight' to 'loose'. In order to adopt an appropriate style, a manager has to consider how far he can trust his subordinates to work well without tight control – and whether they will work well with tight control!

3.4 Trust or control?

The trust-control dilemma

Handy (1987) identified what he called a 'trust-control dilemma' in management relationships. He expressed it as a simple mathematical equation.

$T + C = Y$

where T = the trust the superior has in the subordinate, and the trust which the subordinate feels the superior has in him

C = the degree of control exercised by the superior over the subordinate

Y = a constant, unchanging amount, so that any increase in C leads to an equal decrease in T and vice versa.

If the superior lacks trust (less T) in a subordinate, he will exercise greater control or authority (more C) over his activities, and the subordinate will recognise that he is being trusted less. If the superior wishes to show more trust in the subordinate (more T), he will have to delegate more authority to him, thereby reducing his own control over the work (less C).

As we saw in Chapter 1 (Section 4.2), this can be difficult!

Assumptions about subordinates

To a large extent, the extent to which a manager trusts subordinates and feels able to delegate authority to them will depend on his or her assumptions about how they will behave. *McGregor* (1960) formulated perhaps the best-known framework for talking about this. He described the two extremes of attitude that a manager might have about his subordinates, and labelled them Theory X and Theory Y.

Theory X is the assumption that the average human being dislikes work and will avoid it unless he is coerced, controlled, directed and threatened with punishment. He actually prefers to be directed, since he fears responsibility and wants security above all.

A manager who operates on the basis of Theory X will feel he has to direct and control workers with specific instructions, close supervision and rigid task structures. (This is, to an extent, a self-fulfilling prophecy: if a manager controls his subordinates *as if* they are hostile to work and to the organisation, he will usually create conditions in which they will genuinely become hostile to work and to the organisation!)

Theory Y is the assumption that the ordinary person does not naturally dislike work and does not require tight control in order to put in effort. He is motivated by the desire for personal growth and achievement, and will exercise self-direction and self-control and actively seek responsibility, if he is committed to the task.

A manager who operates on the basis of Theory Y will try to integrate subordinates' needs for development and self-expression with the organisation's objectives, so that both can be achieved together. He will tend to use a democratic or consultative style in order to obtain subordinates' involvement and commitment to the task, and will tend to encourage them to take on more responsibility and more challenging work.

FOR DISCUSSION

'Look to the ant, you sluggard; consider its ways and be wise! It has no commander, no overseer or ruler, yet it stores its provision in summer and gathers its food at harvest.' (The Bible, Book of Proverbs 6: 6–9)

What does this ancient idea suggest about the nature of managerial control?

Activity 7 **(40 minutes)**

Malcolm Ross was head of operations at Disneyland Paris. An article about him in *The Times* described aspects of the culture and mechanisms of management in the 'Magic Kingdom'.

'Ross cuts an impressive figure on first sighting – red shirt, dark green suit, brown slip-ons, and a large white badge bearing the name Malcolm. He wears a gold-plated Mickey Mouse watch and comes laden with electronic gadgets. Keeping tabs on 6,000 theme park employees – "cast members" in Disney-speak – requires an elaborate communications network. "We keep in touch using mobile phones, beepers and a ten-channel radio system," he says, steering me past immaculate flowerbeds and cascading waterfalls. Cast members are equipped with CIA-style black earpieces, and communicate in code. Ross's call-sign is Magic Kingdom. "There is only one Magic Kingdom", he chuckles....

'Ross spends at least an hour a day mixing with the guests, taking in a show, sampling a ride. "It's management by walking about", he says, stooping to pick up a scrap of litter. "It's very important for me to touch and feel the pulse of the park...".

'Anyone about to enter Ross's office is confronted by the words Hakuna Matata, from the film The Lion King. "It means 'No Worries'", says Ross's secretary... "whoever goes through that door had better have good news." '

(a) What type of control is being used here?

(b) Is Malcolm Ross a Theory X or Theory Y manager?

(c) Give at least three effects that his style of management may have on the employees.

(You might like to know that the staff nicknames for the 'Magic Kingdom' are apparently 'Mouseschwitz' – after a notorious Nazi concentration camp – and 'Neuro-Disney' ...)

3.5 Liking or respect?

This is a tough question. It relates to managerial effectiveness: will the team give more to a manager they like, or to one they respect – or even fear? It also touches on the needs of the manager as a person.

(a) On the one hand, a manager has needs for belonging, relationship and approval. (Self esteem depends to a large extent on being liked by others.)

(b) On the other hand, a manager needs to be in control, in order to achieve objectives.

Managers who are responsible for task performance will inevitably have to make decisions that will be unpopular with all or some of their team members. Individuals have different needs and expectations, only some of which will be in harmony with those of others and with organisational goals. Resources are limited, and individuals are in competition for them. So consensus decisions, even moderately pleasing to everybody, will not always be possible – and unpleasant decisions (such as disciplinary action or redundancies) may be required.

Taking a contingency approach, we can see that how a manager resolves this dilemma will depend on:

(a) **The strength of the individual manager's need to be liked**, which in turn will depend on the availability of other supportive, loving relationships in his or her life

(b) **The attitude of the team members** – some may take advantage of a boss who tries to be 'one of the lads'; some may feel insecure with a boss who does not seem to exercise authority or face up to responsibility; others may thrive on being treated as a peer

(c) **The nature of the task or decision** – if the task is basically incompatible with individual/group needs (for example, the work is dangerous or boring), the manager will not be able to fulfil task objectives and stay popular

Activity 8 **(About 1 hour)**

Scott Peck, a well-known American psychiatrist and writer, was appointed director of psychiatry at the US Army Medical Corps. He was responsible for a department of about forty people, mostly professionals, and mainly young. He had never managed anybody before. He later wrote: 'I was perfectly clear in my own mind about what my management style would be: I was going to be just as different from every authoritarian boss who had ever been in charge of me as I could possibly be... Not only did I never make an administrative decision without consulting everyone involved; I did my very best to see that, within the constraints of professional competence, the people under me made their own decisions wherever possible about the matters that affected their own lives... I discouraged them from addressing me as "Major Peck". Soon everyone was calling me Scotty. I was "Mr Nice Guy". And it worked. The mood was euphoric... The department morale was superb.'

After about six months, however, morale began to suffer; petty bickering broke out; tasks began to be neglected. Things came to a head when the department had to plan a move to a new medical complex: there were fights over who got what office, while the packing process fell way behind schedule. In a confrontational meeting about the problem, someone complained that the department was 'all at sea'. Scott Peck reappraised his leadership.

(a) Identify three main reasons for the breakdown in morale.

(b) What suggestions would you make to Scott Peck to get his department performing effectively?

4 SUCCESSFUL CHANGE

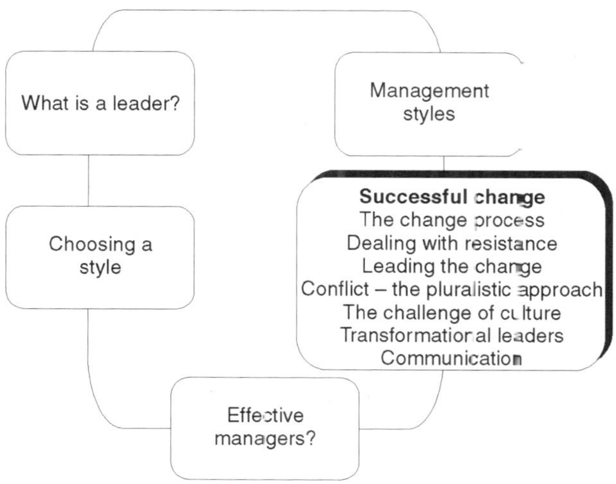

4.1 The change process

Today's business world is highly competitive. Organisations are reshaping themselves to change quickly in order to meet the needs of their customers, changes in economic conditions, rapid developments in technology and globalisation and to do this they need highly committed and flexible workers.

Organisations go through four main stages:

1. **Formative Period** – this is when a new organisation is just getting started. Although there is a founding vision – why the organisation was started, changes of creativity and discovery are needed to overcome obstacles and accomplish breakthroughs.
2. **Rapid Growth Period** – leadership and co-ordination are added to sustain growth and solidify gains. Change is focused on the mainstream business.
3. **Mature Period** – the growth now levels off and changes are only needed to maintain established markets and assure maximum gains are achieved.
4. **Declining Period** – for many organisations it means downsizing and reorganisation. Changes must include tough objectives and compassionate implementation. The goal is to get out of the old and into something new. Success in this period means that the four periods start over again

In Chapter 1 we briefly discussed the two types of change undertaken in organisations. By far the most frequent sort of change is incremental change, eg producing more of something, doing something slightly different and doing things better. Transformational change is an entire change in structure or character.

Nature provides an excellent example of the transformation process in the butterfly. When the caterpillar emerges from it's cocoon a beautiful butterfly capable of flight, it has not merely changed – it has been totally transformed. It will never again be a caterpillar.

There are various ways of responding to these changes. One approach – the least effective – is to simply react to the crisis. Another approach is to deliberately plan the change. This may require new objectives or policies, rearrangements within the organisation or a change in leadership style and organisation culture.

4.2 Dealing with resistance

Most individuals' first reaction to change is to resist it. People get comfortable performing tasks and processes in a certain way. This comfort provides them with the security that they are the masters of their environment. They fear that change could disrupt their lives by making them look like a fool by not being able to adapt and learn, make their jobs harder, lose a sense of control, etc.

There are three important factors for leaders to consider when dealing with resistance:

(a) **The pace of change** – changes should be introduced slowly. The more gradual the change, the more time is available for questions to be asked, reassurances given and retraining organised.

(b) **The scope of change** – total transformation will create greater insecurity but also more excitement than moderate innovation. Leaders need to be aware of how many aspects of their subordinates' lives they are proposing to alter and on how many fronts they are likely to encounter resistance.

(c) **The manner of change** – the climate must be prepared, the need made clear, fears soothed, and if possible the individuals concerned positively motivated to embrace the changes as their own.

- Resistance should be welcomed and confronted, not swept under the carpet. Talking through areas of conflict may lead to useful insights and the adapting of the programme of change to advantage.
- There should be free circulation of information about the reasons for the change, its expected results and likely consequences.
- People must be convinced that their attitudes and behaviours need changing. Objections must be overcome, but it is also possible to get people behind the change in a positive way. If those involved understand that there is a real problem, which poses a threat to the organisation and themselves, and that the solution is a sensible one and will solve that problem, there will be a firm rational basis, for implementing change.
- The effects of insecurity, perceived helplessness, and therefore resentment, may be lessened if people can be involved in the planning and implementation of the change.

4.3 Leading the change

Because of the many sources of resistance to change and the need for organisations to adapt to changing market, cultural and technological conditions, the management of change has become a central managerial problem. The human aspects of the change have to be managed carefully to make sure change is accepted and introduced rapidly and effectively.

Kurt Lewin (1946) developed a programme that involves the management of a three-stage process of behaviour modification:

Unfreezing – is concerned mainly with 'selling' the change, with giving individuals or groups a motive for changing their attitudes, values, behaviour, systems or structures. If the need for change is immediate, clear and perceived to be associated with the survival of the individual or group, the unfreeze stage will be greatly accelerated. Routine changes may be harder to sell than transformational ones, if they are perceived to be unimportant and not survival-based.

Changing – is mainly concerned with identifying what the new, desirable behaviour or norm should be, communicating it and encouraging individuals to 'own' the new attitude or behaviour. This change may occur through assimilation of new information, exposure to new concepts or development of a different perspective.

Refreezing – is the final stage, which stabilises the change, implying consolidation or reinforcement of the new behaviour. Positive reinforcement (praise and reward) or negative reinforcement (sanctions applied to those who deviate from the new behaviour) may be used.

4.4 Conflict – the pluralistic approach

It might be expected that a healthy organisational climate would be reflected by complete harmony in working relationships, and loyalty and common commitment to the goals and objectives of the organisation. Such views appear to imply a **unitary perspective** of the organisation. With the unitary approach, the organisation is viewed as a team with a common source of loyalty, one focus of effort and one accepted leader.

Conflict can be explained, for example, by poor communications, personality clashes or the work of agitators.

Fox, (1999) compared and contrasted the unitary perspective in which the organisation is viewed as a team with a common source of loyalty, one focus of effort and one accepted leader, with the pluralist perspective in which the organisation is composed of a plurality of interest groups with differing goals and allegiances. This view portrays organisations as arenas for conflict on individual and group levels. Members battle for limited resources, status, rewards and professional values. Organisational politics involve constant struggles for control, and choices of structure, technology and organisational goals are part of this process. Individual and organisational interests will not always coincide.

Those who take a pluralist perspective and recognise the existence within organisations of diverse sub-cultures arising from factors such as professional affiliation, status, social or divisional interactions, argue that organisational success springs from the effective leadership and management of diversity, and that cultural change or maintenance efforts have to be undertaken through programmes specifically designed for different segments of the organisation. International companies, with national subsidiaries tied to a parent company, often exhibit distinct cultures interacting with the parent company culture, but so also do many nationally-based companies where, for example, research and development divisions may form a sub-culture quite different from that of marketing divisions.

This constructive conflict view may be the most useful for managers. It neither attempts to dodge the issues of conflict, which is an observable fact of life in most organisations; nor seeks to pull down existing organisational structures altogether. Managers have to get on with the job of managing and upholding organisational goals with the co-operation of other members.

Given that conflict is inevitable, and assuming that organisational goals are broadly desirable, there are two aspects of conflict that are relevant in practice to the leader.

(a) Conflict can be highly desirable. It can energise relationships and clarify issues. *Hunt* (1986) suggests that conflict can have constructive effects.

- It can introduce different solutions to problems.
- Power relationships can be defined more clearly.
- It may encourage creativity and the testing of ideas.
- It focuses attention on individual contributions.
- It brings emotions out into the open.
- It provides opportunity for the release of hostile feelings that have been, or may be, repressed otherwise.

(b) Conflict can also be destructive.

- It may distract attention from the task.
- It can polarise views and dislocate the group.
- Objectives may be subverted in favour of secondary goals.
- It encourages defensive or spoiling behaviour.
- It may result in disintegration of the group.
- Emotional, win-lose conflicts may be stimulated.

4.5 The challenge of culture

An organisation's culture is the general pattern of behaviour, shared beliefs and values that members have in common. It often sets the tone for the company and establishes implied rules for the way people should behave.

Managers create the climate for the organisation. Their values influence its direction and in many successful companies' leaders serve as role models, set the standards for performance, motivate employees, make the company special and are a symbol to the external environment. The culture created by these leaders can result in managerial functions being carried out in quite different ways. Their clear vision of a common purpose elicits commitment. When people participate in the decision-making process and exercise self-direction and self-control, they feel committed to their own plans.

Edwin *Baker*, in 1981, observed twelve corporations that developed unhealthy corporate cultures. He found a common pattern.

(a) The organisation flourished initially under its founder who created, usually without conscious effort, a cohesive group of employees who shared his beliefs and values.

(b) On the founder's retirement the organisation continued to flourish but many employees became rigid and insular in their thinking and behaviour.

(c) Concern for survival faded and, as a result, so did values regarding speed, flexibility, innovation and concern for the customer.

(d) Increased growth led to formalisation and the development of rules and procedures. Divisions occurred between employees and management because of specialisation. Communication and willingness to accept responsibility decreased.

(e) Employees identified with their departments, not with the organisation as a whole.

(f) Corrective action needed to challenge problems of mature products and markets met inertia. It was thwarted by the rigid culture.

'Changing a culture to increase a corporation's effectiveness is a hazardous undertaking,' says *Hampden-Turner* (1990). Changing the distinctive culture of a large, old organisation is enormously difficult and may take years. Most research has shown that, in a large organisation, shifting the value system or culture can take between three and eight years.

If senior managers wish to change a culture, they must know about it in detail. Hampden-Turner suggests six **modes of intervention**: these produce the knowledge about how the culture works.

(a) **Find the dangers ('locate the black sheep')**. In other words, the best way to find out about how a culture works is to violate it, by doing something culturally shocking.

(b) **Bring conflicts into the open**. Interviewing and observation are the principal tools of cultural investigation. Interviews identify what people believe as **individuals**, as opposed to what they affirm as **employees**. The interviewer should uncover dilemmas such as, for example, safety versus performance.

(c) **Play out corporate dramas**. The manager or consultant then discusses the culture with its members. This can result in heated, but hopefully constructive argument.

(d) **Reinterpret the corporate myths**. Corporate stories passed round to recruits indicate something about competing value systems. Sometimes these corporate myths have to change.

(e) **Look at symbols, images, rituals.** . . Rituals are used to celebrate achievement, or to mark changes: 'changing a corporate culture can mean that new symbols, rituals and approaches are devised.'

(f) **Create a new learning system**. Cultures filter and exclude information. They need to be modified to accept new types of data.

The difficult task, obviously, is to establish new and positive norms of behaviour. A consistent approach is needed, requiring the following.

(a) Top management commitment.

(b) Modelling behaviour – management should be seen to be acting on the new norms themselves, not merely mouthing empty words about change.

(c) Support for positive behaviour and confrontation of negative behaviour.

(d) Consistency between the evaluation and reward system and positive behaviour, perhaps by linking pay to acting on positive norms.

(e) Communication of desired norms.

(f) Recruitment and selection of the right people.

(g) Induction programmes for new employees on the desired norms of behaviour.

(h) Training and skills development.

One of the key leadership challenges for the future will be the ability to manage in different countries and cultures. The current models of leadership do not deal with the demand for international competence in working with different country nationals and with different belief and value systems, which is growing more rapidly than in the past. Countless hazards are created by communication problems, cultural differences in motivational and value systems and diverse codes of conduct. Conflicts in culture arise between:

- efficiency and relationships – in parts of South America the quality of interpersonal relationships is considered more important than efficiency, costs, timing and deadlines. Concentrating on efficiency and failing to develop the necessary rapport, trust and mutual understanding can result in lucrative contracts being lost and a lack of understanding between the parties involved.
- truth and face – in Japan they value teamwork and harmony and direct communication of praise and/or criticism can cause great discomfort and loss of face.

4.6 Transformational leaders

Transformational leaders create conditions for followers to want to achieve results and to fulfil themselves. They are thought to engage followers by employing one or more of the 4 'I's' – outlined below – to stimulate voluntary and enthusiastic responses to their influence attempts.

The four 'I's' of transformational leadership are:

(a) **Individualised consideration***:* treats each follower as an individual and provides coaching, mentoring and growth opportunities. It gives personal attention to others, making each individual feel uniquely valued.

(b) **Intellectual stimulation***:* actively encourages a new look at old methods, questions *status quo*, and encourages imagination, creativity, logical thinking and intuition.

(c) **Inspirational motivation***:* increases optimism and enthusiasm, sees problems as opportunities, communicates high expectations, and points out possibilities not previously considered. It provides followers with challenges and meaning for engaging in shared goals and undertakings.

(d) **Idealised influence***:* provides vision and a sense of purpose and sets high standards for emulation. Elicits respect, trust, and confidence from followers. Respected for personal ability.

Activity 9 **(15 minutes)**

Several reactions to change have been proposed:

(a) Acceptance
(b) Indifference
(c) Passive resistance
(d) Active resistance

Give examples of behaviour for each reaction.

4.7 Communication

Although communication applies to all phases of managing, it is particularly important in the function of leading. In its broadest sense, the purpose of communication in an enterprise is to effect change – to influence action toward its welfare.

One key to successful change management is dynamic, responsive and ongoing communication, so transformation depends on these crucial communication tasks:

(a) Creating a compelling change story and communicating objectives to the organisation

(b) Making the transformation vision comprehensive, operational and real

(c) Communicating progress to the organisation and other stakeholders

Good communications can help to minimise conflicts and prevent unnecessary misunderstanding.

Effective communication is a two-way process, perhaps best expressed as a cycle. Signals or 'messages' are sent by the communicator and received by the other party, who sends back some form of confirmation that the message has been received and understood. This is enormously complicated in practice, especially in face-to-face communication: you may send a letter and receive an acknowledgement back, which would correspond to a single cycle of communication, but face-to-face, the workings of two or more minds and bodies (nodding understanding, gesturing and so on) complicate the picture. A basic interpretation of the process of communication might be as follows.

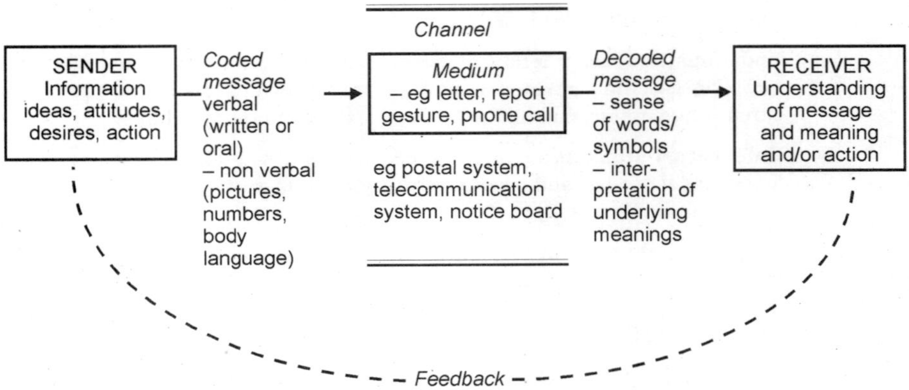

Figure 8.4 Communication loop

As illustrated in Figure 8.4, it is **feedback** that makes communication a two-way process rather than a series of send-receive events. Feedback is a vital and often neglected aspect of the process, which indicates to the sender whether or not his message has been successfully received, understood and interpreted. Failure to seek or offer feedback, or ignoring feedback offered, is one of the major problems in communication.

Further potential problems in the communication process include the following.

(a) **Not** communicating. (Bear in mind that even 'tactful' or 'thoughtful' silences are open to misinterpretation.)

(b) **Pointless** communicating: sending a message that is meaningless, irrelevant or unsuitable to the purpose and recipient of the communication.

(c) **Distortion**: a technical term for the way in which the meaning of a communication is lost in handling. For example, the intention of the sender fails to translate itself accurately into language that is suitable for its purpose and its intended recipient, so that the wrong message is being sent or the language used is not translated properly by the receiver, so the wrong message is being received.

(d) **Noise** refers to distractions and interference in the environment in which communication is taking place. It may be physical noise (passing traffic), technical noise (a bad telephone line), social noise (differences in the personalities, background and attitudes of the parties) or psychological noise (anger, frustration, tiredness and other feelings).

(e) **Non-verbal signals** (gestures, facial expression, appearance, posture are examples) contradicting the verbal message, confusing the recipient. (If someone is saying, 'That's very interesting', as they visibly stifle a yawn, what are you to think?)

(f) **'Overload'** – giving the recipient more information than he can digest or use in the time available – or, on the other hand, insufficient or incomplete information for its purpose.

5 EFFECTIVE MANAGERS?

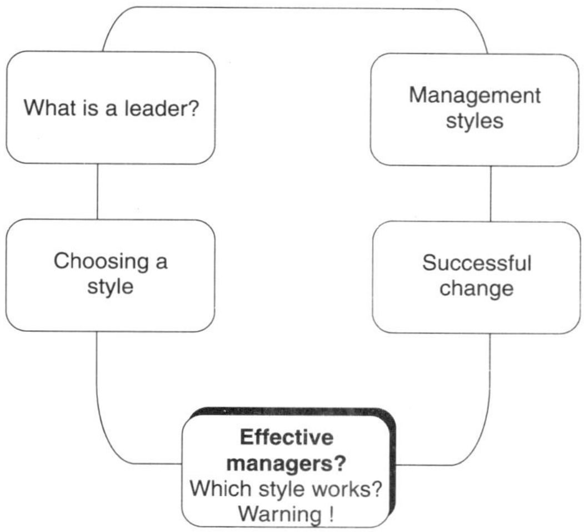

5.1 Which style works?

We have already recommended a contingency approach to this question, which suggests that 'it all depends'. However, it is worth taking note of some major experience-based research into leadership style and effectiveness.

Rensis Likert (1961) asked the question: 'What do effective managers have in common?' He found that four main elements are normally present in any effective manager.

(a) **They expect high levels of performance**. Their standards and targets are high and apply overall, not only to their subordinates' performance, but also to other departments and their own personal performance.

(b) **They are employee-centred**. They spend time getting to know their team and developing trust, so that people feel able to air any problems. When necessary, their actions can be hard, but are always fair. They face unpleasant facts in a constructive manner and help their staff to develop a similar attitude.

(c) **They do not practise close supervision**. Effective managers are aware of their team's capabilities and, within those parameters, help them to define their own performance targets. Once this has been done they monitor the results, rather than the activity. In this way, managers develop their team and free themselves for other managerial functions.

(d) **They operate a participative style of management as a natural style**. This means that if a job problem arises, they do not impose a favoured solution, but put the problem to the people involved. They support the team in implementing whatever solution is agreed.

Likert emphasises that all four features must be present for a manager to be truly effective. For example, a manager who is employee-centred, who delegates and is participative will have a happy working environment – but will not produce the required task results unless (s)he also sets the high performance standards.

Activity 10 **(20 minutes)**

Management style is said to be responsible for subordinates' suffering stress and related health problems – such as high blood pressure, insomnia, coronary heart disease and alcohol abuse.

From your own experience of work, study or even family life, what management behaviours do you think are particularly stressful for employees?

5.2 Warning!

One problem with theories of management approach or style is that studying a concept will not necessarily change an individual's behaviour. Individual managers are unlikely to change their values (which are rooted in past experience, beliefs and attitudes) in response to a theory – especially where it is one of many, often conflicting, frameworks.

Even if a **willingness** to change management style exists, conditions in the organisation may not allow it. It will not necessarily be helpful for managers to model their behaviour on prescriptive formulae which are successful in theory or in a completely different situation: yet more flexible contingency models are difficult to apply in practice.

(a) Managers' personality (or acting ability) may not be flexible enough to utilise leadership theories effectively, by changing styles to suit different situations. A manager who is authoritarian by nature could come across as a hideously stiff and insincere democratic leader, even if the situation demanded it.

(b) Consistency is important to subordinates. If managers practise a contingency approach to leadership, subordinates may simply perceive them to be fickle, or may suffer insecurity, and distrust the unpredictable manager.

(c) 'The essence of leadership is followership' and followers' responses are not necessarily subject to leadership theory, however well supported by research findings from other situations!

FOR DISCUSSION

The Ashridge Studies found that the least favourable attitudes towards work were found – not among subordinates who were subjected to autocratic or 'tells' management styles – but amongst those who were unable to perceive any consistent style of leadership in their boss. In other words, subordinates seemed unsettled by a boss who chops and changes between autocracy, persuasion, consultation and democracy.

Do you think this undermines the basic idea of a contingency approach to management style? What are the main points of value that you have got from your study of management style? Pick at least one thing that you think you could take away and use.

Chapter roundup

- Leadership is the process of influencing others to work willingly towards the achievement of organisational goals.
- Theories of leadership have been based on the following aspects.

  (a) Traits which appear to be common to successful leaders.

  (b) Styles which can be adopted. These are often expressed as a range or continuum, reflecting either the manager's approach to control or the manager's priorities.

  Tells sells ← consults → joins

  Tight ←→ Loose

  Wholly task oriented ←→ wholly people oriented

- A contingency approach to leadership suggests that a style may be appropriate or inappropriate (and therefore effective or ineffective) depending on variables including:

  (a) The structure and demands of the task
  (b) The characteristics and needs of the team and its individual members
  (c) The characteristics and needs of the leader
  (d) The organisational environment.

- A change is only one of several sources of conflict within an organisation. Some consider conflict to be an aberration; others see organisations as political battlefields and conflicts of interest as inevitable.
- Managing change and conflict is thus a vitally important management task.
- People resist change because of uncertainty, fear, lack of confidence, and a sense of dissonance. The success of change can be promoted by taking these factors into account. Only a few are hostile to any change. Change therefore involves structural and behavioural factors.

Quick quiz

1 How do people become leaders in a group or situation?

2 What is the difference between a 'sells' and 'consults' style of management?

3 What might be the disadvantages of a 'tells' style of management?

4 According to Handy, what type of task makes tight control a suitable style?

5 What factors in the environment influence the choice of a tight or loose style?

6 What is the most effective style suggested by Blake's managerial grid, and why is it so effective in theory? Why might it not be effective in practice?

7 Explain the equation T + C = Y.

8 What are Theory X and Theory Y?

9 Do teams need to have a leader? Would they be as effective without one?

10 Why is consistency of management style important – and why might this be a problem?

Answers to quick quiz

1 Through different forms of influence such as vision, inspiration and motivation.

2 'Sells' – the manager still makes all decisions but explains them to subordinates to get them to carry them out willingly. 'Consults' – the manager confers with subordinates, takes their views and feelings into account, but retains the right to make the final decision.

3 'Telling' is one-way, there is no feedback. It does not encourage contributions or initiative.

4 Those which lack initiative, are routine, trivial or have a short time scale.

5 The position of power held by the leader, organisational norms, structure and technology, the variety of tasks and subordinates.

6 9.9. It is effective if there is sufficient time and resources to attend fully to people needs, if the manager is good at dealing with people and if the people respond. It is ineffective when a task has to be completed in a certain way or by a certain deadline even if people don't like it.

7 T = trust in subordinates; C = control by the superior; Y = a constant, unchanging amount.

8 Refer to Section 3.4.

9 Someone has to ensure the objective is achieved, make decisions and share out resources. If everyone on the team is equally able and willing to do these things (unlikely in practice) a good information system is probably all that is needed, not a leader.

10 Inconsistency results in subordinates feeling unsure and distrusting the manager.

Answers to activities

1 You may have come up with excitement, enthusiasm, excellence, endeavour, expenditure, efficiency, effectiveness – and so on, as 'E' words expressing what managers like to see in their staff.

2 Categorisation of different behaviour on smelling smoke in a cinema is as follows.

(a) Behavioural contagion: people are simply copying you, without any conscious intention to lead on your part.

(b) Management. You are dealing with logistics: planning and organising. You are not, however, concerned with influencing the people: they simply respond to the situation.

(c) Leadership. You intend to mobilise others in pursuit of your aims, and you succeed in doing so.

(d) Whatever it is, it isn't leadership – because you have gained no followers.

3 The Ashridge researchers found that:

(a) there was a clear preference for the 'consults' style;

(b) managers were most commonly thought to be exercising the 'tells' or 'sells' styles;

(c) the most favourable attitudes were held by subordinates who perceived their boss to be exercising the 'consults' style.

4 Styles of management in the situations described suggest, using the tells-sells-consults-joins model.

(a) You may have to 'tell' here: nobody is going to like the idea and, since each person will have his or her own interests at heart, you are unlikely to reach consensus. You could attempt to 'sell', if you can see a positive side to the change in particular cases: opportunities for retraining, say.

(b) You could 'consult' here: explain your remedy to staff and see whether they can suggest potential problems. They may be in a position to offer solutions – and since the problem effects them too, they should be committed to solving it.

(c) We prefer a 'joins' style here, since the team's acceptance of the decision is more important than the details of the decision itself.

(d) We would go for 'consult' despite the staff's apparent reluctance to participate. They may prefer you to 'tell' – but may resist decisions they disagree with anyway. Perhaps their reluctance is to do with lack of confidence – or lack of trust that you will take their input seriously, in which case, persistent use of a 'consults' style may encourage them. You could use a 'sells' approach initially, to get them used to a less authoritarian style than they seem to expect.

5 The 'environment' can be improved for leaders if senior management ensure that:

(a) Managers are given a clear role and the power (over resources and information) to back it up

(b) Organisational 'norms' can be broken without fear of punishment – ie the organisation culture is adaptive, and managers can change things if required

(c) The organisational structure is not rigid and inflexible: managers can redesign task and team arrangements

(d) Team members are selected or developed so that they are, as far as possible, of the same 'type' in terms of their attitudes to work and supervision

(e) Labour turnover is reduced as far as possible (by having acceptable work conditions and terms, for example), so that the team does not constantly have to adjust to new members, or leaders

(You were only asked for four suggestions.)

6 Blake's Grid positioning of the given managerial approaches are:

(a) 1.1: low task, low people
(b) 9.1: high task, low people
(c) 1.9: high people, low task

7 Malcolm Ross's control and type of management may be classified as follows. (a) Tight. (b) Theory X. (c) Staff might react by: lack of confidence, demotivation, low opinion of self, fear, lack of trust.

8 (a) Morale has broken down through lack of management control, lack of a cohesive framework, increasing lack of respect for Scott Peck.

(b) To get his department going again, Scott Peck should start laying proper ground rules, take charge and provide a proper structure within which the department would operate.

Scott Peck actually assigned offices to his team and then informed them of his decision. Although this initially caused dismay, morale began to improve almost immediately. His style of leadership remained relatively nonauthoritarian, but not rigidly so. Morale stayed high.

9 Reactions to proposed change:

Acceptance – enthusiastic espousal, co-operation, grudging co-operation or resignation

Indifference – apathy, inaction and lack of interest

Passive resistance – refusal to learn or working to rule

Active resistance – deliberate 'spoiling', go-slows, deliberate errors, sabotage, absenteeism or strikes

10 Stressful management practices identified in employee surveys include:

(a) Unpredictability (staff work with uncertainty, or under threat of an outburst)

(b) Destruction of employees' self-esteem (making them feel insecure or inadequate)

(c) Setting up competitive win/lose situations (turning work relationships into battles for control, making work issues personal conflicts)

(d) Providing too much or too little stimulation (work overload or underload)

(e) Unfairness (not giving credit where it is due)

(f) Failure to define duties and communicate objectives and policies

Chapter 9:
MOTIVATION THEORIES

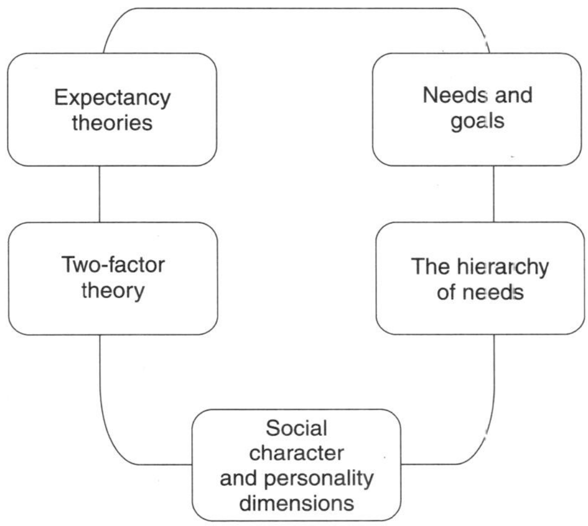

Introduction

The word motivation is commonly used in different contexts to mean:

(a) Goals or outcomes that have become desirable for a particular individual, as in: 'he is motivated by money'

(b) The mental process of choosing a goal and deciding whether and how to achieve it, as in: 'he is motivated to work harder'

(c) The social process by which the behaviour of an individual is influenced by others, as in: 'the manager motivates his team'

In this chapter, we cover some basic motivation theories (which explain the first two meanings). In Chapter 10, we concentrate on 'motivation' in the third sense, which is the practical responsibility of the manager.

Your objectives

In this chapter you will learn about the following:

(a) Motivation

(b) The need theory, two factor theory, expectancy theory of motivation and personality and social character dimensions

1 MOTIVATION THEORIES

One way of grouping the major theories of motivation is by distinguishing between:

(a) *Content theories*
(b) *Process theories*
(c) *Newer approaches to motivation in organisation*

Content theories assume that human beings have an innate package of 'motives' which they pursue; in other words, that they have a set of needs or desired outcomes and will act in such a way as to fulfil them. Maslow's need hierarchy theory (1954) and Herzberg's two-factor theory (1968) are two of the most important approaches of this type.

Process theories explore the process through which outcomes become desirable and are pursued by individuals. This approach assumes that people are able to select their goals and choose the paths towards them, by a conscious or unconscious process of calculation. Expectancy theory is the major approach of this type.

Two of the newer approaches we will be discussing are *Maccoby's* Social Character Theory and *Costa & McRae's* Five-Factor Theory.

We will be looking at all these theories later in this chapter. First, however, we will look briefly at what lies behind motivational theory.

Activity 1 **(10 minutes)**

What do you think is your main 'motive' for studying this module? In other words, what is the main thing you expect to get out of it?

2 NEEDS AND GOALS

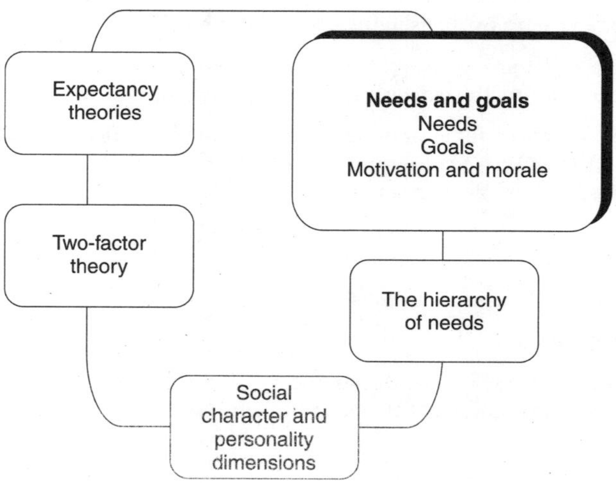

2.1 Needs

Individual behaviour is partly influenced by human biology, which requires certain basics for life: oxygen, food, water, shelter, sleep, self-preservation and so on. When the body is deprived of these essentials, biological forces called needs or drives are activated, and dictate the behaviour required to end the deprivation: eat, drink, flee and so on. We do not learn these drives, we cannot make them go away, and they are very powerful. However, we retain freedom of choice about how we satisfy our drives: they do not dictate specific or highly predictable behaviour. (Say you are hungry: how many specific ways of satisfying your hunger can you think of?)

We also behave in ways that make no direct contribution to our physical survival or health: people study, enjoy art, and make sacrifices for causes they believe in. This suggests that as well as physical drives, we have emotional and psychological needs. The American psychologist Abraham *Maslow* (1954) suggested that people have certain innate needs, as shown in Figure 9.1.

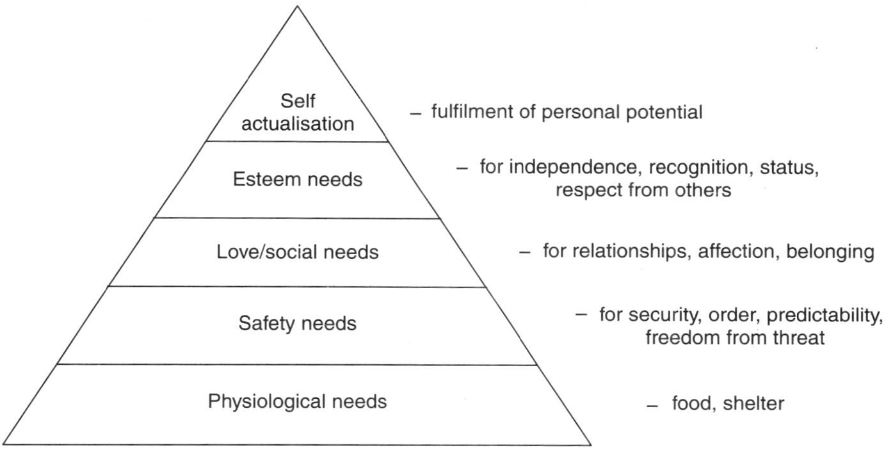

Figure 9.1 Maslow's hierarchy of needs

Maslow also suggested that 'freedom of inquiry' and 'knowledge and understanding' were two further needs and that these were the channels through which we could satisfy all the other needs. Freedom of speech and expression and to gain knowledge, explore and experiment are the bases of satisfaction.

Activity 2 **(20 minutes)**

Decide which of Maslow's categories the following fit into.

(a) Receiving praise from your manager
(b) A family party
(c) An artist forgetting to eat
(d) A man washed up on a desert island
(e) A pay increase
(f) Joining a local drama group
(g) Being awarded the OBE
(h) Buying a house.

It has become fashionable to talk about goals and values rather than needs. People pursue goals which promise to fulfil their needs. For example, if you have a need for achievement, you might have an HNC or HND in Business as your goal. If you have a need for love and belonging, your goal may be to start a family – or join a religious community! As you can see, goals are more specific and more various than needs. Let's look at some of the factors that influence an individual's choice of goals.

2.2 Goals

Each individual has a different set of goals. The relative importance of those goals to the individual may vary with time, circumstances and other factors, including the following.

(a) **Genetic inheritance, childhood environment and education**. Aspiration levels, family and career models and so on are formed at early stages of development.

(b) **Experience**. This teaches us what to expect from life: we will either strive to repeat positive experiences, or to avoid or make up for negative ones.

(c) **Age and position**. There is usually a gradual process of 'goal shift' with age, as well as more radical re-evaluations of one's life, in cases of illness, redundancy, death in the family, birth of a child and so on. Recognition may have high priority for a child, while relationships and exploration may preoccupy teenagers. Career and family goals tend to conflict in the 20-40 age group: career launch and 'take-off' may have to yield to the priorities associated with forming permanent relationships and having children. Power and autonomy goals tend to be essential to an individual's self image in mature years, or 'career peak' time. Retirement usually forces a reappraisal of relationships, purpose in life and security.

(d) **Culture**. Compared to European worker goals, for example, Japanese goals show a greater concern for relationships at work and a lesser preoccupation with power and autonomy.

(e) **Self-concept**. All the above factors are bound up with the individual's own self-image. The individual's assessments of his own abilities and place in society will affect the relative strength and nature of his needs and goals.

You should now be able to identify some of the needs and goals that people might have, where they might come from and why they might change. So why are they relevant to a manager?

2.3 Motivation and morale

We cover motivation in theory and practice below, but the following are some general introductory points.

(a) People behave in such a way as to satisfy their needs and fulfil their goals.

(b) An organisation is in a position to offer some of the satisfactions people might seek: relationships and belonging, challenge and achievement, progress on the way to self-actualisation, security and structure and so on. Pay, or money, does not directly feature in any need lists, but it represents a means of obtaining all sorts of satisfactions of other needs: from food and shelter to personal development courses, power and recognition and so on.

(c) The organisation can therefore influence people to behave in the ways it desires (to secure work performance) by offering them the means to satisfy their needs and fulfil their goals in return for that behaviour. This process of influence is called motivation.

Definition

> **Motivation** (in this context) is the process by which the behaviour of an individual is influenced by others, through their power to offer or withhold satisfaction of the individual's needs and goals.

(d) If people's needs are being met, and goals being fulfilled, at work, they are likely to have a positive attitude to their work and to the organisation. The term **morale** is used to denote the state of mind or spirit of a group, particularly regarding discipline and confidence. Satisfaction at work may thus be associated with high morale. And high morale can (sometimes) be associated with committed performance at work.

FOR DISCUSSION

'Motivation sounds just like "bribery", with a more respectable name.' Do you agree?

We will now examine how needs and goals fit into specific motivational theories.

3 THE HIERARCHY OF NEEDS

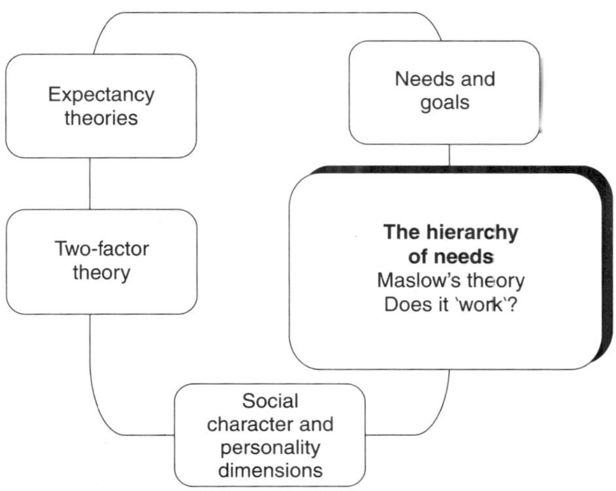

3.1 Maslow's theory

Need theories suggest that the desired outcome of behaviour in individuals is the **satisfaction of innate needs.**

We have already mentioned Maslow's classification of the innate needs of human beings (Section 2 above).

In his motivation theory, Maslow put forward certain propositions about the motivating power of needs. He suggested that Man's needs can be arranged in a 'hierarchy of relative pre-potency'. This means that there are levels of need, each of which is dominant until it is satisfied; only then does the next level of need become a motivating factor. (See Figure 9.1 above)

3.2 Does it work?

There is a certain intuitive appeal to Maslow's theory. After all, you are unlikely to be concerned with status or recognition while you are hungry or thirsty – but once your hunger is assuaged, the need for food is unlikely to be a motivating factor. Unfortunately, research does not bear out the proposition that needs become less powerful as they are satisfied, except at this very primitive level: how much recognition or friendship is 'enough'? The theory is too vague to be used to predict behaviour. Different people emphasise different needs (and some people are clearly able to suppress even their basic physiological and safety needs for the sake of a perceived 'higher cause', or for the sake of other people). Also, the same need may cause different behaviour in different individuals. (Consider how many ways of achieving self-esteem or fame there are!)

Application of the theory in work contexts presents various difficulties. The role of pay is problematic, since it acts as the instrument of a wide range of other rewards – status, recognition, independence and so on. Self-actualisation, too, is difficult to offer employees in practice, since its nature is so highly subjective.

Activity 3 **(10 minutes)**

Where are you, at the moment, in the hierarchy of needs? In other words, which category of needs (if any) is uppermost in your mind and in the way you are directing your activities?

4 TWO-FACTOR THEORY

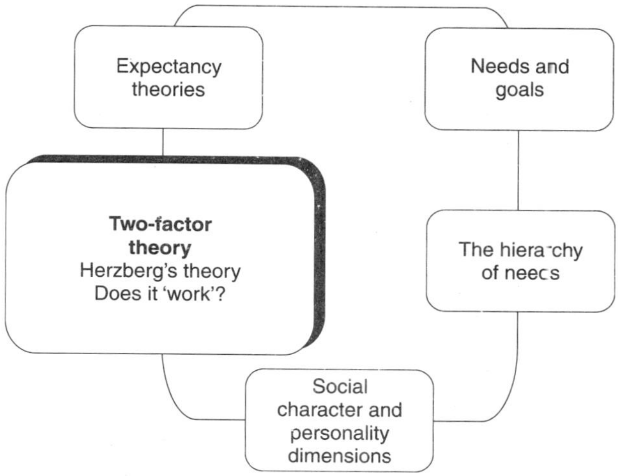

4.1 Herzberg's theory

In the 1950s, the American psychologist Frederick *Herzberg* interviewed 203 Pittsburgh engineers and accountants and asked two 'critical incident' questions. The subjects were asked to recall events which had made them feel good about their work, and others which made them feel bad about it. Analysis revealed that the factors which created satisfaction were different from those which created dissatisfaction.

Herzberg (1968) saw two basic needs of individuals:

(a) The need to avoid unpleasantness, satisfied (temporarily, and in a rather negative way) by 'environmental factors'

(b) The need for personal growth, satisfied at work only by 'motivator factors'

Environmental factors

Herzberg suggests that: 'when people are dissatisfied with their work it is usually because of discontent with the environmental factors'. Herzberg also calls these **'hygiene' factors** because at best they prevent or minimise dissatisfaction but do not give satisfaction, in the same way that sanitation minimises threats to health, but does not give good health.

These environmental, or hygiene, factors include:

(a) Company policy and administration
(b) Salary
(c) The quality of supervision
(d) Interpersonal relations
(e) Working conditions
(f) Job security

Satisfaction with environmental factors is not lasting. In time, dissatisfaction will occur. For example, an individual might want a pay rise which protects his income against inflation. If he is successful in obtaining the rise he wants, he will be satisfied for the time being, but will swiftly take his new level of income for granted, and want more.

Motivator factors

Motivator factors, on the other hand, create job satisfaction and can motivate an individual to superior performance and effort. These factors fulfil the individual's higher need for a sense of self-actualisation or personal growth, and include:

(a) Status (although this may be a hygiene factor as well as a motivator factor)
(b) Advancement
(c) Gaining recognition
(d) Being given responsibility
(e) Challenging work
(f) Achievement
(g) Growth in the job

Activity 4 **(20 minutes)**

Note down:

(a) The things you regard as the 'basics' you would expect from a study course

(b) The things you positively like about studying for a particular course at your college or through another institution

Do the factors you have listed in (a) correspond to Herzberg's 'hygiene' factors: are they things that make studying 'comfortable' but don't really 'switch you on' to extra effort?

Do the factors you have listed in (b) correspond to Herzberg's 'motivator' factors: do they make you want to work harder, for their sake?

4.2 Does it work?

Herzberg encouraged managers to study the job itself (nature of tasks, levels of responsibility) rather than conditions of work. 'Dissatisfaction arises from environment factors – satisfaction can only arise from the job.' If there is sufficient challenge, scope and interest in the job, there will be a lasting increase in satisfaction and the employee will work well; productivity will be above 'normal' levels. The extent to which a job must be challenging or creative in order to provide motivation will depend on each individual, his ability, his expectations and his tolerance for delayed success.

Maslow's hierarchy and Herzberg's two factors are content theories. We will now look at major process theory. There are various theories based on ways of calculating whether extra 'E factors' are worth expending in the pursuit of goals. One of the earliest and most influential is expectancy theory.

5 EXPECTANCY THEORIES

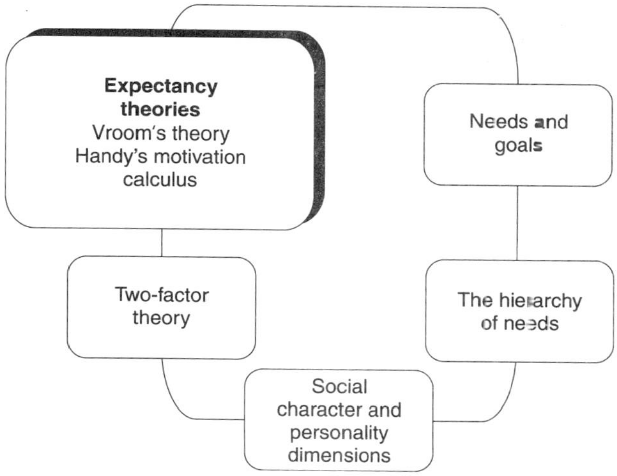

5.1 Vroom's theory

Essentially, expectancy theory states that the strength of an individual's motivation to do something will depend on the extent to which he expects the results of his efforts, if successfully achieved, to contribute towards his personal needs or goals.

In 1964 *Victor Vroom* (another American psychologist) worked out a formula by which human motivation could actually be assessed and measured, based on expectancy theory. Vroom suggested that the strength of an individual's motivation is the product of two factors.

(a) **The strength of his preference for a certain outcome**. Vroom called this **valence**. It may be represented as a positive or negative number, or zero – since outcomes may be desired, avoided or considered with indifference.

(b) **His expectation that that outcome will in fact result from a certain behaviour**. Vroom called this **subjective probability**: it is only the individual's expectation, and depends on his perception of the link between behaviour and outcome. As a probability, it may be represented by any number between 0 (no chance) and 1 (certainty).

In its simplest form, the expectancy equation therefore runs: F = V × E.

Force or strength of motivation to do x	=	Valence (strength of preference for outcome y)	×	Expectation (that doing x will result in y)

This is what you might expect: if either valence or expectation have a value of zero, there will be no motivation.

(a) An employee may have a high **expectation** that behaviour x (increased productivity) will result in outcome y (promotion) – because of past experience, or a negotiated productivity deal for example. So E = 1. However, if he is **indifferent** to that outcome (perhaps because he doesn't want the responsibility that promotion will bring), V = 0. And 0 x 1 = 0: the individual will not be motivated to more productive behaviour.

(b) If the employee has a **great desire** for outcome y (promotion) – but doesn't have high **expectations** that behaviour x (increased production) will secure it for him (say, because he has been passed over previously), E = 0. He will still not be highly motivated.

(c) If V = -1, (because the employee actively fears responsibility and doesn't want to leave his work group), the value for motivation may be negative: the employee may deliberately **under**-produce.

Activity 5 **(15 minutes)**

Read the following statements and analyse the force of each individual's motivations.

(a) Raj has seen how people can progress within the organisation and is studying at evening classes to gain further qualifications.

(b) Mary is good at her job but knows there is little chance of promotion.

(c) John is frightened by new challenges.

Now analyse the force of your motivation to pass this module.

Expectancy theory attempts to measure the strength of an individual's motivation to act in a particular way. It is then possible to compare 'F' (force of motivation) values for a range of different behaviours, to discover which behaviour the individual is most likely to adopt. It is also possible to compare 'F' values for different individuals, to see who is most highly motivated to behave in the desired (or undesirable) way.

5.2 Handy's motivation calculus

Handy (1987) put forward an 'admittedly theoretical' model not unlike the expectancy models, describing 'the way the individual deals with **individual** decisions, to do or not to do something...to apportion or note to apportion his time, energy and talents.'

Handy suggests that for any such decision there is a conscious or unconscious 'motivation calculus' which assesses:

(a) The individual's own needs

(b) Desired results or outcomes (eg job performance)

(c) 'E' factors. Handy suggests that motivational theories have been too preoccupied with 'effort'. He notes that there is a set of words – coincidentally beginning with 'e' – that might be more helpful: energy, excitement, enthusiasm, emotion, expenditure

The 'motivation decision' – how strong the motivation to achieve the desired result will be – depends on the individual's judgement about:

(a) The strength of his needs
(b) The expectancy that expending 'e' will lead to desired results
(c) How far the desired results are expected to satisfy his needs

In practical terms, this suggests that **intended results** or **outcomes** and **feedback on actual results** must be made clear the individual by managers, so that (s)he calculates what is expected, how (s)he will be rewarded, how much 'e' will be needed, and whether the expenditure of 'e' was worth the actual results and rewards.

6 SOCIAL CHARACTER AND PERSONALITY DIMENSIONS

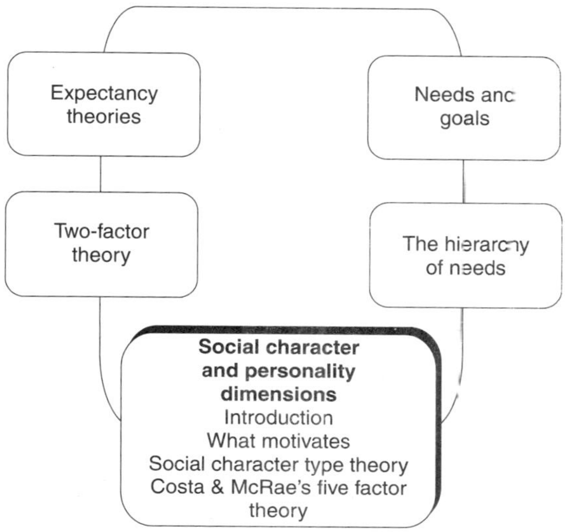

6.1 Introduction

Many theorists over the years have attempted to define what motivates people at work ie, what drives them to be productive and deliver what the organisation wants of them.

As we have noted, theorists such as Maslow believe that motivation is intrinsic. It comes from underlying needs that we all have and it is management's task to diagnose and satisfy those needs if a worker is to perform adequately. Other theorists such as Vroom take the view that motivation is essentially extrinsic – we make a deliberate decision about how hard to work depending on our analysis of costs and rewards.

Herzberg took up Maslow's ideas to develop his 'two factor theory' in which he distinguished between potential satisfiers and dissatisfiers. His ideas were responsible for an emphasis on job enrichment and redesign during the 1950s and 1970s. Although these ideas lost popularity in the 1980s, they re-surfaced as 'Worker Empowerment and high performance work systems' in the 1990s, partly due to the influence of Michael Maccoby's work.

Maccoby (1998) argues that people coming into employment today have different needs from employees of the past. These are due to changes in, for example, the way people are educated (learning is more self-directed) and social relationships (people are less prepared to do as they are told). Therefore, according to Maccoby, work has to match workers' dominant values for them to be motivated. These ideas have helped to make the use of 'empowered' or 'semi-autonomous' teams popular in the workplace. Empowerment is the term given to organisational arrangements that allow employees more autonomy, discretion and unsupervised decision-making responsibility.

Considerable research by *Costa and McCrae* (2003) and others supports the relationship between personality and job performance variables, training efficiency, academic performance, and motivation. According to the Five-Factor Model (FFM), which we outlined in Chapter 6, there are five broad categories at the top of the personality trait hierarchy: neuroticism-emotional stability, extraversion, openness to experience, agreeableness, and conscientiousness

Researchers have linked personality dimensions to a number of industrial and organisational topics, including absenteeism, employee reliability, leadership, organisational climate, employee satisfaction, work motivation, and job scope.

6.2 What motivates

The concept of motivation describes the **impetus to act with energy and purpose**. We are all motivated to: eat, sleep, have fun and work. The challenge for management is to discover what motivates people at work to do what is necessary for the organisation to succeed. In the past, in the industrial-bureaucratic era of rigid hierarchy and electromechanical tools, management's task was to motivate employees to obey orders and perform set tasks. Today, in the age of service industries (and especially information age technoservice), management's task is to motivate employees to take responsibility for: solving problems, responding to customer needs, co-operating with team members, and continuously improving products and services. In the industrial bureaucratic era, motivation for most workers was mostly compliance, showing up on time, and doing what they were told to do. In the technoservice era, this kind of compliance is not enough; another type of motivation becomes essential. The organisation requires people who are motivated, enabled, and empowered to achieve results by exercising judgement.

There are two kinds of motivation. One is **extrinsic motivation**, which has to do with control, getting people to do something they may not want to do. Extrinsic motivation is caused by positive or negative incentives – carrots and sticks. These are most effective when people are in need or afraid. Well-fed people do not jump for carrots, and self-confident people do not allow bosses to beat them. **Intrinsic motivation**, the second kind of motivation, results when internal drives and values are engaged at work.

When employees are asked to rank what they most value in their work, they choose a **combination of extrinsic and intrinsic factors**. Extrinsic factors include better pay and benefits, employment security, opportunity for advancement, and working conditions. Intrinsic factors include challenging work, enjoyable work, meaningful work and above all, opportunity to experience a sense of accomplishment. However, what is challenging, enjoyable, and rewarding depends on employees' individual values (and skills), which differ among people at work.

Sometimes the distinction between intrinsic and extrinsic becomes blurred. Pure intrinsic motivation implies that people would be motivated to work, even if they were not paid, as is the case when people play a game for fun. Pure extrinsic motivation implies that people would not be motivated to do something unless they were paid. In fact, most people need to be paid for their work, even though they may put as much or more of themselves into games and volunteer activities. An increasing number of new generation self-developers take a job for the pay and benefits, but they are intrinsically motivated by other work such as artistic or volunteer activities.

According to Maccoby (1998), motivating employees requires designing jobs that engage their values and provide satisfying rewards. The emphasis will be on skills development, problem solving, continuous improvement, quality products, improved customer service and flexible response to change

This requirement is a challenge not only to managers, but also to employees whose values (intrinsic motivation) are adapted to the bureaucratic-industrial world and not to that of technoservice

6.3 Social Character Type Theory

Maccoby's theory of social character explores the dominant values that determine motivation, and allows us to differentiate five value types: the expert, helper, defender, innovator and self-developer.

Types	Dominant Values	Description
Expert	Mastery, control, autonomy	You approach your work as an expert. Whatever your job, you want to provide high-quality work and to exercise your skill and competence
Helper	Caring for people, relatedness, sociability	You approach your work as a helper. You want to help people.
Defender	Dignity, power, self esteem, protection	You approach your work as a defender. You want to defend against those who do not respect the law, who do harm, or who undermine the values essential to a good organisation.
Innovator	Competition, glory, creating, experimenting	You approach your work as an innovator who knows how to play the game of business. You want to win by making the organisation more successful.
Self-developer	Balancing mastery and play, knowledge and fun	You approach your work as the means to a self-fulfilling life. You want your work to further your own development.

These value types cut across categories of gender, generation, and culture or ethnic group. They describe values that are shared by people everywhere. To understand what motivates ourselves and others, we must identify the dynamic values that determine our needs. Such an understanding leads the way to both organisational productivity and development of our individual potential at work.

Maccoby describes recent historical changes that require a rethinking of what motivates people at work.

(a) The first historical change is that the nature of work continues to shift from manufacturing to service. Over 70 percent of the workforce is now in the service sector.

(b) The second dramatic historical change that affects motivation is that people can no longer count on lifetime careers in a single company.

(c) A third transformation occurring in today's workplace is that the social character of the workforce continues to change from the traditional experts adapted to functional roles in the industrial bureaucracy to the new generation of self-developers who are better adapted to service in the age of information technology.

The new generation of today's self-developers have typically been raised in a family with dual wage earners who share work and child-rearing roles. At an early age, these self-developers learn they cannot always count on their parents to be around when needed. Today's children have to learn interpersonal skills to get along with one another in day care centres and nursery schools and to support each other in the absence of their parents. These childhood experiences form people for whom both self-reliance and teamwork feel natural. Sharing ideas and networking are easy for them. Knowing that they can't count on lifetime employment in an ever-changing market, they naturally put a premium on self-development in order to maintain their employability. This shift in family structure continues. During the 21st century, most employees in the U.S. and Western Europe, at least, will be self-developers, shaped by the combined forces of changing technology, education, and family life.

Maccoby describes this new generation's work needs. They are:

- Clear management commitments on responsibilities and rewards
- Opportunities for expression, challenge and development
- Increased business understanding and development
- Teamwork combined with individual growth
- Fair and meaningful rewards
- Reasons, information, to be included, to know why

6.4 Costa & McCrae's Five-Factor Theory

A personality trait is a stable disposition to behave in a certain way (eg honest, friendly, moody). Personality is used to explain the stability of a person's behaviour and how a person is distinct from other people. In general, it is believed that about 60% of our personality originates from genetic factors while about 40% originates from experiences in the environment. The Five Factor Theory of Personality or 'The Big Five' was developed by *Robert McCrae and Paul Costa* (2003). A person's personality is a combination of these five traits (abbreviated as OCEAN) in various degrees.

(a) **O**penness to experience – people exhibit imaginative, curious, broadminded, intelligent behaviours

(b) **C**onscientiousness – people exhibit dependable, responsible, hardworking, achievement-oriented behaviours

(c) **E**xtraversion – people exhibit sociable, gregarious, assertive and talkative behaviours

(d) **A**greeableness – people exhibit courteous, flexible, good-natured, co-operative behaviours

(e) **N**euroticism or emotional stability – people exhibit anxious, depressed, angry, worried, insecure actions

By describing the individual's standing on each of the five factors, they can provide a comprehensive sketch that summarises the individual's emotional, interpersonal, experiential, attitudinal and motivational style.

The five broad traits, or domains, are represented by several subscales, termed facets.

- **Openness** to experience is made up of the facets: Fantasy, Aesthetics, Feelings, Actions, Ideas, and Values.
- **Conscientiousness** is measured by the facets: Competence, Order, Dutifulness, Achievement-Striving, Self-Discipline, and Deliberation.
- **Extraversion** is measured by the facets: Warmth, Gregariousness, Assertiveness, Activity, Excitement Seeking, and Positive Emotions.
- The **Agreeableness** facets are: Trust, Straightforwardness, Altruism, Compliance, Modesty, and Tender-Mindedness.
- **Neuroticism** comprises facet scales measuring Anxiety, Anger, Hostility, Depression, Self-Consciousness, Impulsiveness, and Vulnerability.

The five factors are summarised in the following table:

Factor	Nature of Factor	Characteristics of High Scorers	Characteristics of Low Scorers
Openness	Toleration for and exploration of the unfamiliar	creative, artistic, curious, imaginative, nonconformist	conventional, down-to-earth, preserving the *status quo*
Conscientiousness	Degree of organisation, persistence, and motivation in goal-directed behaviour	organised, reliable, neat, ambitious	unreliable, lazy, careless, negligent, spontaneous and often unprepared.
Extraversion	Capacity for joy, need for stimulation, interest in other people and external events	talkative, optimistic, sociable, affectionate	reserved, comfortable being alone, stays in the background
Agreeableness	One's orientation along a continuum from compassion to antagonism in thoughts, feelings, and actions	good-natured, trusting, helpful	rude, unco-operative, irritable, aggressive, competitive
Neuroticism	Emotional stability, proneness to distress, excessive cravings or urges, unrealistic ideas	worrying, insecure, high anxiety, easily tempted	calm, secure, relaxed, stable

What do the Big Five predict about our behaviour?

First, having a trait means reacting consistently to the same situation over time, for example, being agreeable or co-operative means consistently going along with reasonable requests, but does not mean always complying with others' wishes.

Second, to respond consistently in the same situation people must have a capacity to respond to situational cues, that is to have the trait to be responsive to situations. For example, if someone purchases a house in the woods, they might want that house because of its secluded location.

Third, behaving differently in a given situation does not mean there is inner inconsistency. For example, someone who likes to attend parties might not often do so because of a stronger desire to work.

Overall, traits are relatively poor predictors of single behavioural acts, but are better predictors of general trends of a person's behaviour. Looking at past behaviour of an individual may be the best predictor of future behaviour.

How might these factors relate to motivation?

Openness is associated with tolerance of ambiguity (which means when something is not clear), a capacity to absorb information, being very focused and the ability to be aware of more feelings, thoughts and impulses simultaneously. The result is deeper more intense experiences. Open individuals are motivated to seek out the unfamiliar and to look for complexity.

Conscientiousness is related to such things as achievement, perseverance, organisation and responsibility. Conscientious individuals are motivated toward achievement through social conformity.

Extraversion has an interpersonal component and is strongly related to positive affect such as being enthusiastic, energetic, interested and friendly. Research found that extraverts show less anxiety over negative feedback. They are highly motivated to seek social situations and to be dominant in those situations. Extraverts are motivated by change, variety in their lives, challenge, and are easily bored. They have more recently been seen as adaptive, ambitious and hardworking.

Agreeableness also has an interpersonal component. Agreeable individuals tend toward conformity in groups, toward modesty, toward not being demanding, and toward being sympathetic. These individuals might be motivated to helping others and to sociable behaviour in general. There may be a link between the motivational processes operating within individuals in regards to this trait, such that agreeable individuals strive for intimacy and solidarity in groups they belong to, which provides emotional rewards.

Neuroticism tends to be viewed negatively and is associated with negative affect, being tense and nervous. A person could be neurotic and conscientious which may have negative health effects but may motivate an individual toward success in work situations.

Chapter roundup

- People have certain innate needs: both physical needs and emotional/ psychological needs. Maslow has categorised needs as physiological, security, love/social, esteem and self-actualisation. People also have goals, through which they expect their needs to be satisfied.
- Content theories of motivation suggest that man has a package of needs: the best way to motivate an employee is to find out what his needs are and offer him rewards that will satisfy those needs.
  - Abraham Maslow identified a hierarchy of needs which an individual will be motivated to satisfy, progressing towards higher order satisfactions, such as self-actualisation.
  - Frederick Herzberg identified two basic need systems: the need to avoid unpleasantness and the need for personal growth. He suggested factors which could be offered by organisations to satisfy both types of need: 'hygiene' and 'motivator' factors respectively.
- Process theories of motivation do not tell managers what to offer employees in order to motivate them, but help managers to understand the dynamics of employees' decisions about what rewards are worth going for. They are generally variations on the expectancy model: $F = V \times E$.
- Maccoby's theory of social character explores the dominant values that determine motivation, and allows us to differentiate five value types: the expert, helper, defender, innovator and self-developer.
- According to the Five-Factor Model (FFM), developed by Costa and McCrae, there are five broad categories at the top of the personality trait hierarchy: neuroticism-emotional stability, extraversion, openness to experience, agreeableness, and conscientiousness

Quick quiz

1 List the five categories in Maslow's Hierarchy of Needs.

2 How do an individual's goals change with age?

3 Define motivation.

4 List three ways in which an organisation can offer motivational satisfaction.

5 List five motivator and five hygiene factors.

6 Explain the formula 'F = V × E'.

Answers to quick quiz

1 Physiological, safety, love/social, esteem, self-actualisation.

2 Increasingly they include forming permanent relationships, having children, power and autonomy.

3 Motivation is the process by which the behaviour of an individual is influenced.

4 Relationships, belonging, challenge, achievement, progress, security.

5 Motivation – status, advancement, recognition, responsibility, challenging work, achievement, growth. Hygiene – company policy and administration, salary, quality of supervision, relationships, job security, working conditions.

6 Force of motivation = Valence × Expectation

Answers to activities

1 Your answer probably indicates that your motives for studying a business qualification are to improve your knowledge, skills and your opportunities.

2 Maslow's categories for the listed circumstances are as follows.

   (a) Esteem needs
   (b) Social needs
   (c) Self-actualisation needs
   (d) He will have physiological needs
   (e) Safety needs initially; esteem needs above in a certain income level
   (f) Social needs or self-actualisation needs
   (g) Esteem needs
   (h) Safety needs or esteem needs

3 We do not usually think consciously about which category of needs we have reached. If you are a student on a low income, your main needs may be in the lower categories such as security and safety. Once those have been taken care of, you will probably move to the need for esteem and recognition.

4 (a) Possibly some of the basics you wish to get from a study course are gaining knowledge, experiencing the 'learning' environment of the college and enjoying the company of colleagues, all of which correspond to Herzberg's hygiene factors.

   (b) Apart from individual subjects which you may particularly enjoy, you might also like the feeling of achievement when you receive good marks, knowing there will be a better opportunity for work or higher education, challenge and growth.

5 The force of motivation in the three situations is:

(a) V = 1, E = 1; F = 1 × 1 = 1 (Highly motivated towards success)

(b) V = 0, E = 1; F = 0 × 1= 0 (Low expectations)

(c) V = –1, E = 0; F = –1 × 0 = 0 (Totally negative and probably under-producing).

Chapter 10: MOTIVATION AND PERFORMANCE

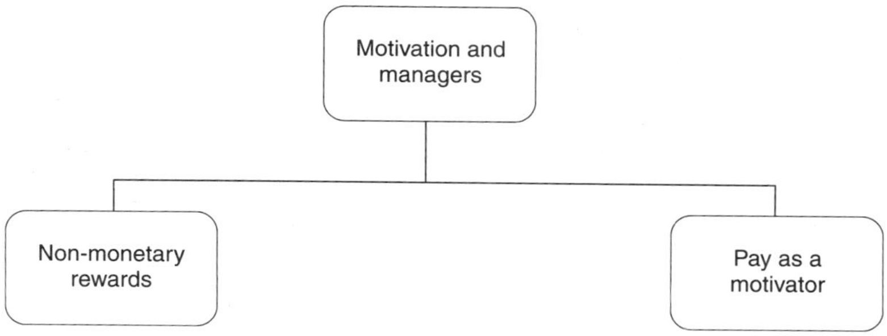

Introduction

Motivation, as it most nearly concerns the manager, is the controlling of the work environment and the offering of rewards in such a way as to encourage extra performance from employees.

As rational purposive beings (who act deliberately in pursuit of goals), employees consciously or unconsciously decide whether it is 'worth their while', or desirable, to put forth 'E factors' – such as energy and effort – in a given work situation. The decision of whether more 'E' is worth putting in is reached by considering what rewards or incentives are available for doing so. We discussed some of the needs and wants of individuals in Chapter 9: effective incentives offer the satisfaction of those needs and wants.

Your objectives

In this chapter you will learn about the following:

(a) The range of rewards and incentives that might act as motivators

(b) How 'job satisfaction' and other non-monetary rewards might be offered to employees

(c) The significance of pay as a motivator

1 MOTIVATION AND MANAGERS

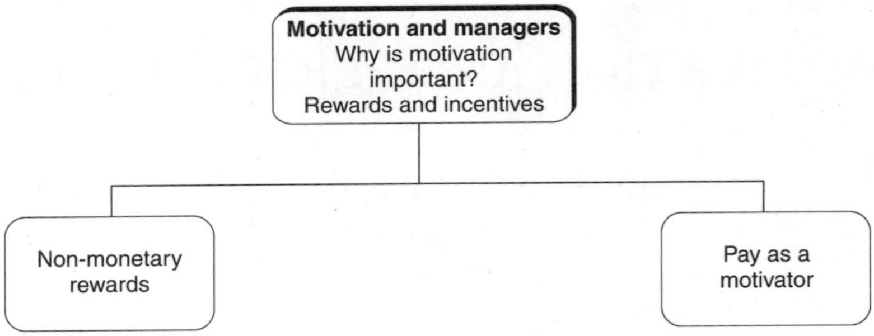

1.1 Why is motivation important?

You may be wondering whether motivation is really so important. It could be argued that if a person is employed to do a job, he will do that job and no question of motivation arises. If the person doesn't want to do the work, he can resign. So why try to motivate people?

Like 'leadership' as opposed to 'management', motivation is about getting extra levels of commitment and performance from employees, over and above mere compliance with rules and procedures.

It is suggested that if individuals can be motivated, by one means or another, they will work more efficiently (and productivity will rise) or they will produce a better quality of work.

FOR DISCUSSION

'If all those who may be considered potential contributors to an organisation are arranged in order of willingness to serve it, the scale descends from possibly intense willingness through neutral or zero willingness to intense opposition or hatred. The preponderance of persons in a modern society always lies on the negative side with reference to any existing or potential organisation.' (Barnard, 1938).

Do you think this is true? What does it suggest about the importance of motivation?

Managers need to be aware, however, that motivation is not an exact science. In particular the case for job satisfaction as a factor in improved performance is not proven. You should be clear in your own mind that although it seems obviously a Good Thing to have employees who enjoy their work and are interested in it, there is no reason why the organisation should want a satisfied work force unless it makes the organisation function better: it is good for human reasons, but it must be (at least plausibly) relevant to organisational efficiency or effectiveness.

1.2 Rewards and incentives

Definitions

> A **reward** is a token (monetary or otherwise) given to an individual or team in recognition of some contribution or success.
>
> An **incentive** is the offer or promise of a reward for contribution or success, designed to motivate the individual or team to behave in such a way as to earn it. (In other words, the 'carrot' dangled in front of the donkey.)

Not all the incentives that an organisation can offer its employees are directly related to **monetary** rewards. The satisfaction of any of the employee's wants or needs may be seen as a reward for past or incentive for future performance.

Different individuals have different goals, and get different things out of their working life: in other words they have different **orientations** to work. There are any number of reasons why a person works, or is motivated to work well.

(a) The 'human relations' school of management theorists regarded work **relationships** as the main source of satisfaction and reward offered to the worker.

(b) Later writers suggested a range of 'higher' motivations, notably:

   (i) **Job satisfaction**, interest and challenge in the job itself – rewarding work

   (ii) **Participation** in decision-making – responsibility and involvement

(c) **Pay** has always occupied a rather ambiguous position, but since people need money to live, it will certainly be part of the reward 'package' an individual gets from his work.

We will now look at some of these in practice.

2 NON-MONETARY REWARDS

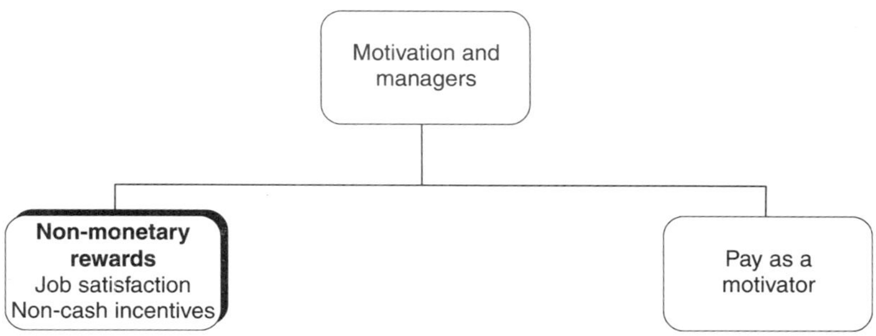

2.1 Job satisfaction

More satisfying job design

Job design is the way in which tasks are fragmented or grouped to form a given job, and what decisions are made about specialisation, discretion, autonomy, variety and other job elements. It acquired its prominence when human relations theorists became interested in the role of job satisfaction in employee performance. It was recognised that jobs made up of low-skilled, repetitive tasks (of which there will inevitably be some in any organisation's operations) could offer little satisfaction to the workers performing them. Such tasks came to be seen as socially isolating, meaningless and monotonous. They were identified as the cause of stress, low morale, fatigue, inattention – causing errors and accidents – and resentment against management.

Activity 1 **(15 minutes)**

How, other than by asking employees (through feedback, interviews or attitude surveys), might an organisation assess whether its employees were satisfied or not?

A systematic approach to job design as a source of job satisfaction was first put forward by Frederick Herzberg, who coined the term 'job enrichment'.

Definition

Job enrichment is planned, deliberate action to build greater responsibility, breadth and challenge of work into a job.

Job enrichment is, in effect, a 'vertical' extension of the job design. It might include:

(a) Removing controls
(b) Increasing accountability
(c) Creating natural work units, teams or client relationships
(d) Providing direct feedback on performance
(e) Introducing new tasks or special assignments

FOR DISCUSSION

'Even those who want their jobs enriched will expect to be rewarded with more than job satisfaction. Job enrichment is not a cheaper way to greater productivity. Its pay-off will come in the less visible costs of morale, climate and working relationships'. (Handy).

Who really gains from job enrichment?

Job enlargement is frequently confused with job enrichment, though it should be clearly defined as a separate technique.

Definition

> **Job enlargement**, as the name suggests, is the attempt to widen jobs by increasing the number of operations in which a job holder is involved.

Arguably, job enlargement is limited in its ability to improve motivation since, as Herzberg points out, to ask a worker to complete three separate tedious, unchallenging tasks is unlikely to motivate him more than asking him to fulfil one single tedious, unchallenging task!

Empowerment

We have already discussed empowerment, in Chapter 1. To recap, in the words of a human resource practitioner (quoted in *Personnel Management*):

'The purpose of empowerment is to free someone from rigorous control by instructions and orders and give them freedom to take responsibility for their ideas and actions, to release hidden resources which would otherwise remain inaccessible.'

The prevailing view of empowerment as a motivator is very much in line with that of the neo-human relations theorists such as Maslow and Herzberg, who believed that organisational effectiveness is determined by the extent to which people's 'higher' psychological needs for growth, challenge, responsibility and self-fulfilment are met by the work that they do. Empowerment is, in effect, a form of job enrichment.

2.2 Non-cash incentives

Incentive and 'recognition' (or reward) schemes are increasingly focused not on cash, but on non-cash awards. Traditionally aimed at sales people, gifts and travel incentives may be offered to staff:

(a) As prizes for workable suggestions on quality improvements or cost reductions

(b) As rewards for performance improvement, achievement, loyalty, teamwork and so on

(c) To encourage internal competition

EXAMPLES

British Telecom – in the wake of large scale voluntary redundancies – launched an up-beat 'Living our values' initiative, including the awarding of gifts to employees exemplifying the organisation's values and being role models to others.

ICL used to offer symbolic awards of bronze, silver and gold medals, but has now replaced these with a gift catalogue (called the 'Excellence Collection') from which nominees choose rewards they value.

Abbey Life's top performers are given the opportunity to attend conventions in exotic foreign locations, with partners (and without an onerous work content): length of stay and luxury of location depend on performance.

Trusthouse Forte has launched a drive to cut employee turnover through an incentive scheme which awards air mileage in return for staff loyalty ... THF is also offering further incentives to staff, including 500 miles for the employee of the month and 1,000 for employee of the year, with another 200 miles for staff receiving a complimentary letter from a guest.

Such schemes can be effective as incentives, team-building exercises, and, perhaps more fundamentally, ways of expressing recognition of achievement – without which staff may feel isolated, undervalued or neglected.

> **Activity 2** **(10 minutes)**
>
> The general secretary of the staff union at *Sun Alliance* has been quoted as saying: 'I have worked for a firm which rewarded its top salespeople with a cruise. I can't imagine anything worse than being trapped on a yacht with a lot of other life assurance salesmen'!
>
> What other demotivating effects may result from non-cash incentive schemes?

3 PAY AS A MOTIVATOR

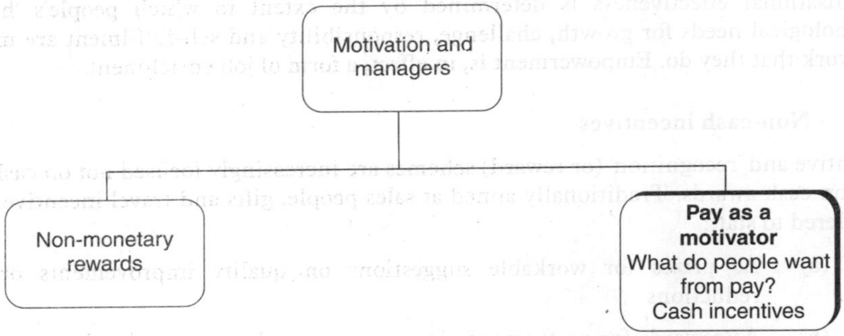

3.1 What do people want from pay?

The most important functions of pay for the organisation are attracting, keeping and motivating staff. But does it work? Pay has a central – but ambiguous – role in motivation theory. It is not mentioned explicitly in any need list, but it may be the means to an infinite number of specific ends, offering the satisfaction of many of the various needs. The assumption that people will adjust their effort if offered money is the basis of payment-by-results schemes, bonuses, profit-sharing and other monetary incentives. However, individuals may have needs unrelated to money, which money cannot satisfy, or which the pay system of the organisation actively denies. So to what extent is pay an inducement to better performance: a motivator or incentive?

Employees need income to live. The size of their income will affect their standard of living. However, people tend not to be concerned to maximise their earnings. They may like to earn more, but are probably more concerned:

(a) To earn **enough** pay

(b) To know that their pay is **fair** in comparison with the pay of others both inside and outside the organisation

Payment systems then have to tread the awkward path between equity (the perceived fairness of pay rates and structures) and **incentive** (an offered reward to stimulate extra effort and attainment by particular individuals and groups).

Pay as a hygiene factor

Pay is one of Herzberg's hygiene rather than motivator factors. It gets taken for granted, and so is more usually a source of dissatisfaction than satisfaction. (In the absence of information about how much colleagues are earning, individuals tend to guess – and usually over-estimate. This then leaves them dissatisfied because they resent earning less than they think their colleagues are getting!)

However, pay is the most important of the hygiene factors. It is valuable because:

(a) It can be converted into a wide range of other satisfactions (perhaps the only way in which organisations can – at least indirectly – cater for individual employee's needs and wants through a common reward system)

(b) It represents a consistent measure of an individual's worth or value to an employer, allowing people to compare themselves with other individuals and occupational groups inside and outside the organisation

The only reason to work?

The Affluent Worker research of Goldthorpe, Lockwood *et al* (1968) investigated highly-paid Luton car assembly workers who experienced their work as routine and dead-end. The researchers concluded that they had made a rational decision to enter employment offering high monetary reward rather than intrinsic interest: they were getting out of their jobs what they most wanted from them.

The Luton researchers, however, did not claim that all workers have this kind of orientation to work, but suggested that a person will seek a suitable balance of:

(a) The rewards which are important to him
(b) The deprivations he feels able to put up with

Most people have limits to their purely financial aspirations, and will cease to be motivated by money if the deprivations – in terms of long working hours, poor conditions, social isolation or whatever – become too great: in other words, if the 'price' of pay is too high.

FOR DISCUSSION

How do you (and others) feel personally about pay as a motivator? Where would you draw the line between extra money and the hardships required to earn it?

Organisations are obliged to reward or remunerate employees for the amount and standard of work agreed in the contract of employment: to give a fair day's pay for a fair day's work. In addition, the organisation may wish to offer monetary incentives (or 'carrots') to employees, if they will work longer or more productively. Monetary incentives include performance-related pay, bonuses, and profit-sharing. So do they work?

3.2 Cash incentives

Following our discussion of the limitations of pay as a motivator, you should be aware of a number of difficulties associated with incentive schemes based on monetary reward.

(a) Workers are unlikely to be in complete control of results, because of other variables such as resource availability, or market conditions. The relationship between an individual's efforts and a results-related reward may therefore be indistinct. This will affect the expectancy calculation, and reduce the motivating effect of the incentive.

(b) Increased earnings simply may not be an incentive to some individuals. An individual who already enjoys a good income may be more concerned with increasing his leisure time, for example.

(c) Even if employees are motivated by money, the effects may not be altogether desirable. Individual bonuses, for example, may encourage self-interest and competition at the expense of teamwork. Payment by results may encourage attention to output at the expense of quality, and the lowering of standards and targets (in order to make bonuses more accessible).

(d) Workers often suspect that if they regularly achieve high levels of output (and earnings), they will make it look too easy (and costly) so that management will set higher performance targets to reduce future earnings. Work groups therefore tend to restrict output to a level that they feel is 'fair', but 'safe'.

Chapter roundup

- Various means have been suggested of improving job satisfaction but there is little evidence that a satisfied worker actually works harder.
- Pay is the most important of the hygiene factors, but it is ambiguous in its effect on motivation.

Quick quiz

1 What is the difference between a reward and an incentive?

2 Distinguish between job enrichment and job enlargement.

3 What is 'empowerment'?

4 Give two examples of non-cash incentives and two examples of monetary incentives.

5 'People will work harder and harder to earn more and more pay.' Do you agree? Why (or why not)?

6 List three potential problems of cash incentives.

Answers to quick quiz

1. A reward is given for some contribution or success. An incentive is a promise or offer of reward.
2. Job enrichment is planned, deliberate action to build greater responsibility, breadth and challenge of work into a job. Job enlargement is the widening of a job by increasing the number of things an employee does.
3. Empowerment frees staff from rigorous control to let them take responsibility for their ideas and actions.
4. Non-cash incentives include gifts, awards, travel. Cash incentives include bonuses, results related rewards, profit sharing.
5. People work to earn enough pay which can then be converted into other satisfactions. If they enjoy a good income, they become more concerned with increasing leisure time.
6. Workers are not in control of results, individual bonuses can encourage self-interest, payment by results emphasises output rather than quality.

Answers to activities

1. (a) There is little evidence that a satisfied worker actually works harder – so increased productivity per se will not imply satisfaction on the part of the work force. They may be motivated by fear, or work methods may have been improved.

   (b) There is, however, support for the idea that satisfied workers tend to be loyal, and stay in the organisation.

   (i) Labour turnover (the rate at which people leave an organisation) may therefore be an indication of dissatisfaction in the workforce – although there is a certain amount of natural wastage.

   (ii) Absenteeism may also be an indication of dissatisfaction, or possibly of genuine physical or emotional distress.

   (c) There is also evidence that satisfaction correlates with mental health – so that symptoms of stress or psychological failure may be a signal to management that all is not well.

2. Non-cash incentive schemes can be regarded as manipulative, irrelevant (awards may be seen as being given for things that ought to be part of the job, with no special effort required), or just plain gimmicky.

Part D

Working with Others: Teamwork, Groups and Group Dynamics

Chapter 11: GROUP BEHAVIOUR AT WORK

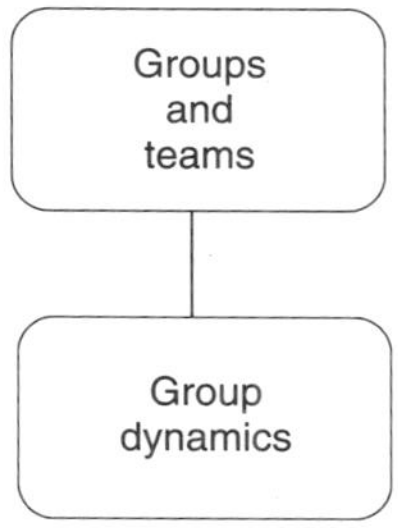

Introduction

We have already studied how individuals behave in and by themselves (intra-personal behaviour) and in relation to other individuals (interpersonal behaviour). You may, however, have noticed yourself that people behave differently in a group or crowd than they do on their own or when talking to one or two others: think about a gang of friends on an outing, or a crowd of people at a football match. The interplay and influences within groups that create this behaviour are called 'group dynamics'.

Groups in business organisations are, in effect, sub-organisations, and they require management for 'controlled performance of collective goals': not only their own collective goals, but those of the business organisation as a whole. This is especially important if the organisation wishes to empower work teams. This chapter looks at what goes on, and why, when people work together in teams.

Your objectives

In this chapter you will learn about the following:

(a) Formal and informal groups

(b) Areas in which teamworking may be more or less effective

(c) How to identify which stage of development a team has reached, and predict what comes next

(d) The dynamics of groups, with regard to behavioural norms, communication and decision-making

(e) The positive and negative (dysfunctional) aspects of group cohesion

1 GROUPS AND TEAMS

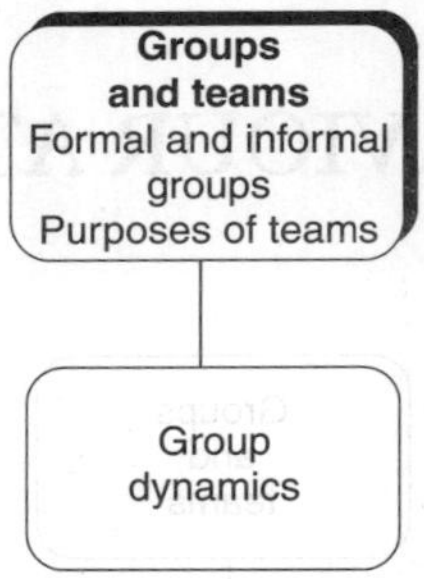

1.1 Formal and informal groups

Definition

> A **group** is any collection of people who perceive themselves to be a group.

The point of this definition is that there is a difference between a random collection of individuals and a 'group' of individuals who share a common sense of identity and belonging. Groups have certain attributes that a random 'crowd' does not possess.

(a) **A sense of identity**. Whether the group is formal or informal, its existence is recognised by its members: there are acknowledged boundaries to the group which define who is 'in' and who is 'out', who is 'us' and who is 'them'.

(b) **Loyalty to the group,** and acceptance by the group. This generally expresses itself as conformity, or the acceptance of the norms of behaviour and attitudes that bind the group together and exclude others from it.

(c) **Purpose and leadership**. Most groups have an express purpose, whatever field they are in: most will, spontaneously or formally, choose individuals or sub-groups to lead them towards the fulfilment of those goals.

You should bear in mind that although an organisation as a whole may wish to project itself as a large group, with a single identity, loyalty and purpose, any organisation will in fact be composed of many sub-groups, with such attributes of their own. People will be drawn together into groups by a preference for smaller units, where closer relationships can develop and individual contributions are noticed; by the combined power of a group which individuals may not possess; and by the opportunity to share problems and responsibilities.

(a) **Informal** groups will invariably be present in any organisation. Informal groups include workplace cliques, and networks of people who regularly get together to exchange information, groups of 'mates' who socialise outside work and so on. The purposes of informal groups are usually related to group and individual member satisfaction, rather than to a task.

(b) **Formal** groups, put together by the organisation, will have a formal structure and a function for which they are held responsible: they are task oriented, and become teams. Leaders may be chosen within the group, but are typically given authority by the organisation.

A primary working group is the name given to the immediate social group of an individual worker: in other words, the people (s)he works with directly and most of the time. This group is the smallest unit of the organisation: the close relationships on which it depends cannot be formed among more than about a dozen people. People tend to be drawn into groups of this size, and if the organisation does not formally provide for them, informal primary groups – whose aims will not necessarily be in harmony with those of the organisation – will spring up. It is only comparatively recently that organisations have realised the importance of primary working groups for harnessing the energy and team-spirit of employees. With the concept of empowerment, attention is being given to enhancing the purpose and leadership of such groups.

Activity 1 **(20 minutes)**

Anthony Jay has identified a primary workgroup of ten people as the descendant of the primeval hunting band, working together for mutual survival. He suggests that such a small band balances:

(a) the individuality which is necessary to generate new ideas; with

(b) the support and comradeship necessary to develop and put those ideas into action.

What primary groups are you a member of in your study or work environment(s)? How big are these groups? How does the size of your class, study group, work-team – or whatever – affect your ability to come up with questions or ideas and give you the help and support to do something you couldn't do alone?

We have suggested that a small group can allow people to generate ideas, and encourage action. How might the organisation utilise these benefits? What might it use teams for?

Definition

A **team** is a formal group established to achieve particular objectives.

1.2 Purposes of teams

From the organisation's point of view, the advantages of teams may be as follows.

(a) Teams allow the performance of tasks that require the skills and time of more than one person, without involving co-ordination across structural boundaries. They are mechanisms for co-ordinating the efforts of individuals within a controlled structure.

(b) Teams encourage exchange of knowledge and ideas, and the creation of new ideas through 'hitchhiking': one person's idea or information sparks off an idea in someone else's head. They are thus particularly useful for:

(i) Increasing communication

(ii) Generating new ideas

(iii) Evaluating ideas from more than one viewpoint

(iv) Consultation, where a cross-section of views may help to produce better, or more acceptable, decisions

(v) Job-related training, since they allow the testing of ideas in a realistic work-group context

(vi) Resolving conflict, since argument can lead to agreement, compromise or consensus which will be reinforced by the group's sense of solidarity

(c) The power of the team over individual behaviour can be both:

(i) A method of control – or, better still, self control

(ii) A powerful motivator, if the aims of the group can be harmonised with the aims of the organisation.

All of these factors have encouraged the empowerment of teams, as opposed to individuals.

Examples of teamworking

Specific applications of teamworking may include the following.

(a) *Brainstorming groups*

Definition

Brainstorming is a process whereby people produce spontaneous, uncensored ideas, sparked off by a particular problem or task.

A brainstorming group would typically involve six to twelve people. The idea of brainstorming is to 'throw out' ideas, however irrelevant or impractical they may seem. The ideas are not, at this stage, criticised or examined, so people are free to think creatively and take risks, and to feed or 'hitchhike' on each other's ideas. The next stage would be for the ideas to be considered individually, and a decision made. Such an approach might be used to solve specific production problems, for example, or to come up with marketing or new product ideas.

FOR DISCUSSION

In a small group, imagine you are the advertising agency creative team given the task of recommending a new name for the charity Oxfam. (This was a real task set by The Spastic Society, who felt that the word 'spastic' for sufferers of cerebral palsy has taken on unfortunate connotations. Also, the name does not sound dynamic enough, and does not express the Society's purpose: to raise awareness of prejudice against sufferers, to emphasise their underutilised potential in the workplace, and to support their aspirations.)

Oxfam may feel their title, although well known, is misunderstood (where's the famine in Oxford?). Brainstorm some ideas for a catchy and expressive new name. If you do this in class, you might like to have 'competing' groups of 6-10 people, and get each to present what it considers its best idea. Remember to look for quantity, not quality, at the brainstorming stage, though: the real job candidates were observed spending too much time discussing single ideas, with not enough ideas on the table.

(The Spastic Society changed its name to SCOPE. Do you think this is a good name?)

(b) *Quality circles*

Definition

> **Quality circles** are groups of (typically 6-10) employees from different levels and/or disciplines, who meet regularly to discuss problems of quality and quality control in their area of work.

In these days of **empowered teams**, quality improvement is only one area in which responsibility is given to groups of employees – but it is still one of the most important. Quality circles are said to result not only in improved product quality, but also in higher morale among employees, higher productivity and a better level of awareness about organisational issues.

(c) *Project or product/service teams,* set up to handle:

(i) Strategic developments, such as new product development, or the introduction of computer systems

(ii) Tasks relating to particular 'cases' or customer accounts, products or markets

(iii) Tasks relating to a particular process within the production system (design, purchasing or assembly of components, say)

(iv) Special audits or investigations of current procedures or potential improvements and opportunities

(d) *Training or study groups*

Training groups (sometimes called 'T-groups') are often used to develop individuals' awareness of how they behave in relation to others, and particularly within a team: members are encouraged to observe and give feedback on the group's behaviour and how they respond to it. T-groups develop skills in identifying and controlling group dynamics in a 'live' context and are sometimes used when new groups are formed due to reorganisation.

(e) *Employee representative committees,* such as the local branch of a trade union or staff association, or less formal groups which meet to discuss matters of interest or concern to staff. Such groups may meet jointly with representatives of management for the purposes of consultation and negotiation.

(f) *Other committees and 'panels'* – for example, employee selection panels; investigatory panels for disciplinary or grievance procedures; task forces set up to investigate and/or make decisions on a particular task or problem; advisory committees on specialist areas (a legal team, say) and so on.

What makes group behaviour different from individual or interpersonal behaviour? More people 'play off' each other in different ways and combinations. This is called 'group dynamics'.

2 GROUP DYNAMICS

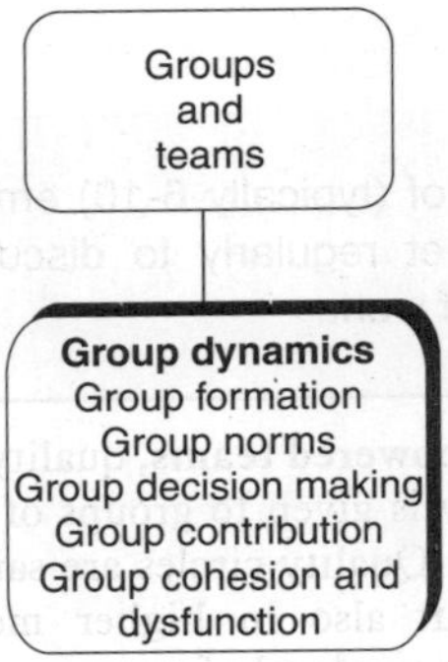

2.1 Group formation

Groups 'mature'. Tuckman (2001) identifies four stages in this development, which he gives the catchy names: forming, storming, norming and performing.

(a) **Forming**. The group is just coming together, and may still be seen as a collection of individuals. Each individual wishes to impress his or her personality on the group, while its purpose, composition, and organisation are being established. Members will be trying to find out about each other, and about the aims and norms of the group, without 'rocking the boat'.

This settling down period is essential, but may be time-wasting.

(b) The second stage is called **storming** because it frequently involves more or less open conflict. Changes may be suggested in the group's original objectives, leadership, procedures and norms. Whilst forming involved toeing the line, storming brings out team members' own ideas and attitudes. This may encourage disagreement, as well as creativity.

(c) The third or **norming** stage is a period of settling down. There will be agreements about work sharing, output levels and group customs. The enthusiasm and creativity of the second stage may be less apparent, but norms and procedures may evolve which enable methodical working to be introduced and maintained. This need not mean that new ideas are discouraged, but that a reasonable hearing is given to everyone and 'consensus' or agreement (often involving compromise) is sought.

(d) Once the fourth or **performing** stage has been reached the group concentrates on its task. Even at earlier stages some performance will have been achieved, but the fourth stage marks the point where the difficulties of growth and development no longer get in the way of the group's task objectives.

It would be misleading to suggest that these four stages always follow in a clearly-defined progression, or that the development of a group must be a slow and complicated process. Particularly where the task to be performed is urgent, or where group members are highly motivated, the fourth stage will be reached very quickly while the earlier stages will be hard to distinguish. Some groups never progress beyond storming, however, because their differences are irreconcilable.

It is often the case that after a team has been performing effectively for a while it becomes complacent. In this phase, which has been called 'dorming' (so that it sounds like the other phases in Tuckman's model), the team goes into a semi-automatic mode of operation, with no fresh energy or attention focused on the task – even if it changes – and with efforts devoted primarily to the maintenance of the team itself.

Activity 2 **(10 minutes)**

Read the following statements and decide to which category they belong (forming, storming, norming, performing, dorming).

(a) Two of the group arguing as to whose idea is best.
(b) Progress becomes static.
(c) Desired outputs being achieved.
(d) Shy member of group not participating.
(e) Activities being allocated.

2.2 Group norms

Work groups establish norms or common patterns of behaviour, to which all members of the group are expected to conform. Norms develop as the group learns what sorts of behaviour work and don't work, in terms of maintaining the group and protecting its interests. There may be norms of interpersonal behaviour (the way the members speak to each other and so on), dress, timekeeping, attitudes (towards management, for example) and/or work practices and productivity. In other words, group norms are 'the way we do (or don't do) things round here'.

Norms may be reinforced in various ways by the group.

(a) **Identification with the group** may be offered as a reward for compliance, through marks of belonging, prestige and acceptance.

(b) **Sanctions or penalties** of various kinds may be imposed as a deterrent to non-conforming behaviour: ostracising or ignoring the member concerned ('sending him to Coventry'), ridicule or reprimand, even physical hostility. The threat of expulsion from the group is the final sanction.

In other words the group's power to influence an individual depends on the degree to which he values his membership of the group and the rewards it may offer, or wishes to avoid the negative sanctions at its disposal.

Activity 3 **(20 minutes)**

How might group norms:

(a) Cause problems for a new manager?
(b) Adversely affect performance?
(c) Help in the process of management control?
(d) Help in the process of change management?

2.3 Group decision-making

As we have noted, empowerment involves groups in decision-making. This can be of benefit where:

(a) Pooling skills, information and ideas – perhaps representing different functions, specialisms and levels in the organisation – could increase the quality of the decision; groups have been shown to produce better evaluated (although fewer) decisions than individuals working separately: even the performance of the group's best individual can be improved by having 'missing pieces' added by the group

(b) Participation in the decision-making process makes the decision acceptable to the group, whether because it represents a consensus of their views, or simply because they have been consulted. Acceptance of the decision by the group may be important if it affects them, and/or they are responsible for carrying it out

How group decisions are made

However, it is worth considering *how* a group arrives at a decision. Depending on the personalities of its members and of its leader, and the nature of the task (for example whether it needs to be completed within a short or long time-frame), a team may arrive at decisions in a number of ways.

- Does it allow itself to be persuaded by its leader, or another dominant member?
- Does it defer to the member most qualified to make a particular decision?
- Does it collect information and views from all its members – but allow the leader/dominant member/qualified member to make the decision?
- Does it collect information and views from all its members and try to reach general consensus or agreement, however much discussion that takes?
- Does it collect information and views from all its members and take a democratic vote on the decision?
- Does it keep any dissenting views or contradictory information quiet, to allow consensus to prevail?
- Does it insist on dealing with dissenting views and contradictory information, even if it takes longer to reach a decision?

Depending which behaviour is adopted, there is clearly a trade-off between:

(a) The speed of the decision
(b) The acceptability of the decision to all group members, and
(c) The quality of the decision from the point of view of results

Activity 4 **(20 minutes)**

If you were team leader in the following situations, what kind of decision-making behaviour would you encourage?

(a) The computer expert in your team has suggested that the team should change over to a different, more efficient software package. Some of the team have only just mastered the current software, after quite a struggle. The new software will, however, iron out some very frustrating problems in the work.

> (b) The office manager has offered you a choice of yellow or blue, when the offices are redecorated next month, but she needs to do the purchasing almost immediately. What would your team prefer?

Problems with group decision-making

There are problems in group decision-making.

(a) **Group decisions take longer to reach than individual decisions** – especially if the group seeks consensus by working through disagreement. (This is the preferred practice in Japan.)

(b) **Group decisions tend to be riskier than individual decisions**. This may be because:

  (i) Shared responsibility blurs the individuals' sense of responsibility for the outcome of the decision

  (ii) Contradictory information may be ignored, to protect the group's consensus or pet theories

  (iii) Cohesive groups tend to feel infallible: they get over-confident

  (iv) Group cohesion and motivation may be founded on values like innovation, boldness and flexibility – which support risk-taking

(c) **Group decisions may partly be based on group norms and interests** – the group's own 'agenda' – rather than organisational interests: group maintenance is itself a powerful *raison d'être.*

2.4 Group contribution

One way of analysing the functioning of a team is to analyse the frequency and type of individual members' contributions to group discussions and interactions. This is a relatively simple framework, which can revolutionise the way you behave in groups – as well as your understanding of the dynamics of a given team.

Who contributes?

The team leader should identify which members of the team habitually make the most contributions, and which the least. You could do this by taking a count of contributions from each member, during a sample 10-15 minutes of group discussion. (Count any spoken remark addressed to the discussion, not asides to other members, or mutters to self.) For example:

Robbie	/
Martha	
Jason	卌 /
Mary	卌 卌
Gary	卌 卌 /
Paul	
Mark	卌 卌 /

If the same general pattern of high contribution (Mary, Gary), medium contribution (Mark) and low contribution (Robbie, Martha, Jason, Paul) tends to be *repeated*, irrespective of the matter being discussed, you might suspect that Mary, Mark and Gary are 'swamping' the other members, or that the other members have a problem communicating, or are not interested, or have nothing to contribute, or *feel* they have nothing to contribute. This team has a problem that needs to be addressed. Confronting the team with its contribution count may spark off an honest discussion of the problem – if group relationships are strong enough to support the conflict that may be required.

How do they contribute?

Consultants Neil Rackham and Terry Morgan have developed a helpful categorisation of the types of contribution people can make to team discussion and decision-making.

Category	Behaviour	Example
Proposing	Putting forward suggestions, new concepts or courses of action.	Why don't we look at a flexi-time system?'
Building	Extending or developing someone else's proposal.	'Yes. We could have a daily or weekly hours allowance, apart from a core period in the middle of the day.'
Supporting	Supporting another person or his/her proposal.	'Yes, I agree, flexi-time would be worth looking at.'
Seeking information	Asking for more facts, opinions or clarification.	'What exactly do you mean by "flexi-time"?'
Giving information	Offering facts, opinions or clarification.	There's a helpful outline of flexi- time in this BPP Study Text.'
Disagreeing	Offering criticism or alternative facts or opinions which contradict a person's proposals or opinions.	'I don't think we can take the risk of not having any staff here at certain periods of the day.'
Attacking	Attempting to undermine another person or their position: more emotive than disagreeing.	'In fact, I don't think you've thought this through at all.'
Defending	Arguing for one's own point of view.	'Actually, I've given this a lot of thought, and I think it makes sense.'
Blocking/difficulty stating	Putting obstacles in the way of a proposal, without offering any alternatives.	'What if the other teams get jealous? It would only cause conflict.'
Open behaviour	Risking ridicule and loss of status by being honest about feelings and opinions.	'I think some of us are afraid that flexi-time will show up how little work they really do in a day.'
Shutting-out behaviour	Interrupting or overriding others; taking over.	'Nonsense. Let's move onto something else – we've had enough of this discussion.'
Bringing-in behaviour	Involving another member; encouraging contribution.	'Actually, I'd like to hear what Fred has to say. Go on, Fred.'

Category	Behaviour	Example
Testing understanding	Checking whether points have been understood.	'So flexi-time could work over a day or a week; have I got that right?'
Summarising	Drawing together or summing up previous discussion.	'We've now heard two sides to the flexi-time issue: on the one hand, flexibility; on the other side, possible risk. Now ...'

Each type of behaviour may be appropriate in the right situation at the right time. A team may be low on some types of contribution – and it may be up to the team leader to encourage, or deliberately adopt, desirable behaviours (such as bringing-in, supporting or seeking information) in order to provide balance.

You might draw up a **contribution profile**, by following the same procedure as a contribution count, but adding behavioural categories (perhaps a few at a time, at first). If you were worried about interpersonal conflict in your team, for example, you might look specifically for attacking, defending, blocking/difficulty stating, shutting-out and disagreeing: are such behaviours common in the team? Are particular individuals mainly at fault? Are attacks aimed at a particular person, who is forced to defend: a purely interpersonal conflict? Or is disagreement constructive and based on real objections – not linked to attacking or shutting-out?

Contribution profile	*Mary*	*Martha*	*Paul*	*Gary*	*Mark*	*Jason*	*Robbie*
Attacking					𝍸	///	
Defending	𝍸			𝍸			
Blocking					//		
Supporting	𝍸			𝍸			/
Shutting out				/	////	///	

Activity 5 **(10 minutes)**

What problems can you identify in the contribution profile give above?

2.5 Group cohesion and dysfunction

Problems may arise in an ultra close-knit group because:

(a) The group's energies may be focused on its own maintenance and relationships, instead of on the task

(b) The group may be suspicious or dismissive of outsiders, and may reject any contradictory information or criticism they supply; the group will be blinkered and stick to its own views, no matter what; cohesive groups thus often get the impression that they are infallible: they can't be wrong – and therefore can't learn from their mistakes

(c) The group may squash any dissent or opinions that might rock the boat. Close-knit groups tend to preserve a consensus – falsely if required – and to take risky decisions, because they have suppressed alternative facts and viewpoints

This phenomenon is called '**groupthink**'. In order to limit its effect, the team must be encouraged:

(a) Actively to seek outside ideas and feedback
(b) To welcome self-criticism within the group
(c) Consciously to evaluate conflicting evidence and opinions

Activity 6 **(15 minutes)**

Can you see any dangers in creating a very close-knit group? Think of the effect of strong team cohesion on:

(a) What the group spends its energies and attention on

(b) How the group regards outsiders and any information or feedback they supply

(c) How the group makes decisions

What could be done about these dangerous effects?

Chapter roundup

- A group is a collection of people who perceive themselves to be a group. A group with a strong sense of collaborating towards the fulfilment of their collective goals is a team.
- Collections of individuals develop into groups or teams through the stages of forming, storming, norming, performing (and possibly dorming).
- Groups 'behave' differently from individuals. Some of the dynamics of groups of which a manager should be aware include:
  - The tendency of groups to develop norms of behaviour
  - The ways decision-making behaviour affects team performance and satisfaction
  - The way in which personal, interpersonal and task factors influence the contributions of team members
  - The tendency of very cohesive groups to risky behaviour

Quick quiz

1 What is (a) brainstorming? and (b) a quality circle?

2 Outline what happens in the 'storming' stage of team development.

3 Why do individuals comply with group norms?

4 Why are groups particularly (a) useful and (b) risky for decision-making?

5 List six of Rackham and Morgan's categories of contribution to group discussion.

6 What is 'cohesion', and what effect does inter-group competition have on it?

Answers to quick quiz

1 (a) A process by which people produce spontaneous ideas, sparked off by a problem or task.

(b) Usually 6–10 employees from different levels and disciplines meeting to discuss problems related to quality or quality control in their area of work.

2 Storming brings out members' own ideas and attitudes. There may be conflict as well as creativity.

3 To be accepted and to avoid sanctions or penalties.

4 (a) More ideas, suggestions, and participation usually make the decision more acceptable.

(b) Decisions take longer and may be based on group norms and interests.

5 Proposing, building, supporting, seeking information, giving information, disagreeing. For other categories refer to Section 2.4.

6 Solidarity. Faced with competition it causes a group to close ranks, focuses its energies and makes the group concentrate on objectives.

Answers to activities

1 The primary groups are probably your tutor group or class. If at work, it would be the section in which you work. If the groups are large, you may feel reluctant to put forward ideas or ask questions, but even within a large group you should feel there is support and that help is at hand if you need it.

2 Categorising the behaviour of group members in the situations described results in the following: (a) storming, (b) dorming, (c) performing, (d) forming, (e) norming.

3 Group norms might have the effect of:

(a) 'Freezing out' a new manager who wants to change group behaviour

(b) Limiting output to what the group as a whole feels is fair for what they are paid: over-producing individuals are brought into line with the group output norm, so as not to make the group look bad

(c) Aiding management control by a process of self-regulation, if the group norms can be aligned with task objectives; under-producing individuals, for example, are brought into line by group pressure to pull their weight

(d) Aiding management in changing attitudes: if a manager can involve some individuals in accepting and communicating change, the rest of the group may be brought into line with the adjusted norm

4 (a) The new software is clearly desirable for the task. You could make a decision yourself, supported by the expert advice of the relevant team member. However, there does not seem to be a time limit on the decision (it is only a suggestion) and there does seem to be a good reason for

taking the time to consult the rest of the group. The change is something that will affect them all, and you can anticipate conflict (from the members who find technology a struggle); it should be brought into the open and worked through into consensus if possible. Agreement will make implementing the change much easier later on.

(b) This decision is more about acceptability than about quality: the colour is entirely a matter of taste, and the group will have to live with it, so they should be invited to share the decision. On the other hand time is short, and it is the sort of argument that could go to and fro for ever: you are unlikely to persuade people that one colour or the other is 'better', if they prefer the other one! A quick, democratic vote may show clear support one way or the other: if opinion is tied, the leader should make an authoritative casting vote, without wasting time over it.

5 You may have noticed that Mark spent most of his communication time attacking and blocking – being difficult – and Jason also attacked. This clearly forced Mary and Gary into defending but also supporting each other: this may be positive for them, but is likely to polarise the group. Meanwhile, Mark and Jason's shutting out behaviour and the tension in the group effectively prevent the others from contributing altogether.

6 For ideas, if required, see Section 2.5.

Chapter 12:
BUILDING EFFECTIVE TEAMS

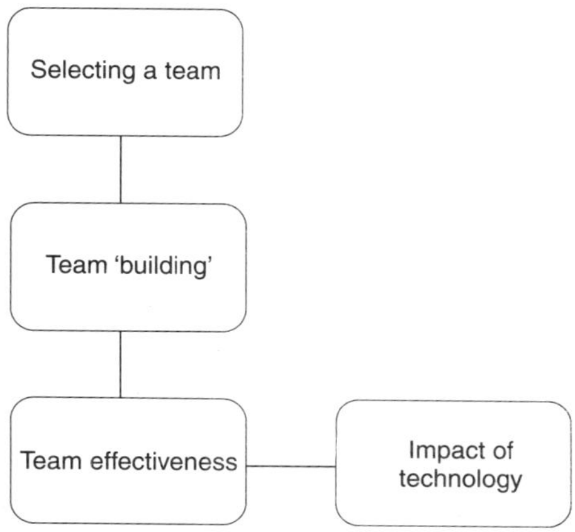

Introduction

In Chapter 11, we looked at how individuals behave in groups, and (which is slightly different) how groups behave. In this chapter, we look at the practical implications for managers who wish to create effective teams.

Your objectives

In this chapter you will learn about the following:

(a) The types of people and behaviour required for an effective team

(b) Techniques for teambuilding

(c) Factors influencing the effectiveness of teams, and take a contingency approach to team management

(d) How to assess the effectiveness (or otherwise) of a team

(e) The impact of technology on team functioning

1 SELECTING A TEAM

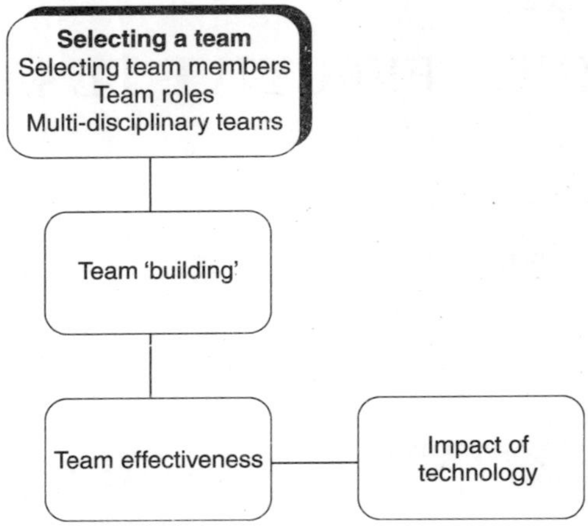

1.1 Selecting team members

Team membership may already be dictated by:

(a) **Existing arrangements**: a long-standing committee, section or department

(b) **Organisation**: a task force or project/product team may require a representative from each of the functions involved in the task, for the sake of co-ordination

(c) **Politics**: representatives of particular interest groups in the organisation might need to be included, so that they feel their interests are protected and so that decisions reached (if any) are likely to find broad acceptance

(d) **Election**: for example in the case of a staff association committee

Where a manager is able to select team members, however, (s)he should aim to match the attributes or resources prospective members are able to bring to the group with the requirements of the task.

(a) **Specialist skills and knowledge** may be required, from different areas in the organisation (or outside it).

(b) **Experience** may be helpful, especially if other team members are relatively inexperienced, and are therefore less likely to anticipate and know how to handle problems.

(c) **Political power in the organisation** may be a useful attribute in a member, particularly if the team is in competition for scarce resources, or its collective authority is unclear. The team leader may, for example, wish to co-opt a senior manager as the team's 'champion' in the organisation.

(d) **Access to resources**, such as use of equipment in other departments or information through specialist or personal contacts, may be helpful.

(e) **Competence** in the tasks likely to be required of the team member will be desirable, whatever other resources (s)he brings to the team.

In addition, both task performance and team maintenance (keeping the group together and satisfied) will require a mix of personalities and interpersonal skills.

Activity 1 **(10 minutes)**

Before reading on, list five 'types' of people that you would want to have on a project team, involved (say) in organising an end-of-term party.

1.2 Team roles

RM Belbin researched business-game teams at the Carnegie Institute of Technology. He developed a picture of the character-mix in a team, which many people find a useful guide to team selection and management. Belbin suggests that an effective team is made up of people who fill, between them, the following eight roles.

(a) The **co-ordinator** – presides and co-ordinates; balanced, disciplined, good at working through others.

(b) The **shaper** – highly strung, dominant, extrovert, passionate about the task itself, a spur to action.

(c) The **plant** – introverted, but intellectually dominant and imaginative; source of ideas and proposals but with disadvantages of introversion (unsociability, inhibition, need for control).

(d) The **monitor-evaluator** – analytically (rather than creatively) intelligent; dissects ideas, spots flaws; possibly aloof, tactless – but necessary.

(e) The **resource-investigator** – popular, sociable, extrovert, relaxed; source of new contacts, but not an originator; needs to be made use of.

(f) The **implementer** – practical organiser, turning ideas into tasks, scheduling, planning and so on; trustworthy and efficient, but not excited; not a leader, but an administrator.

(g) The **team worker** – most concerned with team maintenance; supportive, understanding, diplomatic; popular but uncompetitive; contribution noticed only in absence.

(h) The **finisher** – chivvies the team to meet deadlines, attend to details; urgency and follow-through important, though not always popular.

Belbin has also identified a ninth team-role, the specialist, who joins the group to offer expert advice when needed. Examples are legal advisers, PR consultants, finance specialists and the like.

FOR DISCUSSION

What role would you, and each of your study group or class-mates, fill in a working group, do you think?

1.3 Multidisciplinary teams

There are two basic approaches to the organisation of team work.

Multi-disciplinary teams

Multi-disciplinary teams bring together individuals with different skills and specialisms, so that their skills, experience and knowledge can be pooled or exchanged. To an extent, this goes on in any case, at organisational level, but then it requires more elaborate mechanisms for communication and co-ordination. The following chart shows a multi-disciplinary structure, cutting across traditional functional boundaries. In effect, each team member has two bosses: the functional department manager who has line authority over him, and the project manager who has authority over his activity on the project. (This is called a matrix structure, see Figure 12.1.)

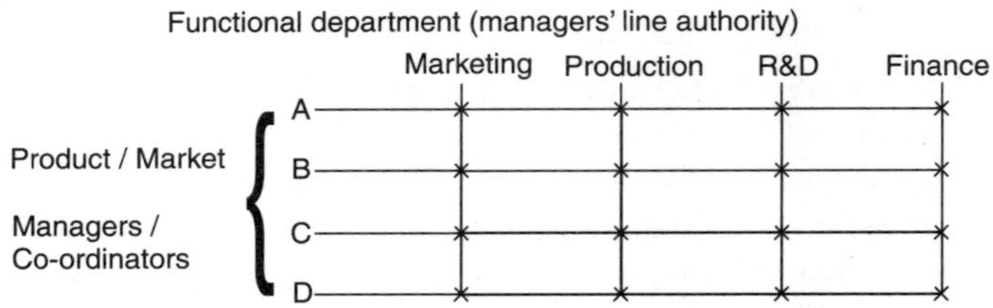

Figure 12.1 Matrix structure

We first saw the matrix structure back in Chapter 3.

Teamworking of this kind encourages freer and faster communication between disciplines in the organisation, which:

(a) Increases workers' awareness of their overall objectives and targets

(b) Aids co-ordination, and

(c) Helps to generate solutions to problems, and suggestions for improvements, since a multi-disciplinary team has access to more 'pieces of the jigsaw'

Multi-skilled teams

Instead of pooling the skills and knowledge of different specialists, a team may simply bring together a number of individuals, each of whom is functionally versatile or multi-skilled, and who can therefore perform any of the group's tasks. These tasks can then be shared out in a more flexible way between group members, according to who is available and best placed to do a given job at the time it is required.

2 TEAM 'BUILDING'

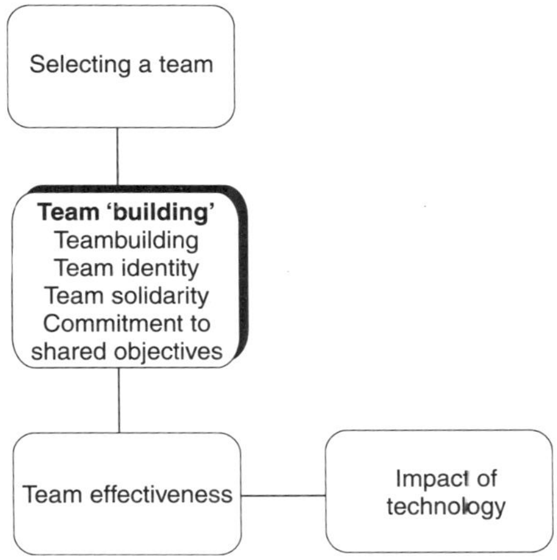

2.1 Teambuilding

Teambuilding involves:

(a) Giving a group of people a greater **sense of their identity as a team**; this is sometimes called '*esprit de corps*' or 'team spirit'

(b) Encouraging group **loyalty or solidarity,** so that members put in extra effort for the sake of the group

(c) Encouraging the group to commit themselves to **shared work objectives,** and to co-operate willingly to achieve them

Activity 2 **(30 minutes)**

Why might the following be effective as team-building exercises?

(a) Sending a project team (involved in the design of electronic systems for racing cars) on a recreational day out 'karting'.

(b) Sending a project team on an 'Outward Bound' style course, walking in the mountains from A to B, through various obstacles (rivers to cross and so on).

(c) Sending two sales teams on a day out playing 'War Games', each being an opposing combat team trying to capture the other's flag, armed with paint guns.

(d) Sending a project team on a conference at a venue away from work, with a brief to review the past year and come up with a 'vision' for the next year.

These are actually commonly-used techniques. If you are interested, you might locate an activity centre or company near you which offers outdoor pursuits, war games or corporate entertainment and ask them about team-building exercises and the effect they have on people.

2.2 Team identity

A manager may be able to increase his work group's sense of itself as a team by any or all of the following means.

- **Giving the team a name**. A group name or nickname can express a lot about the team and encourage its members to identify with it: if the nickname naturally emerges from the group, as the way it refers to itself, even better. What sort of qualities of a group do names like 'The Monarchs', 'The Crazy Gang', 'The Gangstas' or 'The A Team' express?
- **Giving the team a badge or uniform**. 'Uniform' may sound offputting – but basically suggests any kind of shared dress norms. If a team has a distinctive identifying style or insignia, it will be expressing its boundaries: who is out and who is in. Think about how teams you know use baseball caps or T-shirts, badges or ties in this way. What do you notice about the crews in MacDonalds, say, or the Guardian Angels?
- **Expressing the team's self-image**. One way of doing this is by identifying key phrases which tend to be repeated in the group, and turning them into group mottoes, or slogans. Think about the effect of slogans such as: 'You don't have to be crazy to work here, but it helps', or 'The impossible takes a bit longer'.
- **Building a team mythology**. Collecting and repeating stories about past successes and failures (funny or heroic) develops the group's self-image in the same way that experience shapes an individual's. Classic cock-ups make just as good team-building myths as hard-won successes or lucky breaks, as long as there is the sense that the team came through it together.

Activity 3 **(45 minutes)**

Consider the group of people you are studying with. Do you feel you are a team? Appoint a leader – someone you think is a 'co-ordinator' type, who will keep the discussion on track and under control – and try another brainstorming session. This time you are going to organise the end of term party.

2.3 Team solidarity

Another term for solidarity is 'cohesion' (literally, sticking together). Here, again, are some practical suggestions.

- **Expressing solidarity**. This is one of the more important uses of a team slogan. 'One for all and all for one' and 'United we stand' may be clichés now, but they caught on, to good effect, in their day. If you were a Polish trade union leader, why might you want to call a movement 'Solidarnosc' ('Solidarity')?
- **Encouraging interpersonal relationships**. Team members need to trust each other and be willing to work together – at the very least. Informal relationship-building activity should be encouraged and even provided (within reason, obviously: the main everyday focus of the group should be on its work objectives). Rallying round in times of need can be particularly powerful – but a team leader might want to pay attention to comparatively trivial things like members' birthdays, too.

- **Controlling conflict**. Personality clashes and disagreements should be dealt with immediately, and in the open – not left to fester and infect the whole team. The team leader needs to mediate between conflicting members, not to act as judge between them. In other words, (s)he needs to guide them in expressing and understanding their disagreement, and in finding ways of resolving the conflict that will be acceptable to both, if at all possible: a win-win situation.

- **Controlling intra-group competition**. Team members should all feel that they are being treated fairly and equally. The team leader should not show favouritism – which means that if there are inequalities of status, pay or 'say' in decisions, all members should be able to see that they are both reasonable and necessary to the success of the team as a whole. (You might give more of a say to someone who is an acknowledged expert.) Getting team members competing among themselves for bonuses and so on may spur them to better individual performance, but will not build the team.

- **Encouraging inter-group competition**. Competition with other teams, however, has been shown to increase cohesion within the competing groups, as they face what they perceive to be a threat from outside. The team closes ranks, and submerges its differences, demanding loyalty: it also focuses its collective energies more closely on the task. If a team lacks cohesion, or a task is particularly demanding of effort and loyalty, the team leader might pull the team together by finding an 'enemy', competitor or other perceived threat to face them with. (Warning: don't try this if it is important to the organisation as a whole to have teams working together!)

Remember, however, to keep your cohesive group open to new information, to avoid 'groupthink' (see Chapter 11, Section 2.5).

2.4 Commitment to shared objectives

The purpose of teambuilding is, ultimately, not to have a close-knit and satisfied team, but to have a close-knit and satisfied team that fulfils its task objectives. In fact, a cohesive and successful task-focused team may be more supportive and satisfying to its members than a cosy group absorbed only in its own processes and relationships.

Getting a team behind its objectives involves:

(a) Clearly setting out the team's objectives, and their place in the activity of the organisation as a whole

(b) Involving the team in setting specific targets and standards, and agreeing methods of organising work, in order to reach the objectives

(c) Providing the right information, resources, training and environment for the team to achieve its targets – involving the team in deciding what its requirements are

(d) Giving regular, clear feedback on progress and results – including constructive criticism – so the team can celebrate what they have achieved, and be spurred on by what they have not yet achieved

(e) Encouraging feedback, suggestions and ideas from the team, and doing something about them: helping team members believe that they can make an impact on their work and results, and that that impact is appreciated by the organisation

(f) Giving positive reinforcement (praise or reward) for creativity, initiative, problem-solving, helpfulness and other behaviour that shows commitment to the task

(g) Visibly 'championing' the team in the organisation, fighting (if necessary) for the resources it needs and the recognition it deserves

Assuming that we've now gathered and built a group of people into a close-knit, performing team, how do we know whether they are actually effective?

3 TEAM EFFECTIVENESS

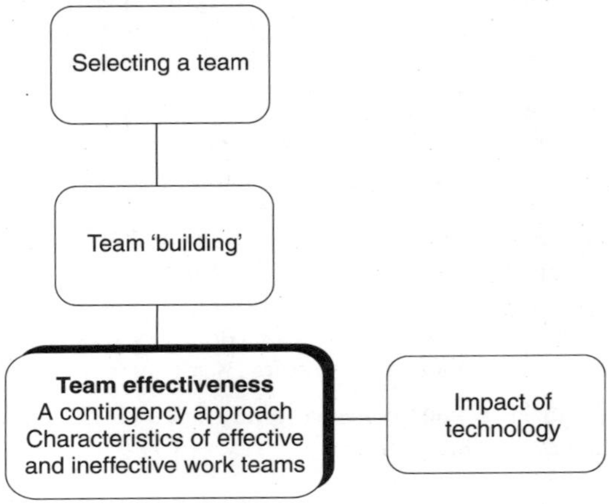

3.1 A contingency approach

An effective team is one which does two things.

- Achieves its task objectives
- Maintains co-operative working through the satisfaction and interrelationships of its members

Unfortunately, no two groups of people are the same – and they may also be doing different work in different organisational set-ups. So the team leader will need to take a contingency approach. How much supervision does the team need? Should you let the team make the decisions? Do more team members need to contribute to group discussions? Should you discourage disagreement in the group? Answer: it all depends.

Charles Handy suggested the framework shown in Figure 12.2 as a guide to the factors that influence a group's effectiveness. The intervening factors are those that the team manager can manipulate in order to alter the outcomes, according to the situation (s)he has been given to start with.

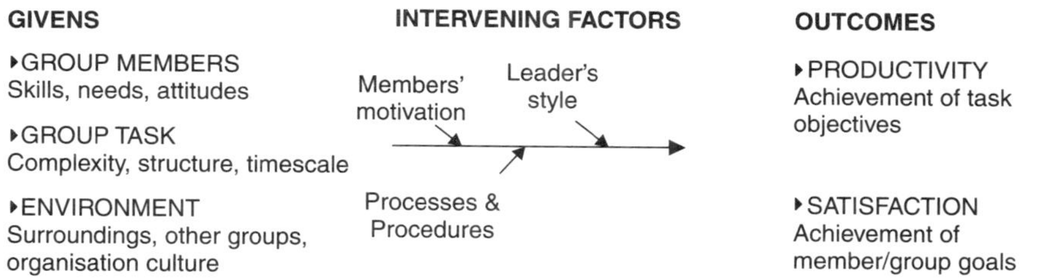

Figure 12.2 Group effectiveness

As an example, if the members have a high need for structure, but the task is very complex and ambiguous, and the organisation culture is intolerant of failure (all givens), the manager may need to adopt a relatively authoritarian management style, motivate team members by rewards for results, and establish 'safe' control procedures (intervening factors) if the team is to succeed without too much stress (outcomes).

If a manager is to improve the effectiveness of the work team (s)he must have some idea of what an effective or ineffective group is like.

3.2 Characteristics of effective and ineffective work teams

Some pointers to group efficiency are **quantifiable** or numerically measurable factors; others are more **qualitative** factors, which can be observed, but are less easily measured. No one factor on its own is significant, but taken collectively they present a picture of how well or badly the group is operating.

Quantifiable factors

Effective work group

(1) Low rate of labour turnover
(2) Low accident rate
(3) Low absenteeism
(4) High output and productivity
(5) Good quality of output
(6) Individual targets are achieved
(7) Few stoppages and interruptions to work

Ineffective work group

(1) High rate of labour turnover
(2) High accident rate
(3) High absenteeism
(4) Low output and productivity
(5) Poor quality of output
(6) Individual targets are not achieved
(7) Time is wasted owing to disruption of work flow
(8) Time is lost owing to disagreements between superior and subordinates

Qualitative factors

Effective work group

(1) High commitment to the achievement of targets and organisational goals

(2) Clear understanding of the group's work

(3) Clear understanding of the role of each person within the group

(4) Trust and open communication between members

(5) Idea sharing

(6) New-idea generation

(7) Mutual help and encouragement, if necessary, through constructive criticism

(8) Group problem-solving, addressing root causes

(9) Active interest in work decisions

(10) Consensus of opinion sought, through argument and mutual adjustment

(11) Desire for self-development through work and career

(12) Motivation and ability work in the leader's absence

Ineffective work group

(1) Little understanding of organisational goals or the role of the group

(2) Low commitment to targets

(3) Confusion and uncertainty about the role of each person within the group

(4) Mistrust between group members, and suspicion of leaders

(5) Little idea sharing

(6) Few new ideas generated

(7) Competition, self-interest and hostile criticism within the group

(8) Superficial problem-solving, addressing symptoms, not causes

(9) Passive acceptance of work decisions

(10) Interpersonal hostility, grudges and attempts to dominate

(11) Boredom and uninterest in work

(12) Need for leadership to direct and control work

Activity 4 **(20 minutes)**

Try to interview somebody who manages a work team, who would be willing to talk to you for just 10 or 15 minutes. Run through the checklist of factors given above, asking your interviewee to give a 'Yes' or 'No' to each of the statements. Put a question mark (?) where it was difficult for the respondent to answer, because the factor was not easy to define or measure. You might want to reconsider some of our factors, or the way they are phrased, in the light of the answers you get. What conclusions can you draw from your survey?

4 IMPACT OF TECHNOLOGY

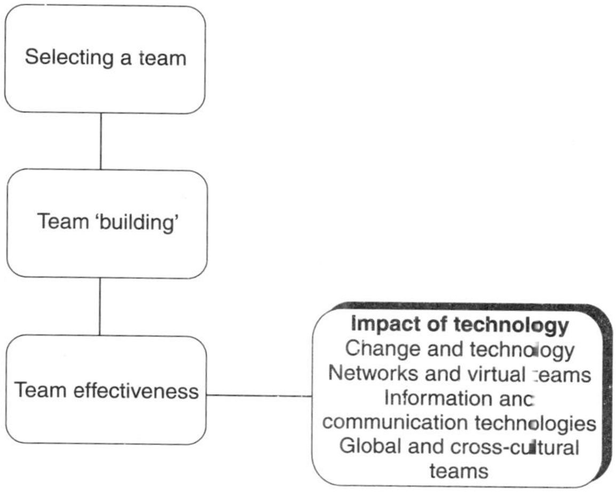

4.1 Change and technology

In an increasingly global, fast moving, knowledge-based economy, organisations must react to change by processing information and making decisions quickly. At the same time, they must cut the costs of doing business as the global slowdown maintains its stranglehold and travel becomes more difficult, more complex, and less convenient.

Today's business environment is more tightly connected and more complex than it has ever been before. The increased connectivity has increased volatility within industries and across the economy as a whole. Increased complexity has made it increasingly difficult to ever have all of the information in one place.

Connectivity and complexity taken together are causing organisations to find new ways of working and working together to survive. These new ways are characterised by a new set of values and a different set of technologies.

One response is the push towards networks, virtual workers and virtual teams. Virtual teaming and collaboration are changing how people work and learn. They are changing how we think about work and management of work. It is not just about increasing productivity in the workforce but also giving people control of their work environment and their work preferences.

To give employees that control not only requires changing how we view the nature of what work is and how it gets done, but also new values based on trust.

4.2 Networks and virtual teams

Until recently, when you said you worked with someone, you meant by implication that you worked in the same place for the same organisation. Now people do not need to be located in the same place to work together. They can work in virtual or network organisations, either as members of 'virtual teams' or as teleworkers.

Definition

> A **Virtual Team** – also known as a Geographically Dispersed Team (GDT) – is a group of individuals who work across time, space, and organisational boundaries with links strengthened by webs of communication technology. They have complementary skills and are committed to a common purpose, have interdependent performance goals, and share an approach to work for which they hold themselves mutually accountable.

Geographically dispersed teams allow organisations to hire and retain the best people regardless of location.

A virtual team does not always mean teleworkers. Teleworkers are defined as individuals who work from home. Many virtual teams in today's organisations consist of employees both working at home and small groups in the office but in different geographic locations.

There are seven basic types of virtual teams

1. **Networked Teams** consist of individuals who collaborate to achieve a common goal or purpose; membership is frequently diffuse and fluid.
2. **Parallel Teams** work in the short term to develop recommendations for an improvement in a process or system; they have a distinct membership.
3. **Project or Product-Development Teams** conduct projects for users or customers for a defined period of time. Tasks are usually non-routine, and the results are specific and measurable; the team has decision-making authority.
4. **Work or Production Teams** perform regular and ongoing work usually in one function; they have a clearly defined membership.
5. **Service Teams** support customers or the internal organisation in typically a service/technical support role around the clock.
6. **Management Teams** work collaboratively on a daily basis within a functional division of a corporation.
7. **Action Teams** offer immediate responses activated in (typically) emergency situations.

A virtual team is an evolutionary form of a network organisation enabled by advances in information and communication technology. Global competition, the computer age, and excessive travel expenses have evolved to make working across continents and countries an easy, practical way to achieve superior results. Using a combination of technology and teams, many companies are pursuing virtual teams to increase technology and knowledge transfer, increase the speed of solutions and decrease bottlenecks or delays between customers and suppliers or geographically dispersed employees.

Virtual teams are like project or natural work teams with added components. The latter may consist of members with cross-functional backgrounds from the same company, in the same location. They work together to solve problems in their day-to-day jobs. However, teams become virtual when you add any of the following three components:

1. **Different geography or locations of team members**: Virtual team members can be located in different parts of a city or in different parts of the world.

2 **Team members from different organisations or parts of the organisation**: Team members can be from different organisations or from different parts of the same organisation.

3 **Different durations or lengths of time that members work together as a team**: Depending on its mission, a virtual team may unite for a project that lasts a few days, months, or years.

Activity 5 **(30 minutes)**

Outline some advantages and disadvantages of teleworking.

4.3 Information and communication technologies

Virtual teams are supported by both hardware and software. General hardware requirements include telephones, PCs, modems or equivalent, and communication links such as the public switched network (telephone system) and local area networks. Software requirements include groupware products such as electronic mail, meeting facilitation software, and group time management systems.

The following matrix illustrates some of the information and communication technologies that support virtual teams – working together with anyone, at anytime, from anywhere:

	Same place	**Different place**
Same time	• Face-to-face Meetings • Open Space Technology	• Virtual Meetings • Distance Learning • Help Desks • Telework • Group Authoring • Video Conferencing • Open Space Technology
Different time	• Team Rooms	• Electronic Mail • Group Time Management • Distance Learning • Computer Conferencing

The kinds of technology that can assist in making work co-ordination for virtual teams relatively simple and highly effective include the following:

Conferencing

There are three basic forms of conferencing:

(a) Audio conferencing
(b) Data conferencing
(c) Video conferencing

Microsoft's NetMeeting and Interwise conferencing are good examples of multimedia group conferencing products. NetMeeting, for example, allows team members to share and collaborate using applications such as Word and Excel, and any other Windows based application. Chat and whiteboard are other supported functions. In desktop video-conferencing, a camera is mounted on the top of a person's computer monitor and team members are able too see and hear one another, as though they were gathering informally in a colleague's office

Groupware software enables teams of people to work on the same document at different times. Software programs such as Lotus Notes allow team members to share ideas and information, work together on projects, and take part in group discussions with all team members. It also allows team members to create and share documents that include text, presentation graphics, scanned images, sound, video and more. Most importantly, this software offers several levels of security so that sensitive information is not compromised when collaborating with people outside of the organisation

Newsgroups, bulletin boards and **electronic mail** on the Internet linking to a world-wide, networked computing community with millions of users from government, business, research, industry and education. Microsoft Outlook is the primary electronic mail systems for most organisations. Security is an important consideration for virtual teams especially if transmitting sensitive information over a network. Many email and conferencing products support various types of encryption or other security methods

Intranets are essentially communication tools that operate by linking an organisation's computers in a way similar to the Internet. It is a closed network, however, which is accessible to people within the organisation (and maybe approved outsiders). Like the Internet, its users access it by means of a piece of software called a 'browser', which allows them to look at pages of text and images which are hosted on a company server. The user clicks on links written into these pages to go to other pages. The potential for collaborative work is enhanced by Intranets, it provides a means for team members to have a 'window' on each others' progress and assist each other in troubleshooting.

Electronic whiteboards – are very useful in meetings for collaboration on ideas and capturing them electronically. Ideas, once captured can be distributed electronically to meeting attendees.

Projectors – that connect to PCs are very useful in meetings. Slide presentations can be displayed from the PC without the requirement for making transparencies. Electronic copies are easily distributed to team members via electronic mail. Finally electronic presentations can be modified during the meeting and agreement reached.

Time management systems – are useful in co-ordinating team members schedules. Many time management systems show free and busy times and some also allow meetings to be scheduled and conference rooms and other resources reserved.

Websites – the work of virtual teams can also be enhanced by use of a website. It can be a useful place to store and distribute graphic materials, schedules, flowcharts, reference materials, and more.

4.4 Global and cross-cultural teams

The current trend towards globalisation and cross-cultural encounters is becoming a part of daily business. People from different national backgrounds are joined together in work groups and teams in order to get things done across geographical boundaries. Organisations are reaching out to conquer the world markets aiming at the best resources available, the ultimate goal being a strategic advantage in producing value for customers. This brings many challenges to the corporate world but it is good to keep in mind, that not only corporate giants are moving towards multinational business environments. Most middle-sized companies are looking at international markets in order to survive.

With trends of business becoming more global the people who are to make things happen are moving closer into contact with colleagues, partners and customers from different parts of the world. As a reaction to the rapid expansion of global business local perspectives on business are also being highlighted. Terms such as globalocalisation – taking into consideration the 'glocal' aspect of business – have been coined to emphasise the importance of being able to cope with the demands of international business without undermining the power of the local labour and market potential

A global virtual team can be defined as 'a temporary, culturally diverse, geographically dispersed, electronically communicating work group'. The notion of temporary in the definition describes teams where members may have never worked together before and who may not expect to work together again as a group. The characterisation of virtual teams as global implies culturally diverse and globally spanning members that can think and act in concert with the diversity of the global environment. Finally, it is a heavy reliance on computer-mediated communication technology that allows members separated by time and space to engage in collaborative work.

A cross-cultural work group or team is one in which variety in terms of cultural and national origins exist in addition to those inherent in definitions of work groups and teams. When trying to describe cross-cultural work groups we assume that the following attributes are present concurrently:

- They are social entities embedded in larger social systems.
- They perform one or more tasks relevant to their organisation's mission.
- Their task performance has consequences that affect others inside or outside the organization.
- They are made up of individuals whose work roles require them to be interdependent.
- They have membership that is identifiable not only to those in the group but also to those outside it.

Chapter roundup

- Team building involves attention to:
  - Team member selection
  - Team identity
  - Team solidarity
  - Shared beliefs and objectives
- An effective team is one that achieves its tasks and satisfies its members.
- A contingency approach to team effectiveness includes attention to:
  - The givens: the group, the task and the environment
  - Intervening factors which the manager can manipulate: leadership style, motivation, processes and procedures
  - The outcomes: group productivity and member satisfaction.
- A Virtual Team is a group of individuals who work across time, space, and organisational boundaries with links strengthened by webs of communication technology. The characterisation of virtual teams as global implies culturally diverse and globally spanning members in which variety in terms of cultural and national origins exist.

Quick quiz

1 What should a manager look for when selecting team members?

2 What are Belbin's eight roles for a well-rounded team?

3 Suggest five ways in which a manager can get a team 'behind' task objectives.

4 Suggest five quantifiable characteristics of effective teams and five qualitative characteristics of ineffective teams.

5 What are:

(a) The 'givens'
(b) The 'intervening factors'

in a group's performance?

Answers to quick quiz

1 Skills, knowledge, experience, political power in the organisation, access to resources, competence.

2 Co-ordinator, shaper, plant, monitor-evaluator, resource-investigator, implementer, team worker, finisher.

3 Set clear objectives, get the team to set targets/standards, provide information and resources, give feedback, praise and reward, and champion the team in the organisation.

4 *Quantifiable characteristics of effective teams*

Low rate of labour turnover
Low accident rate
Low absenteeism
High output and productivity
Good quality of output

(see Section 3.2 for more)

5 *Qualitative characteristics of ineffective teams*

Little understanding of organisational goals
Low commitment to targets
Confusion about the role of individuals
Mistrust and suspicion
Little idea sharing

(see Section 3.2 for more)

5 (a) Members, task, environment
(b) Motivation, leadership, processes/procedures

Answers to activities

1 For your ideal team, you might have listed: a person with originality and ideas; a 'get up and go' type, with energy and enthusiasm; a quiet logical thinker who can be sensible about the ideas put forward; a plodder who will be happy to do the routine leg-work; and a team player who can organise the others and help them reach agreement on ideas.

2 (a) Recreation helps the team to build informal relationships: in this case, the chosen activity also reminds them of their task, and may make them feel special, as part of the motor racing industry, by giving them a taste of what the end user of their product does.

(b) A team challenge pushes the group to consider its strengths and weaknesses, to find its natural leader, to co-operate and help each other in overcoming obstacles.

(c) This exercise creates an 'us' and 'them' challenge: perceiving the rival team as the enemy heightens the solidarity of the group.

(d) This exercise encourages the group to raise problems and conflicts freely, away from the normal environment of work, and also encourages brainstorming and the expression of team members' dreams for what the team can achieve in future.

3 You may have found it easier to work as a team this time. The group has probably generated a number of ideas as to what form the party should take. Activities may have been allocated (drinks, food, music) and decisions made on how to publicise the event. Hopefully, you have not yet reached the 'dorming' stage.

4 Hopefully, you found the checklist in Section 3.2 effective. If not, change the wording. From the answers you received you should be able to judge how effective the team/group is.

5 The advantages of working from home are mainly the savings of office space and the elimination of travelling time with consequent reduction in stress, expense, fatigue etc. Other factors and considerations are:

- Saving on providing special 'office' clothes
- Sense of independence and freedom to plan own schedule
- Potential for development of own business enterprises
- Unfettered use of skills and expertise in projects which interest the employee without interference of employer
- Reduction or removal of typical interruptions in office (from colleagues, telephone calls, visitors), enabling the employee working from home to concentrate and complete work more quickly and effectively
- Opportunity of employment for individuals who might otherwise be unable to work (eg parent at home with children, carers for sick and elderly, disabled, chronically sick, people living in remote locations who could not reasonably travel to work)

The disadvantages may relate to working environment, equipment or social factors.

Working environment:

- The costs of office accommodation are largely transferred from the company/employer to the individual at home.
- Some homes may not offer suitable opportunities for the administrative work and the allocation of space and facilities for this purpose may be detrimental to other occupants.
- Neighbours may object to business activities in a residential area and the business use of the premises may incur charges and taxes.

Equipment:

- The problem of power cuts or breakdown of equipment (which may cause loss of income through inability to carry on working) is much more likely to affect the homeworker than the conventional office employee.
- A freelance worker will need to ensure having the financial resources to provide power, telephone link, equipment and consumables (failure to pay BT for example could mean an end to business).
- People working from home lack immediate access to the technician support provided in many offices and may suffer delay (and loss of earning opportunities) if equipment breakdowns occur.
- The homeworker will need to ensure that work is safeguarded from the danger of hacking, espionage, sabotage, loss/corruption of essential data etc and maintain security and back-up systems.
- Valuable equipment could be vulnerable to loss by theft or vandalism.

Social factors:

- There is loss of face-to-face contact, which can be very important in meetings and negotiations and is not fully compensated for by mail or phone calls.
- The joys of freedom from the tyranny of the office and the journey to work may be offset by the loss of social contact with colleagues at work.

- The home worker may lack stimulus from the traditional working environment and direct contact with new developments and methods, as well as the benefits of group activities.
- The employee working from home requires strong self discipline, motivation and the ability to organise his or her own work schedule, priorities and systems. They should not be diverted by other (domestic) demands or succumb to taking too frequent days off.
- There may be a sense of never being able to get away from work or, for the workaholic, the temptation to keep going to the detriment of other activities.

Glossary

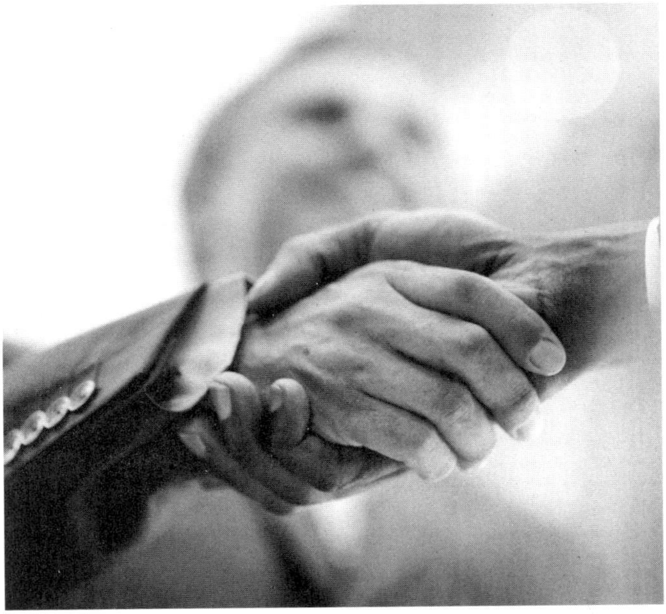

Accountability The duty of the individual to report to his superior to account for how he has used his delegated authority and fulfilled his responsibilities.

Added value An accounting term for the difference between the cost of raw materials and the sales price of the finished product: in other words, the value that is perceived to have been added to inputs by processing within the organisational system.

Attitude A mental and neural state of readiness exerting a directive or dynamic influence upon the individual's response to all objects and situations with which it is related.'

Authority The right to do something, or to get others to do it.

Bias is a mental tendency or inclination to see things in a particular way. It is used mainly to refer to irrational preferences or dislikes, usually a form of prejudice.

Brainstorming A process whereby people produce spontaneous, uncensored ideas, sparked off by a particular problem or task.

Budget A statement of desired performance, usually expressed in financial terms (expenditure, revenue, profit and so on).

Centralisation The concentration of authority for making most decisions at the top levels of the organisation.

Communication The transmission or exchange of information.

Conflict Any personal divergence of interests between groups or individuals. Organisational conflict arises from behaviour intended to obstruct the achievement of some other person's goals.

Control The overall process whereby goals and standards are defined, and performance is monitored, measured against the goals and adjusted if necessary, to ensure that the goals are being accomplished.

Co-operation Working or acting together.

Co-ordinate To plan or take action to improve, the interrelationships (especially of timing and methods of communication) between a number of various activities, which contribute to the achievement of a single objective, so that they do not conflict and the objective is achieved with a minimal expenditure of time and effort (*Dictionary of Management*).

Counselling A purposeful relationship in which one person helps another to help himself. It is a way of relating and responding to another person so that that person is helped to explore his thoughts, feelings and behaviour with the aim of reaching a clearer understanding. The clearer understanding may be of himself or of a problem, or of the one in relation to the other.' (*Rees*).

Criterion (plural: criteria) A factor or standard by which something can be judged or decided.

Culture (in the sense of organisational 'climate'). The collective self-image and style of the organisation; its shared values and beliefs, norms and symbols.

Decentralisation The dispersion of authority to make decisions throughout all levels of the organisation.

Delayering The reduction of the number of management levels from bottom to top.

Delegation The process whereby superior A gives subordinate B authority over a defined area which falls within the scope of A's own authority.

Diagnosis is the thorough analysis of facts or problems in order to gain understanding. (A diagnosis is the opinion reached as a result of such analysis.) In medical terms, diagnosis is the identification of diseases through the examination of symptoms.

Discipline A condition in an enterprise in which there is orderliness in which the members of the enterprise behave sensibly and conduct themselves according to the standards of acceptable behaviour as related to the goals of the organisation.

Dysfunction Any disturbance in a person (or system) which prevents it from functioning or fulfilling its intended role of purpose.

Empowerment The current term for making workers (and particularly work teams) responsible for achieving, and even setting, work targets, with the freedom to make decisions about how they are to be achieved.

Flat organisation An organisation which, in relation to its size, has a small number of hierarchical levels. This implies a *wide* span of control.

Formal organisation An organisation which is deliberately constructed to fulfil specific goals. It is characterised by planned division of responsibility and a well-defined structure of authority and communication. The organisation structure provides for consistent functions and roles, irrespective of changes in individual membership.

Grievance Occurs when an individual feels that (s)he is being wrongly treated by a colleague or supervisor: picked on, unfairly appraised or blocked for promotion, or discriminated against on grounds of race or sex.

Group Any collection of people who perceive themselves to be a group.

Human resource management is 'a strategic and coherent approach to the management of an organisation's most valued assets: the people working there who individually and collectively contribute to the achievement of its objectives for sustainable competitive advantage'. *(Armstrong)*

Incentive The offer or promise of a reward for contribution or success, designed to motivate the individual or team to behave in such a way as to earn it. (In other words, the 'carrot' dangled in front of the donkey!)

Influence The process by which an individual or group exercises power to determine or modify the behaviour of others.

Informal organisation One which is loosely structured, flexible and spontaneous, fluctuating with its individual membership. Examples of an informal organisation are colleagues who tend to lunch together and 'cliques'. Informal organisations always exist within formal organisations.

Internal customer concept Any unit of an organisation whose task contributes to the work of other units can be regarded as a supplier of services, like any other supplier used by the organisation. The 'receiving' units are thus customers of that unit. The service unit's objective thus becomes the efficient and effective identification and satisfaction of customer needs – as much within the organisation as outside it.

Job A grouped set of tasks allocated to a given worker.

Job enlargement The attempt to widen jobs by increasing the number of operations in which a job holder is involved.

Job enrichment Planned, deliberate action to build greater responsibility, breadth and challenge of work into a job.

Learning The process of acquiring, through experience, knowledge which leads to changed behaviour.

Motivation The process by which the behaviour of an individual is influenced by others, through their power to offer or withhold satisfaction of the individual's needs and goals.

Network A contemporary organisational structure that is founded on a set of alliances with other organisations that serve a wide variety of functions.

Organisational conflict Arises from behaviour intended to obstruct the achievement of some other person's goals.

Organisations 'Social arrangements for the controlled performance of collective goals'. *(Buchanan and Huczynski).*

Perception The psychological process by which stimuli or in-coming sensory data are selected and organised into patterns which are meaningful to the individual.

Personality The total pattern of characteristic ways of thinking, feeling and behaving that constitute the individual's distinctive method of relating to the environment.

Policy A general statement or understanding which provides guidelines for management decision making.

Power The ability to do something, or get others to do it.

Prejudice A 'pre-judgement', an opinion formed before all the relevant facts are known – particularly an unfavourable opinion.

Quality circles Groups of (typically 6-10) employees from different levels and/or disciplines, who meet regularly to discuss problems of quality and quality control in their area of work.

Reward A token (monetary or otherwise) given to an individual or team in recognition of some contribution or success.

Responsibility The liability of a person to be called to account for the way he has exercised the authority given to him. It is an obligation to do something, or to get others to do it.

Span of control The number of subordinates immediately reporting to a superior official. In other words, if a manager has five subordinates, the span of control is five.

Stakeholders All those individuals, groups and institutions who have a legitimate interest or 'stake' in the organisation's activities and performance.

Tall organisation One which, in relation to its size, has a large number of levels of management hierarchy. This implies a *narrow* span of control.

Team A formal group established to achieve particular objectives.

Bibliography

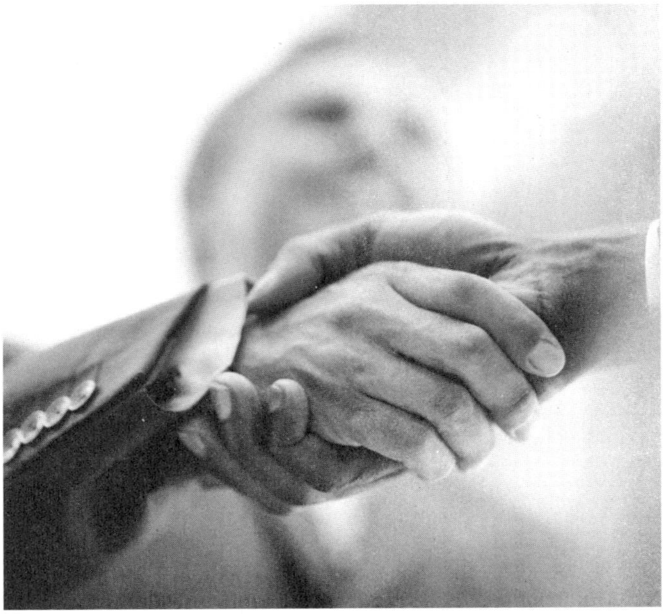

Armstrong, M. (1997) *A Handbook of Personnel Practice*, London: Kogan Page

Barnard, C, (1938) *Functions of the executive* Boston: Harvard University Press

Belbin, M. (1993) *Team Roles at Work*, Oxford: Butterworth-Heineman

Blake, R. and Mouton J, (1964) *The Management Grid*, Houston, Texas: Gulf Publishing

Bridges, W. (1995) *Jobshifts: How to Prosper in a workplace without jobs*. Reading: Addison-Wesley

Buchanan, D. and Huczynski A, (1991) *Organisational Behaviour: An Introductory Text*, Hemel Hempstead: Prentice Hall

Crichton, A, (1968) *Personnel Management in Context*: Batsford

Cuming, M (1985), *The Theory and Practice of Personnel Management* Oxford: Butterworth-Heinneman

Daft, R (2001) *Organisation Theory and Design*. 7th ed. London: Pearson

Drucker, P. (1993) *Management: Tasks, Responsibilities, Practices*. Harper Business

Drucker, P. (1989) *The Practice of Management*, Oxford: Butterworth-Heinemann

Fayol, H. (1967) *General and Industrial Management*, London: Pitman

Fox, A. (1999) *Readings in Contemporary Employment Relationship*, ed. Mortimer, D., Leece, P. and Morris, R. Marrickville: Harcourt Bruce

Goldthorpe, J. Lockwood, D. Bechhofer, F and Platt, J. (1968) *The Affluent Worker: Industrial attitudes and behaviour* Cambridge: Cambridge University Press

Goleman D, (2000) Leadership that gets results. *Harvard Business Review*, Mar-Apr

Guest, D. (2002) Human resource management, corporate performance and employee well-being: building the worker into HRM. *Journal of Industrial Relations*

Hampden-Turner, C. (1990) *Corporate Culture*. London: Economist Books

Handy, C. (1987) *Gods of Management*, London: Souvenir Press

Handy, C. (1993) *Understanding Organisations*, 4th ed. Harmondsworth: Penguin

Herzberg, F. (1968), *Work and the Nature of Man*, Cleveland: World.

Hunt, J. (1986) *Managing People at Work*, Basingstoke: McGraw-Hill

Johns, T. (1994) *Perfect Customer Care*, London: Arrow Business Books

Kolb, D. (1984) *Experiential Learning*. New York: Prentice Hall

Lewin, K. (1946) *Field Theory in Social Science*, London: Tavistock

Likert, R. (1961) *New Patterns of Management*

Lupton, T. (1963) *On the Shop Floor* Oxford: Pergammon Press

Lupton, T. (1971) *Management and the Social Sciences* Harmondsworth: Penguin

Maccoby, M. (1998) *Why work: motivating and leading the new generation*, New York: Simon & Schuster

Maslow, A. (1954) *Motivation and Personality*, New York: Harper and Row

Mayo, A. (1998) *People Management*, 22 January

Mayo, E. (1975) *Social Problems of an Industrial Civilization*. London: Routledge

McCrae R. and Costa P, (2003), *Personality in Adulthood, a Five-factor Theory Perspective*, Guildford: Guildford Press

McGregor, D. (1960) *The Human Side of Enterprise*. New York: McGraw Hill

Mead, G.H. (1934) *Mind, Self and Society* ed. C.W. Morris. University of Chicago

Mintzberg, H. (1979) *The Structuring of Organisations*. New Jersey: Prentice Hall

Mintzberg, H. (1980) *The nature of managerial work*, Prentice Hall

Pedler, Burgoyne and Boydell (1991) *The Learning Company* London: McGraw-Hill

Peters, T. (1992) *Liberation Management* New: York Alfred A. Knopf

Peters, T. and Waterman R. (1982), *In Search of Excellence*. New York: Harper and Row

Reddin, B. (1997) *Groups at Work*, Oxford: Blackwell Publishers

Rooke and Torbert (1998) *Organisational Transformation as a Function of CEO's Developmental Stage*. Boston: Edge/Work Press

Schein, E. (1985) *Organisational Culture and Leadership*. San Fransisco: Jossey-Bass

Stacey, R. (2000) *Strategic Management and Organisational Dynamics: the Challenge of Complexity*. 3rd ed. Harlow: Pearson Education

Taylor, F, (1911), *The Principles of Scientific Management* (reprinted 1947) New York: Harper and Row

Trist E and Bamforth K (1951) 'Some logical and pyschological consequences of the longwall method of goal getting' *Human Relations*, Vol. 4 pp. 6-27 and 37-38 Cited in Stacey (2000)

Tuckman, (2001) *Learning and Motivation Strategies*, Harlow: Prentice Hall

Vroom, V. (1964) *Some Personality Determinants of the Effects of Participation* Englewood Cliffs, New Jersey: Prentice Hall

Yoder, D. (1958) *Handbook of personnel management and labor relations* New York: McGraw-Hill

Yoder, D. (1952) *Personnel principles and policies*, Englewood Cliffs: Prentice Hall

Weber, M. (1947) *The Theory of Social and Economic Organisation*. Free Press. Translated and edited by Henderson, A. and Parsons, T.

Index